THE GREAT BEAR

CONTEMPORARY WRITINGS ON THE GRIZZLY

THE GREAT BEAR

CONTEMPORARY WRITINGS ON THE GRIZZLY

EDITED BY
JOHN A. MURRAY

Alaska Northwest Books™
Anchorage • Seattle

All royalties from the sale of this book will be donated to The Nature Conservancy's Pine Butte Swamp Grizzly Bear Preserve near Choteau, Montana, with the exception of Doug Peacock's portion, which he has requested be donated to Vital Ground, a Nature Conservancy branch devoted to acquiring new grizzly bear habitat.

Library of Congress Cataloging-in-Publication Data
The great bear: contemporary writings on the grizzly/edited by
    John A. Murray.
            p. cm.
        Includes bibliographical references and index.
        ISBN 0-88240-392-3
        1. Grizzly bear. I. Murray, John A., 1954–   .
QL737.C27G738 1992   91-40629
599.74'446—dc20   CIP

Book and cover design by Cameron Mason
Cover illustration by Margaret Chodos-Irvine

Alaska Northwest Books™
A division of GTE Discovery Publications, Inc.
22026 20th Avenue S.E.
Bothell, WA 98021

Printed on acid-free, recycled paper in the United States of America

*To the grizzlies of Denali—Ragged Ear, Blondie,
Queen Gertrude, Columbus, Big Stony, the Twins, Frisky,
the Eielson Sow, and others—who have so patiently tolerated
my presence in their world and who have given me so many
hours of happiness. Long may they, their descendants, and
their cousins elsewhere freely roam the wilds of North
America.*

CONTENTS

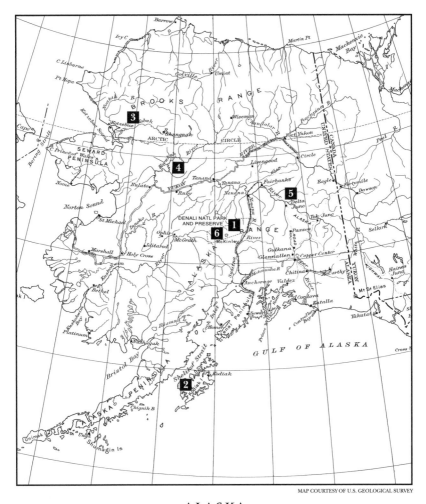

MAP COURTESY OF U.S. GEOLOGICAL SURVEY

ALASKA

Chapter number, author, and location:
  1 Adolph Murie, Denali National Park and Preserve
  2 Roger A. Caras, Kodiak Island
  3 John McPhee, Kobuk River drainage
  4 Richard Nelson, Koyukuk River drainage
  5 John Haines, Tanana River drainage
  6 Rick McIntyre, Denali National Park and Preserve

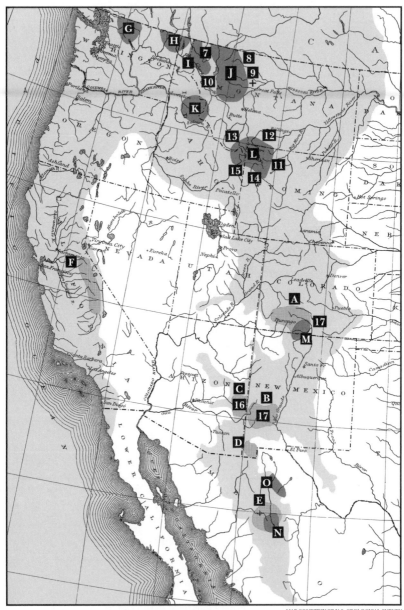

LOWER 48

MAP COURTESY OF U.S. GEOLOGICAL SURVEY

☐ Approximate distribution of grizzlies, 1850
+ Approximate location of The Nature Conservancy's Pine Butte Swamp
Grizzly Bear Preserve near Choteau, Montana

Chapter number, author, and location:
  7 Edward Abbey, Northern Rockies
  8 William Kittredge, Northern Rockies
  9 A. B. Guthrie, Jr., Northern Rockies
  10 Doug Peacock, Northern Rockies
  11 Frank C. Craighead, Jr., Yellowstone National Park
  12 Paul Schullery, Yellowstone National Park
  13 Thomas McNamee, Yellowstone National Park
  14 Jim Carrier, Yellowstone National Park
  15 Rick Bass, Yellowstone National Park ecosystem
  16 Aldo Leopold, Southwest—Arizona
  17 John A. Murray, Southwest—Colorado and New Mexico

Possible grizzly bear restoration areas:
  A The San Juan Mountains of southwestern Colorado. Over 900 square miles of designated wilderness area available for the sanctuary. Grizzlies possibly present in the area (see "M" below).
  B The Gila Wilderness of southwestern New Mexico. Over 1,000 miles of designated wilderness area available for the sanctuary. Last grizzly killed here in 1931.
  C The Blue Range Primitive Area of southcentral Arizona. Over 300 square miles available for the sanctuary. Last grizzly killed in this region in 1935.
  D The Gray Ranch of southwestern New Mexico, recently acquired by The Nature Conservancy. Over 500 square miles available for the sanctuary. Last grizzlies killed here by Ben Lilly in 1911.
  E The Rio Yaqui headwaters of Mexico's Sierra Nevada Mountains. Wilderness acreage unknown. Grizzlies possibly present in the area (see "N" below).
  F The Sierra Nevada Mountains of central California. Over 3,600 square miles available for the sanctuary. Last grizzly killed in the state (which has the grizzly on its flag) in 1922.

Areas in which grizzlies are known or thought to exist, 1992:
  G North Cascades grizzly bear ecosystem. Grizzlies confirmed but rare.
  H Selkirk Mountains grizzly bear ecosystem. Grizzlies present but in small numbers; as of 1989 there were 19 grizzlies wearing active radio collars.
  I Cabinet Mountains/Yaak River grizzly bear ecosystem. After five years of intensive research, scientists estimate there are fifteen or fewer grizzlies present here.
  J Northern Continental Divide grizzly bear ecosystem. Scientists estimate there are from 440 to 680 grizzlies present in this region; grizzly hunting currently permitted under strict regulations.
  K Bitterroot Mountains grizzly bear ecosystem. Grizzlies confirmed but rare; no population estimates available.
  L Yellowstone National Park grizzly bear ecosystem. Scientists estimate there are approximately 200 bears at present in and around the park.
  M San Juan grizzly bear ecosystem. Adult grizzly killed here in 1979; unconfirmed sightings and reports of grizzly activity persist.
  N Rio Yacqui grizzly bear ecosystem. Scientific studies inconclusive; reports of grizzlies persist.
  O Sierra del Nido grizzly bear ecosystem. Scientific studies inconclusive; grizzly was killed here in 1960.

"In 1909, when I first saw the West, there were grizzlies in every major mountain mass, but you could travel for months without meeting a conservation officer. Today there is some kind of conservation officer 'behind every bush,' yet as wildlife bureaus grow, our most magnificent mammal retreats steadily toward the Canadian border. Of the 6,000 grizzlies officially reported as remaining in areas owned by the United States, 5,000 are in Alaska. Only five states have any at all. There seems to be a tacit assumption that if grizzlies survive in Canada and Alaska, that is good enough. It is not good enough for me. The Alaskan bears are a distinct species. Relegating grizzlies to Alaska is about like relegating happiness to heaven; one may never get there."

—Aldo Leopold
"Wilderness for Wildlife,"
A Sand County Almanac, with Essays on Conservation from Round River, 1949

PREFACE

THIS ANTHOLOGY HAD its genesis about a year ago as I was reorganizing my home library and decided to put all the grizzly bear books on one shelf. Previously, these titles were scattered through several regional and author sections, and often could not be found when needed, like a set of valuable tools distributed among a variety of drawers. When the job was done, twenty-three books filled the new shelf. As I pulled up a chair and paged through these books, admiring essays here and there, it occurred to me that no anthology existed that gathered together contemporary essays on the grizzly, that is to say, those written after Aldo Leopold's seminal 1949 essay "Escudilla." At about the same time, I joined The Nature Conservancy and began to learn more about its many fine preserves, including the 18,000-acre Pine Butte Swamp Grizzly Bear Preserve near Choteau, Montana. *The Great Bear* was born out of a desire to materially help The Nature Conservancy in its efforts to save grizzly habitat, by donating the book's royalties directly to the Montana preserve, and to publish under one cover some of the most recent essays on the species, so that grizzly lovers everywhere might find their favorite authors in one convenient volume.

Anyone who has visited Yellowstone or Glacier or Denali National Park lately knows from the overcrowding that our national parks are insufficient in size and number for the recreational needs of the growing American population, not to mention the habitat requirements of wide-ranging mammals like the grizzly. In the twenty-first century we are going to need many more parks, forests, and refuges; the land now set aside is simply not adequate. What The Nature Conservancy is doing—in an era of fiscal austerity—is essentially what the federal government formerly did, namely, buy land for the purpose of wildlife preservation. Obtaining land with scenic or natural values is not easy, but already, The Nature Conservancy has, in addition to their many other projects around the world, purchased the 30-square-mile Pine Butte Swamp Grizzly Bear Preserve in Montana as well as the 500-square-mile Gray Ranch in the bootheel of New Mexico where grizzlies lived up to 1911. Much more needs to be done. For example, it will be essential to either purchase outright or procure a conservation easement on the 77,000-acre Banded Peak Ranch located on the Navajo River east of Chromo, Colorado, if the much-discussed restoration of grizzlies to the San Juan Mountains is to succeed. This is the core of existing habitat in which a grizzly was killed in 1979 and possibly contains the last few southwestern grizzlies. Either way, the project will take millions of dollars. The federal government has substantial funds in the form of royalties designated for conservation accounts from oil and gas leases, but these dollars are difficult to pry loose. Working together with The Nature Conservancy, a relatively small number of people who share a common conservation philosophy can pool their resources and make wonderful things happen.

The Nature Conservancy's Pine Butte Swamp Grizzly Bear Preserve was established to protect critical spring habitat for the bears along the Rocky Mountain Front of northern Montana. This is also the last area in North America where grizzlies still venture out on the high plains; the species once ranged about as far east as the one-hundred-third meridian in the Killdeer Mountains of North Dakota, the prairie rivers of eastern Colorado, and the Davis Mountains of west Texas. Pulitzer Prize–winning novelist A. B. Guthrie, who grew up along the Rocky Mountain Front, loved the area so much he placed its mountains and rivers in his best-selling novel *The Big Sky* in 1947. Each spring, around a dozen grizzlies come down into the preserve to forage on overwintered berries, fresh spring grass, and roots and tubers before returning to the high mountains. The food resources of areas like Pine Butte Swamp Grizzly Bear Preserve can mean the difference between life and death for grizzlies, whose nutritional banks are low from a winter of deep sleep. This is particularly the case for sows with nursing cubs.

I have learned much about the natural history of the grizzly bear from those people who were technical readers on my earlier book *Wildlife in Peril: The Endangered Mammals of Colorado* (1987), which focused primarily on grizzly reintroduction in the San Juan Mountains of southwestern Colorado. These individuals taught me as much about grizzlies as they did about public policy and fair and felicitous writing: Tom Beck, Dave Armstrong, Paul Schullery, Chris Servheen, Steve Bissell, and Judy Shepard. Also very helpful were John Craighead, Dave Brown, Ernie Wilkinson, Al LeCount, Jim Halfpenny,

Karen Meany, Sandy Binker, Bob Ralston, Jim Ruch, and Tim Schultz. Here, in Alaska, I owe a considerable debt to my friends at Denali National Park and Preserve, who have greatly facilitated my study of grizzly bears: Ralph Tingey, George Wagner, Bill McDonald, Tom Griffith, Russ Berry, Ken Kehrer, Ralph Cunningham, and Fred Dean. I extend a special word of appreciation to park naturalist Rick McIntyre, for his always enjoyable companionship in the field and for a place to get out of the weather now and then, and also to Montana writer Rick Bass, who made a 1990 photosafari to Denali so memorable. Thanks to fellow photographers Michio Hoshino of Tokyo and Bob Landis of Billings, who have shared many grizzly sightings with me. Thanks also to Jimmy Miller, who made a 1991 grizzly trip so enjoyable, and to David Rains Wallace, for a 1989 excursion up the Savage River that I will always remember. The authors and their publishers have been exceedingly helpful in securing permissions for this book; no anthology can be successfully undertaken without such eager assistance, and I thank them all for their enthusiasm and cooperation. The chance to talk over the phone with ninety-year-old A. B. Guthrie, in the course of securing permissions, and to tell him how much *The Big Sky* had changed my life, alone made the project worthwhile. My gratitude goes to the editors at Alaska Northwest Books™— Marlene Blessing, Maureen Zimmerman, and Ellen Wheat—who recognized the value of the book and who have offered every form of assistance possible in bringing it to fruition.

I would like to thank my family: my mother, who read Ernest Thompson Seton's *Biography of a Grizzly* to her three sons so long ago; my father, who took my brother and me up to Yellowstone in the park's centennial year of 1972 and showed us grizzly country; my grandfather, who never tired of relating the story of how he drove a Model T Ford on unpaved roads all the way from Cincinnati to Yellowstone in 1929 just to show everybody a bear, and who told the saga of how *his* grandfather took the Northern Pacific to Miles City in 1882 to see the park bears, but had to turn back when his leg, crippled from the Civil War, could not take the 250-mile stagecoach ride. To paraphrase the first sentence of Norman Maclean's *A River Runs Through It,* in our family, there was no clear line between religion and bears. And my love and appreciation go to my wife and son, for their patience with my many absences each year as I visit the grizzlies of Denali. This summer will be the first time I take my two-year-old boy out of the back carrier and plant his little scampering feet on a mountain trail with fresh grizzly tracks on it. No better place for a father and son to walk.

—John A. Murray
Fairbanks, Alaska
June 3, 1991

Should you wish to visit the Pine Butte Swamp Grizzly Bear Preserve, write Pine Butte Guest Ranch, HC 58–Box 27, Choteau, Montana 59422. The telephone number is (404) 466-2621. From mid May through September, workshops in the preserve feature such activities as wildlife observation, hiking, birding, horseback riding, photography, horse-packing, animal tracking, and fossil hunting. For information regarding programs and membership, write The Nature Conservancy, 1815 North Lynn Street, Arlington, Virginia 22209.

PART I
ALASKA

"The sight of the [grizzly] bear stirred me like nothing else the country could contain. What mattered was not so much the bear himself as what the bear implied. He was the predominant thing in that country, and for him to be in it at all meant that there had to be more country like it in every direction and more of the same kind of country all around that. He implied a world. He was an affirmation to the rest of the earth that his kind of place was extant."

—John McPhee
"The Encircled River,"
Coming into the Country, 1977

ALASKA IS PRIME GRIZZLY COUNTRY, FROM fog-drenched Kodiak Island through the forested Interior to the cold, barren tundra of the North Slope. Authorities estimate that there are around 5,000 grizzlies in the state. Those brown bears inhabiting the coastal regions of Pacific Alaska—including such islands as Kodiak, Shuyak, Afognak, and Admiralty—are designated as a separate subspecies, *Ursus arctos middendorffi*, because of their significantly larger body size. Brown bears, or grizzlies, found elsewhere in Alaska are known by the common Latin appellation, *Ursus arctos horribilis*. The two subspecies can, and do, interbreed easily. Hunting seasons for grizzly bears in Alaska currently permit an individual to take one brown or grizzly every four years. Bear populations are managed by the government so that the resource is not depleted, as happened with uncontrolled hunting in the Lower 48 states. Because there is little livestock grazing in Alaska, and because population growth and economic development are held in check by the severe climate, future prospects for the species in the state are good.

There are five locations in Alaska where grizzlies can be observed in the wild on a regular basis: (1) Denali National Park and Preserve* offers shuttle bus tours along the 88-mile-long road that bisects the northern half of the park. Around 90 percent of all visitors to Denali Park see a grizzly in the wild. Passenger cars were outlawed in the park in 1972, which is probably the chief reason that bears are still seen near the road. (2) McNeil River State Game Sanctuary on the Alaska Peninsula offers visitors the chance to view up to sixty bears at one time feeding on salmon at McNeil River Falls. All visitors must apply for permits through a lottery system and are confined to several viewing platforms in the vicinity of the falls. (3) Brooks Falls in Katmai National Park and Preserve on the Alaska Peninsula offers a situation similar to that at McNeil River. Reservations are necessary and Brooks Camp is becoming a more competitive and restrictive experience, as visitor use increases. (4) Stan Price State Wildlife Sanctuary at Pack Creek on Admiralty Island is similar to both Brooks Camp and McNeil Falls, as bears are observed fishing for sea-run salmon in Pack Creek

---

*Mount McKinley National Park was established in 1917. In 1980, the park was renamed Denali National Park and Preserve, to acknowledge that the Natives of Alaska had always called the mountain *Denali*, The Great One.

and in the marshy intertidal areas. (5) Fraser River on Kodiak Island, which like the other coastal sites can only be reached by floatplane or boat, provides an opportunity to watch the bears catching salmon on the Fraser River. For these last four sites, the best time to visit is from early July through mid to late August during salmon spawning season.

No person should consider his or her outdoor experiences complete without having seen a grizzly in the wild, and Alaska is the best place to accomplish that goal. Whereas national parks elsewhere were formed in often bizarre geometric configurations bearing no relationship to ecosystem boundaries, the national parks and other conservation areas in Alaska were created with that prior deficiency in mind. Denali National Park is larger than the state of Massachusetts, and the contiguous Arctic–Yukon Flats National Wildlife Refuges are greater in size than New England. Hunting is forbidden in all of Alaska's national parks to ensure that the species will have a safe future in the forty-ninth state. Here people will forever be able to see North America as it was in the beginning, before the Indians came, when the grizzlies roamed wild and free.

LIKE MOST NATURALISTS who have worked in Alaska—
Georg Steller, John Muir, Robert Marshall—Adolph Murie came
from elsewhere. After a brief visit to Alaska in 1922 to assist his
older half-brother, Olaus Murie, with a caribou research project,
"Ade" returned to the state in 1939 to begin an intensive two-year
study of the relationship between wolves and Dall sheep in Mount
McKinley National Park. His research culminated in *The Wolves
of Mount McKinley* (1944), a work Barry Lopez has called "a classic
. . . the first unbiased ecological treatise on wolves." Murie's
masterpiece, *A Naturalist in Alaska* (1961), was awarded the John
Burroughs Medal for nature writing.

"The Ways of Grizzly Bears," one of the most memorable
essays in that book, captures the essence of Alaskan grizzly
country. Murie notes humorously that "a bear a long distance
from a scale always weighs the most," and vividly describes an
incident in which a single male attends to two adult females
during the height of the early summer breeding season. The
strength of Murie's narratives is that, like works of science, they
are deeply rooted in fact, while, like works of literature, they are
enlivened by artistry and craft. Murie's special gift as a writer was
the ability to put aside the specialized language of the scientific
monograph and bring the nonspecialist closer to the subject. The
influence of his characteristic anecdotal approach can be seen in
the essays of some nature writers of the seventies and eighties,
particularly those of the West who seem to be more familiar with
Murie's writing.

Murie held strong philosophical views about the study
of wildlife in national parks. He was an advocate of passive
observation and nonintrusive methods of scientific study, and
believed marked or collared animals were incompatible with the
national park experience. The results of Murie's research in
Denali National Park were published in 1980 as *The Grizzlies of
Mount McKinley,* a work edited by his son, Jan Murie, a zoologist at
the University of Alberta in Edmonton.

*"The Ways of Grizzly Bears," taken from Adolph Murie's A Naturalist in
Alaska (Devin Adair, 1961), is reprinted by permission of Louise Murie-
MacLoed.*

1. THE WAYS OF GRIZZLY BEARS

ADOLPH MURIE

T H E NORTH SIDE OF THE ALASKA RANGE IS GRIZZLY country. Old bruin may be found from the partially wooded terrain along the north boundary of the park to the glaciers at the heads of the many parallel river valleys. The entire country is his home, and one may meet bears anywhere from the river bars to the ridgetops. Regardless of where one camps, one is sure to have grizzly neighbors. Even in remote areas such as McGonnagal Pass they are ever on hand to utilize unguarded food caches. One group of climbers up toward Anderson Pass thought grizzlies "sure plentiful" there. When we were camping at the head of Savage River in 1922 and 1923, we saw bears so frequently that we assumed we were in the very choicest bear country.

In spring and fall one is especially likely to see bears on river bars digging roots, and they follow the same occupation on mountain slopes. In summer, high passes such as Sable Pass are especially fre- quented for grazing, and, in season, berry chomping may take the bears anywhere. Always they wander freely over their ranges, with few worries, taking care chiefly to avoid proximity to other bears.

The grizzlies vary in color from "straw color" to rich chocolate and black. A Sourdough told me one day that he had seen a mother with three cubs—"one lemon, one orange, and a chocolate!" Some of the faded straw-colored bears appear quite whitish when the sun is reflected at a certain angle, for a moment being taken sometimes for Dall sheep. The face is dark brown or blackish, and the feet and legs are blackish. In the fall of 1959 I saw an unusual cream-colored bear. The black legs and brown face contrasted sharply with the rest of the coat.

The head is large and broad. The facial profile is "dish-faced," that is, the forehead rises so abruptly that it is not in a straight line with the muzzle. The eyes are small and the nose somewhat squared off. The hump over the shoulder, along with the dish face, is useful in distinguishing the grizzly from the black bear. The claws on the front feet are long and slightly curved, in contrast to the shorter and more tightly curved claws of the black bear. The long claw length shows up clearly in the track. Grizzly feet always have, relatively speaking, a dainty appearance, perhaps because they are covered with shorter hair than the legs. The hips are wide and solid; the stomach sometimes sags.

The weights of grizzlies have often been estimated, but few bears have been weighed. A bear a long distance from a scale always weighs most. One well-known bear hunter in Alaska, who had three dead bears in the hills at one time and was taking a naturalist out to see them, had all their weights estimated. But when he learned that the naturalist carried steelyards with him, the hunter began to hedge, and the closer they approached the bears, the lower fell the estimates. The actual weights of all three bears were far below even the reduced estimates. A very old black male, with much-worn teeth, that was shot as he was raiding a construction camp kitchen at Savage River weighed, after loss of blood, 650 pounds. Dressed weight (without head, hide, and innards) was 439. He was not very fat, having only a thin layer over his body. His live weight was probably close to seven hundred pounds. If he had been really fat, he might have weighed fifty to a hundred pounds more.

I recall the first bear track I ever saw. It was my initial day afield in McKinley Park and my brother and I were crossing from Jenny Creek over a rise to Savage River, on our way to the head of the river. One lone track in a patch of mud is all we saw. But the track was a symbol, and more poetic than seeing the bear himself—a delicate and profound approach to the spirit of the Alaska wilderness. A bear track at any time may create a stronger emotion than the old bear himself, for the imagination is brought into play. You examine the landscape sharply, expecting a bear on every slope as your quickened interest becomes eager and enterprising. The bear is somewhere, and may be anywhere. The country has come alive with a new, rich quality.

The track of the front foot is diagnostic because of the long claws, which leave their marks about two inches beyond the toe pad (this distance is about one inch in the black bear track). The front-foot track frequently shows a small rounded depression back of the main pad mark; this is the impression made by the small posterior pad, which is so situated that it does not always touch the ground.

Although grizzlies generally travel about at random, they occasionally develop a characteristic trail. Short pieces of such trails have been noted in McKinley Park in woods bordering streams. I found a very deeply worn trail along Wood River in the mountains several miles east of the park. This definite trail was used by bears because of the lay of the land. The main channel of the river was flowing at the base of high, steep banks, and bordering the banks was a dense stand of spruce. Bears traveling up and down the river on the side I was on found it convenient to follow a trail through the woods. In using the trail the bears had characteristically stepped in the same tracks until two rows of deep track depressions had been worn into the hard ground. That the trail was much used was indicated not only by the track depressions but also by numerous rubbed "bear trees."

There is probably considerable individual and sexual variation in the home ranges of grizzlies, and females with cubs probably behave differently from those without. Some of the variations would be due to the lay of the land and the distribution and abundance of food plants. The range in spring, when roots are the chief food, is slightly different from what it is later in the summer, when the diet has shifted to grass or berries. But the changes due to diet would usually be rather local. My impression is that in the spring, when bears emerge from winter quarters, they travel more widely than later. A male probably wanders far during the mating period in search of a mateable female.

The females with cubs often confine their movements for most of the summer to an area less than a dozen miles in diameter. At Sable

Pass we have seen females with cubs at short intervals for weeks in an area only six or seven miles across. Sometimes a bear will feed several days in an area and then climb over a high ridge to feed in another valley for a time. Thus, bears in Sable Pass or along Igloo Creek may move over into Big Creek, or they may go to the Teklanika River for a few days. Lone bears were known to occupy a limited area for a few days and then wander away, appearing and disappearing during the season. Their identification was uncertain, and data on them are not extensive. Several females that were in an area with spring or yearling cubs occupied the same area the following year. One female with three cubs was recognized in the Polychrome area during three successive summers; the third year she was followed closely by the two-year cubs.

The home ranges of bears overlap broadly, some bears having practically identical home ranges at least for most of the summer. Three mothers, each with yearlings, spent one summer on Sable Pass (a favorite grizzly area) and I once saw a fourth female with yearlings there; I saw a female with spring cubs a few times and another family of yearlings only three or four miles away. In addition to these, two large males and at least two breeding females were in the area for several weeks. In 1950 two females, one with three cubs, the other with two cubs, spent the summer on Sable Pass. They kept apart as much as possible but often were near enough together to be acutely conscious of one another. Usually both females cooperated in keeping apart, like similar poles of a magnet. The presence of these two females on the same range was the cause of a tragedy, which I shall describe later. (In a garbage dump at Yellowstone Park I have seen thirty grizzlies wallowing together with bodies practically touching. Here, apparently, wild natural habits are being lost, and the dump is making of our lone philosopher bears a bunch of gregarious characters. They perhaps are gregarious, however, only at the dump. Along the Alaska coast the brown bears sometimes congregate loosely to feed on the migrating salmon, but are not congested as at a garbage dump.) A certain amount of hostility is perhaps one factor in keeping bears widely distributed over McKinley Park. I assume that a bear finding an area bearless or sparsely populated might tend to remain there, for they are "lone wolves" rather than gregarious under natural conditions.

Mating in McKinley Park takes place during May, June, and early July, when one may occasionally see in the distance a bear followed by a much larger bear with long legs and a stiff, long stride. It is the male following the female who at long last (unless this happens to be her first experience) is ready to breed again. Mating behavior seems to be quite varied, as the following observations indicate.

About May 10, 1941, I saw a female grizzly at Toklat River, near a small road camp. She spent most of the day digging roots and fed on garbage thrown away near the camp. About a week later she was joined by a young, lighter-colored male, slightly smaller. I saw them breeding on May 20. They were together most of the time and were often playing together and hugging, much like the two bears I have just spoken of. On May 22 it became a triangle affair, for a huge dark male appeared on the scene. He endeavored to drive the small male away, chasing him far up the mountainside, back to the bar, and up the mountain a second time. When the large male followed the female, she also ran away from him. On May 23, at 9:00 A.M., I saw the female digging roots. A little later, a half-mile away, the large male was following the small male across the broad river bar. The large male grunted at intervals. The bears climbed up a slope, where they fed on roots, the smaller one keeping an eye on his rival. Later he descended to the bar and started across to the female. But the watchful bigger male hurried down the slope and on the bar came to within two hundred yards of him. Both bears then galloped away, disappearing behind a patch of woods, and then reappearing four or five hundred feet up the slope on the other side of the bar. The small male returned to the bar, started to cross it, but changed his mind and came back to the female. The big bear, seeming to be winded by the exertion, rested high on the slope for a long time, then came down and was lost to view in the trees. The female and small male wrestled, then fed close together on roots. Later they wrestled again and the male grabbed the female with his jaws back of an ear and tried to mount her, but she rolled over. They continued to wrestle and play for some time, then resumed feeding on roots. When I left at 2:30 P.M., the pair was crossing the bar. I did not see the big male after he came off the mountain and disappeared in the woods. It appeared that the female was being true to her first love and that the stronger bear was unable to win her affections.

On May 24 the small male was in the woods. Later he was joined by the female, who apparently had been chased, for not long after she arrived the large male came through the woods on her trail, grunting and bawling loudly at intervals. At his approach the other two bears ran away together. On June 2 I again saw the small male mating with the female.

The large male continued following the pair of bears at Toklat. On June 8, when I saw the three moving toward Mile Sixty-six, the large male was chasing the female. On June 9 I saw the three bears two miles from Mile Sixty-six, fourteen miles from Toklat. All three were sleeping only a few feet apart, on a point of rock. They lay sprawled on their backs, stomachs, and sides, occasionally changing positions or stretching a leg. Most of the time they lay on their sides. When I returned three hours later, they had moved to the gravel bar, where they were sleeping on their sides on the wet mud. The persistence of the large male had been rewarded to the extent of sharing the female. (In a report on the Kenya Parks of Africa, it is said that two male lions shared a single female, behavior said to be unusual.) It was reported that the large male mated with the female on June 10. Soon after this date the mating activities of the bears apparently terminated.

These grizzlies had mated over a period of several weeks. The small male and the female were together for at least twenty-three days.

On June 12, 1953, I saw three bears on the north slope of Cathedral Mountain. A male was in possession of a female, and a bear slightly smaller than the male was hanging on the outskirts. This third bear appeared to be another male. I first noticed one of the bears at 4:00 P.M., as it lay on the slope, quite alert, for every few minutes it raised its head to look around. At 8:00 P.M. I noted that three bears were in the area; earlier, two of them had apparently been hidden by the alder and willow brush, which was quite tall. The large, dark male walked up to another bear, apparently a female, and they touched noses. Then the male covered her for about an hour. Much of the time the female wriggled about, apparently trying to escape while he held her with his paws in front of her hips and his head lying along her neck. Once she escaped but ran only ten or fifteen yards and stood, and the male again covered her. The third bear approached to within about twenty yards of the pair when the male first covered the female, but later went off a short distance, moving about a little as he watched the pair. The following two days the three bears remained in the area, much of the time hidden from view. On the fifteenth they were reported moving toward Igloo Creek.

It is interesting to watch a pair maneuvering on a slope. On June 3, 1953, I saw a large, dark male, with a huge, shaggy head, following a much smaller, straw-colored female. He kept herding her from below, as though his objective were to keep her up on the slope. When she traveled, he traveled on a contour below her. Once, when a sharp ridge hid her from him, he galloped forward and upward to intercept her, but she seemed to have anticipated this and had doubled back. When he saw her again she was two or three hundred yards away. He galloped after her, his hoarse panting plainly audible half a mile away. But she made no real effort to escape, and he was soon herding her from below again. At noon they lay down about twenty yards apart, and a little later, when he went into a dip to feed, she hurried away as though she were playing a coy game with him. When he returned and found her missing, he galloped a short distance in two directions and, not seeing her, went back to where she had rested and from there followed her track. She was on a prominence, moving slowly, and after a gallop he was again directly below her. The chase continued all day. In the evening, as they were lying near each other, I saw the male get up and slowly approach her, but she quickly moved away.

Another pair I observed on Divide Mountain on June 30, 1947, went through a similar performance, the male herding the female from below. Once, when they stood facing each other about twenty yards apart, she raised her paws above her head and struck the ground stiffly, as bears do when bluffing. When she wandered among some large boulders, one of them was dislodged and would have struck the male as it bounced down the slope if he had not jumped aside. (I took this to be accidental.) The following day they were still in the same area, maneuvering as before.

A big shaggy male grizzly in the summer of 1959 kept company with two females. He was always recognizable by the limp in his front left foot. A limp is hard to analyze sometimes, but the left leg seemed stiff, raising his body a little as he walked. The left elbow seemed to protrude outward excessively. The long, unkempt hair over the eyes gave him an ancient, patriarchal look. I first saw him on June 13 as he was making his way with long, deliberate strides down a ridge in the Sable Pass area. He surprised a mother and two spring cubs that were foraging near a bank in a swale and galloped lumberingly toward them, but they hurriedly galloped up the slope away from him and did not stop until they topped the ridge and went out of sight. He continued to the main draw, where a miniature creek a few feet wide wound down through a narrow strip of tall willow brush. The huge fat hindquarters seemed to have an excessive sidewise wobble, and this, along with the hitch of the lame front leg, gave him a characteristic gait. I measured the tracks he left when he crossed a snowbank in the draw and found the hind track to be about ten-and-a-half inches long. He was especially picturesque silhouetted against some of the snowbanks he followed.

A week later, on June 20, I saw this male walking far behind a very blonde female. On the twenty-sixth, in the morning, he was following the blonde closely, and at times she was following him. That same evening this male was in pursuit, at a deliberate walk, of a very dark female that hopped along on three legs. She carried her right hind foot, on which she had a round bare spot just above the heel. I had first seen her in the area on June 17. He followed her to a point near the top of a ridge where at times he was only about fifty yards from her. They maneuvered about the ridge for some time before they both lay down. A little later the crippled female had moved far below, to the base of the ridge. The next day, June 27, the male was breeding with the blonde when I discovered them. He held her for about ten minutes. When she escaped, she sat down a few yards away. The crippled female was at the time resting about twenty yards away; soon she moved over a ridge out of sight. The male followed and the blonde brought up the rear. The male continued following the crippled female for about fifteen minutes and she kept moving well ahead of him. Later in the day I saw this same procession.

On the twenty-eighth, the three bears were together and the male was breeding with the crippled female. Earlier in the day the crippled female had been very coy and at one time was half a mile from the other two bears; I saw her lying on her back, kicking all four legs in the air. Twice, when the blonde was only a few yards from the male, he made a few bluffing jumps toward her, hitting the ground hard with his front paws. But both times she returned at once to him after retreating a short distance.

This miscellaneous maneuvering continued for the following few days, the male following one or the other of the females. On July 1, the male followed the blonde part of the time but paid more attention to the crippled female. Her foot, by the way, was much improved;

although she still carried it when loping, she used it in walking. The blonde, after July 1, wandered farther away from the other two bears, but she was near them on July 4 when I again saw the other two breeding.

On July 8, when I discovered the two crippled bears about ten o'clock in the evening, he was holding her as she squirmed. After five minutes she broke away, moved off twenty-five yards, and waited while the male overtook her again. This time he held her for twenty-five minutes and for much of the time she continued squirming in his grasp. When I left they were resting about five yards apart.

The last day I saw the crippled pair together was July 10. The blonde had left a few days earlier. I continued to see both crippled bears in the Sable Pass area for a few weeks, the male until July 26 and the female until August 4. (They probably moved away in search of berries, the crop on Sable Pass being below par.) The blonde female, I did not definitely recognize during this period.

I saw a second large male in the area during the mating period, on June 12 and 28 and July 4, but he was not near the mating bears, usually being a mile or more from them. During the mating period, the females paid no attention to each other. Each one had been in the company of the male for at least two weeks, but I observed the blonde with the male about a week before the cripple was with him; apparently the blonde left him about a week before the cripple departed.

Observations on nursing yearlings and two-year cubs are significant in regard to the breeding interval of female grizzlies in the park.

In 1953 I was surprised to see a yearling cub nursing. On a few occasions in the literature a yearling black bear and brown bear cub had been reported nursing, but it was assumed that these instances were exceptions. Since my first observation of the nursing yearling, I have had opportunities to check on thirteen mothers that were followed by yearlings. In every case these one-and-a-half-year cubs were nursing; the interval and duration were similar to what I had observed in spring cubs.

My observations suggest that cubs also regularly nurse the early part of their third summer abroad. In the seven families I have been able to check in this regard, the females nursed their large two-and-a-half-year cubs. The latest nursing noted was July 12. All observations indicate that families generally break up during the third summer between late May (one record) and September.

The observations of nursing yearlings and two-year cubs suggest a minimum breeding interval of females with cubs of at least three years. In some cases in which I have observed females followed by two-year cubs throughout the breeding period, the interval appears to have been at least four years. It is also significant that, of the two dozen or more mated females I have observed, none was followed by a yearling, and only one by a cub older than a yearling.

The one, two, or three cubs (the usual numbers) are born in mid-winter in the hibernation den. They are extremely small, weighing only about one and a half pounds. They still seem very tiny when one sees them abroad with the mother in the early spring.

Grizzlies in McKinley Park go into hibernation in October and emerge in early April. In 1939 I saw bear tracks on April 17, the first day I was in the field; and in 1941 I saw the first bear tracks on April 8.

On October 11, 1939, when there was a foot of snow on the ground, I saw a grizzly digging a den on a steep slope far up a mountain. In digging, the bear disappeared into the hole, then came out tail first, pawing the dirt out of the entrance. At intervals he pawed back the pile of dirt at the entrance, and dirt rolled far down the slope over the snow. The entrance was just large enough to permit the bear to enter. The following spring I saw fresh tracks leading away from the den; undoubtedly it was used by the bear for his winter sleep. When I climbed to the den later in the summer the chamber had caved in, so it could not be used a second year. The chamber was four feet from the entrance and was about five feet in diameter. The floor of the burrow led upward at an angle of about ten degrees. Where the den was dug, the mountain sloped at a forty-five degree angle. Other dens, also caved in, were in similar situations.

A bear may have a den in mind long before denning time. On July 22, 1953, I found a freshly dug den on a slope. The bear had recently dug a tunnel with a slightly upward slant, twelve feet long, just under the sod. The entrance was about twenty-four inches wide and twenty-seven inches high. A chamber at the far end had not yet been dug. When a companion and I visited the den again on August 23, we learned that the bear had been back and dug a chamber at the far end that measured four by three feet, the longer dimension being at right angles to the burrow. The chamber may not have been finished at this time. A quarter of a mile from this den was the fresh beginning of another burrow that was only about five feet long.

Six years later I again visited this den and found it still usable. The sod roof was especially firm and no doubt accounted for the long preservation of the den. In front of the entrance a number of cinque-foil bushes had been nipped off in past years and brought into the chamber for bedding. Also in the chamber were remnants of dry grass and herbaceous material. Apparently the den had been used at least once, and possibly oftener, since it was dug in 1953.

On another slope, quite steep, I found an old den whose roof had caved in some years ago. The broad mound of dirt at the den entrance was now covered solidly with herbaceous dogwood. When I visited this den in 1959, I learned that a bear had more recently started a den just below this old one. It was unfinished, but extended six feet, and part of this distance was under the dirt mound of the old den. Had the former occupant of the old den returned some years later? Or perhaps another bear recognized the old den as an old den and it had suggested den digging to him.

Bears do not go into a comatose state during hibernation as do ground squirrels, but can be activated readily at all times. They emerge from the den fat but are said to lose weight later. Food resources may be limited when they first emerge, so it seems logical that they should lose some weight then. Bears seem to be traveling a good deal at this time, a way of life which also would be conducive to loss of weight in the spring.

ROGER CARAS IS WELL KNOWN to most readers both for his
many distinguished nature books and his highly visible work as a
special wildlife correspondent for ABC-TV, where he appears
regularly on the evening news and presents documentary features
on wildlife and conservation issues. Among Caras's books are *The
Custer Wolf* (1966), *The Endless Migrations* (1985), and *Animals in
Their Places* (1988). One of his most highly regarded books,
Monarch of Deadman Bay: The Life and Death of a Kodiak Bear (1969),
was awarded the John Burroughs Medal for nature writing. Roger
Caras also received the Joseph Wood Krutch Medal in 1977 and
Israel's Oryx Award for Wildlife Conservation in 1984. Caras is the
Ernest Thompson Seton of contemporary nature writing; no
other nature writer is quite as skilled at showing us the lives of
wild animals from their perspective.

No anthology on the North American grizzly bear would be
complete without a selection representing the subspecies of
coastal Alaskan brown bears. These bears, which inhabit the
coasts and islands of Alaska and British Columbia and grow to
enormous proportions (1,000-plus pounds) as a result of their
resource-rich environment, are genetically identical to the inland
grizzly. The only difference is that the big brownies feast regularly
on sea-run salmon and the bumper berry crops that flourish in
the cool, wet climate. The bears of Kodiak Island are currently
threatened by cattle ranching and overhunting. In this selection
from Roger Caras's *Monarch of Deadman Bay* we see the great
patriarch of Kodiak Island in his maturity, being stalked here
not by a big-game hunter but by a wildlife photographer, who
employs all of the skills of the former but leaves the behemoth
undisturbed for others to enjoy at a later time.

2. MONARCH OF DEADMAN BAY

ROGER A. CARAS

AT SEVENTEEN, MONARCH HAD ALL BUT STOPPED growing. His weight rose and fell with the seasons, the texture of his shaggy coat varied according to the time of year, and there were periods when he seemed bigger than at others, but basically he had leveled off. Indeed, a few hairs along the line of his lower lip and others near the outer corners of his small, intense eyes were gray at their tips.

In the years of his maturity he had known seven sows and had fathered fourteen cubs. One mating had produced a single cub and another triplets. Eleven of the fourteen cubs had survived; two females and one male among his offspring had already reproduced themselves. The chocolate boar was thus immortal.

Despite his advancing years his senses remained sharp. He was still noble breeding stock and worth Nature's attention. When he could no longer instill the future with his strength she would dull his senses until they would no longer sustain him. When Nature had used him up she would abandon him to perform in solitude his last service within the great cycle: he would die and give his chemistry back to the land. Everything in his physical makeup was on loan, nothing more. Nature may be the creator of all that is beautiful, all that stirs the poet's soul; she may brush our cheeks with gentle summer winds; she may teach the birds to sing and give flowers their perfumed glory. But any sentimentality about these wonders is on the part of the beholder. Nature may be many things, but she is not sentimental. For every life she gives, she demands an ultimate payment in used chemicals. For every life she maintains, she exacts a promise of future life. For her, that is all that matters. Sentimentality is *our* projection, based on our emotional needs. Man is slowly learning not to anthropomorphize, but he may never learn to accord Nature the same objectivity. In order to do so he would have to slay a goddess, or at least recognize a queen of his pantheon for what she is.

From our studies of contemporary primitive man, and from our fractional knowledge of ancient man, we can surmise that the hunting of the bear has often had a quasi-religious significance. Man has always coexisted with bears. Assyrian amulets picture the bear wielding a club, although the precise significance of the symbol escapes us. The Eskimos within the envelope of their frozen latitudes evolved a bear-god at an early stage of their history and called him Nanuq. Rhpisunt was the bear-mother-goddess of the Haida Indians along the mainland coast not far from Monarch's island range. She was an awesome figure with supernatural powers. When the hunters of the southwestern deserts finally found the elusive House of the Sun they found it guarded by a bear and a serpent. When Estanatlehi, the greatest of the Navajo deities, created new clans to repopulate the world, she sent a bear to them as a protector and as one who could teach them how to hunt. Caves in other parts of the world have yielded stone bear figures, and rock and cave paintings have further attested to the role the great shaggy animal has played in the mysteries of man. The hunter who would take the life of a bear today and ask the taxidermist to create from its salvaged carcass a testimonial of manhood is the inheritor of this ageless magic. His is a ritual honestly come by, surprisingly still extant.

Man has developed the ability, if not the universal will, to control or at least redirect his atavistic drives. And so many men have taken to hunting not to kill, but to record. The hunter with the camera is slowly replacing the hunter with the gun. Theirs is an art requiring the greater skill, and in exercising their mastery of it the practitioners often run the greater risks.

The stories of the colossal bear that lived around Deadman Bay had reached the ears of many men. One among them determined to trace the stories to their source, not to cancel its life, but to see it, record it, and experience it as vividly as possible.

The photographer was no less skilled in the ways of the wild than the hunter. His equipment was, if anything, more sophisticated and complex. His Nikon F cameras were the best the genius of the Japanese optical industry had to offer, their many and varied lenses masterpieces of scientific craftsmanship. They had the power to reach out to the bear, snatch away his image, yet deprive him of nothing, and to freeze a moment of his life for posterity. To capture and hold a fraction of cosmic evolution was what fascinated the photographer. He heard and responded to the intriguing if obviously exaggerated tales about the giant bear. He would have him as surely as a hunter, yet he would leave him unharmed.

Monarch had abandoned his habit of approaching campsites. He was no less curious about mankind, but he had become far more cautious. He had reached and passed the point that comes to all great bears who survive their early years; he was a trophy animal of particular interest. When conscious involvement between man and bear becomes mutual, the bear must retreat or perish. Monarch had been tracked so many times, had so often been forced to alter his course because of the scent or sound of man, that he had become hypersensitive. Each of these experiences had been violently disturbing to him, and there had been two bullets to emphasize the lesson he had learned while still a cub with his mother.

Eleven times hunters had actually tracked Monarch's fresh spoor, and eleven times he had outwitted them. On two other occasions he had chosen to stand and fight, although on neither occasion was he their specific target. No experience he had ever had at the hands of man had been rewarding, no contact profitable. He was not really afraid of man, but in the wisdom of his age he generally sought a quick escape when humans arrived and began their blundering invasion of his cherished solitude. It is almost surprising that his victims numbered only two. At least half a dozen times since he had taken a second human life he had been given opportunities to kill again.

In the truly wild places of our planet a guide is needed not only to help the stranger kill, but to save him from being killed. The photographer, like the hunter, needed an expert with him in bear country. The professional welcomed the change. The killing of a bear no longer held any fascination for him and he had come secretly to despise many of the men for whom he worked. He saw in their eyes something he did not like and heard in their voices something he could not fathom. He admired a man who will take a hunter's chances, suffer a killer's hardship, yet will take nothing away from the land. As a man who had himself killed too much, he welcomed this refreshing sanity. However, a bear cannot respond to the gentler nature of the photographer and cannot be relied upon to remain calm simply because he has not been wounded. And so the photographer's guide must carry a rifle.

They were three days' march from the Bay when they first picked up Monarch's spoor. The guide assured his client that no other bear in the area left quite that kind of sign. The enormous hind foot had been planted several inches in front of the forepaw on the right side. Unlike a human foot, the bear's big toe is on the outside, and a track can always be oriented to the bear's position by this means. The tracks that the guide pointed to in the soft mud by the bank of the small inland lake did not differ in kind from other bear tracks they had seen, but they differed dramatically in size. Further on, when they encountered a clear stretch of track, the photographer tried to walk in the bear's footsteps. He had to waddle like a duck, for the side-to-side spread was far greater than a human can comfortably approximate. The photographer tried to emulate Monarch's stride and nearly went flat in the mud. The track sets were fifty-five inches apart.

As they passed beyond the recently flooded area the ground became firm again and they lost the trail in a stretch of exposed rock. The direction the giant had taken seemed clear enough, however, and they continued on until the guide grasped the photographer by the arm and pulled him to a stop. They knelt together beside a clump of brush to examine a recently occupied bed. Moss and leaves had been raked together and a crude mattress formed. The furrows the bear's claws had made in the raking process were still clear on the surrounding ground. As the two men stood and peered intently ahead, the guide slipped the safety off his rifle and moved up until he was abreast of the photographer. "I'll lead from here on in. He might not recognize the fact that you're the friendly type." The photographer fell behind the guide and they started toward the ridge that lay directly ahead.

About ten feet short of the ridge the guide went down on all fours and began creeping forward, always shifting his rifle so that it was ahead of him. The photographer checked the film advance lever on both cameras, depressed the button that allowed the meter to register the light intensity and took a quick reading off an area of neutral density supplied by sun-dried grass. He selected a shutter speed of one five-hundredth of a second to freeze whatever action he might encounter and rotated the stop ring on his lens until the indicator needle settled dead center on the dial. He then moved up to where the guide hunched just below the ridge.

The guide's whisper was clipped and barely audible. "Biggest goddam bear I've ever seen. Just take it slow and he's all yours." The photographer started toward the ridge an inch at a time. He was certain the bear on the other side could hear his heart pounding. He could feel it thudding against his chest wall, noted it pulsing in his right temple. When the downslope was within his range of vision he almost gasped aloud. Monarch was less than twenty-five feet away, methodically digging an enormous hole in the side of the hill. The photographer could sense the guide moving up beside him. Slowly he eased his camera up through the grass until the lens emerged into the clear. Moving with excruciating care, he brought his eye level with the viewfinder. Again with exaggerated slow motion he moved his hand forward and twisted the focusing ring on the lens. He selected the bear's ear as a target and rotated the ring until the two halves were joined in the split-image circle in the center of the viewing field. The whole scene came into focus and the photographer's hand slipped back from the lens to locate the button on top of the camera body.

Monarch had smelled out the new fox den site an hour before and for lack of anything better to do had begun to dig it out. The chances that he would realize any real profit from his labors were slim and yet he dug. As a born plunderer and hopeless drudge it was the kind of simple mechanical activity that he seemed to like. It was repetitive and energy-consuming and satisfied some need within him, a sort of motor response which no one quite understands but which can often be observed and must be significant. Monarch had already moved close to a hundred pounds of dirt when he heard the focal plane shutter slap across within the camera body, giving the sensitive color film its split second of sun. He looked up, sniffed around in a great circle, first facing up the slope and then down.

As he quartered away from the ridge the photographer advanced the film so slowly and deliberately that Monarch missed the slight sound. Momentarily satisfied that he was not in danger, he returned somewhat indifferently to his chores. The second time the shutter slipped past the opening and the reflex mirror swung out of the way, Monarch rose to his hind legs and began to cast around in earnest. The guide alongside the photographer was worried about the short expanse of open land that separated them from the now thoroughly alerted giant. He squeezed the photographer's arm firmly, a signal to hold off until the animal had settled down. One more picture could give their position away and a charge could follow with very little time for a clear, defensive shot. In order to bring his rifle up to ready and still keep the bear in view, the guide would have to reveal himself. He was not anxious to do that.

Monarch woofed several times. Each time the two men could see him hunch and push the sound forth. As long as he was only woofing, the guide felt that things would remain short of the danger point. But if he chopped his jaws just once, or coughed, the guide was determined to shoot. They were too close, the bear too big, and his reputation too bad. For surely this was the bear they called Monarch, the man-killer.

After several minutes of testing the air, the bear sank again to all four feet and shuffled toward his excavation. He was totally uninterested in it now and did no more than push at a little earth before sitting on his heavy haunches to stare down the hill toward the stream and brush that clustered together at the bottom. The afternoon sun slanted across the valley and caught the bear's chocolate fur in its yellowing rays. It was a magnificent moment, one the photographer would probably never know again. He couldn't resist and the shutter and mirror slapped again. In an instant the bear was on his feet facing uphill, thoroughly alert now, and angry.

All of the guide's instincts told him to shoot before the bear could charge, but something held him back. He didn't want to take that life. Something would be destroyed that might never be replaced. This was undoubtedly the outlaw bear, the one men spoke of almost as if he were an ancient legend. A charge seemed imminent and the distance could be covered by the bear on an uphill gallop in a matter of seconds. The hunter didn't even have the advantage of a rifle at the ready. In a way, it was a moment of truth for man and bear alike.

Monarch had located the sound, but the wind was still at his back so he couldn't quite get the scent. If the wind had shifted, his already short temper would have been inflamed by the man-smell and the charge would surely have come. Perhaps because the wind was from the wrong quarter, or for reasons we can never know, Monarch did not charge. He turned instead and shuffled down the hill. When his back was to them the two men eased forward and the photographer got three more shots of the retreating giant. They heard him in the brush after he was lost from view. He ripped a tree to the ground and roared once. Then all was quiet.

Both men sat on the ridge and stared into the little valley. The photographer turned to the guide, who was wiping the sweat from the band inside his cap, "Were you scared?" The guide looked at the man and smiled. "I got an image to maintain." The photographer smiled back and took out his own handkerchief. He felt a slight chill as the perspiration that had soaked his shirt began to evaporate. The wind had shifted and was now blowing from behind them.

JOHN McPHEE WAS BORN in Princeton, New Jersey, and later attended Princeton University and Cambridge University. As a staff writer for *The New Yorker,* he has traveled widely and written on a variety of subjects. His many books include *A Sense of Where You Are, The Pine Barrens, The Crofter and the Laird, The Survival of the Bark Canoe, The Curve of Binding Energy, Encounters with the Archdruid,* and *The Control of Nature.* In 1977 he was awarded an Academy-Institute Award for Literature from the American Academy and Institute of Arts and Letters. McPhee is currently Ferris Professor of Journalism at Princeton University and teaches a course entitled "The Literature of Fact."

In this selection from "The Encircled River," one of three sections in his Alaska book, *Coming into the Country* (1976), McPhee describes an encounter with a Barren Ground grizzly bear north of the Arctic Circle. Seeing the wild bear at home in its natural habitat profoundly moves McPhee, and provides him with an opportunity to reflect on bears: "This was [the grizzly's] country, clearly enough. To be there was to be incorporated, in however small a measure, into its substance—his country, and if you wanted to visit it you had better knock." The area through which John McPhee traveled on that trip—the Salmon and Kobuk river drainages—was set aside in 1980 as the Kobuk Valley National Park. "This was," McPhee wrote reverently, ". . . the most isolated wilderness I would ever see. . . ." The author leaves little doubt here but that the high point of the trip was the encounter with a grizzly in the wild.

3. THE ENCIRCLED RIVER

JOHN McPHEE

T H E RIVER WAS LOW, AND PAT POURCHOT HAD picked a site as far upstream as he judged we could be and still move in boats. We were on an island, with the transparent Salmon River on one side—hurrying, scarcely a foot deep—and a small slough on the other. Deeper pools, under bedrock ledges, were above us and below us. We built our fire on the lemon-sized gravel of what would in higher water be the riverbed, and we pitched the tents on slightly higher ground among open stands of willow, on sand that showed what Bob Fedeler called "the old tracks of a young griz." We would stay two nights, according to plan, before beginning the long descent to the Kobuk; and in the intervening day we would first assemble the kayaks and then be free to disperse and explore the terrain.

There was a sixth man with us, there at the beginning. His name was Jack Hession, and he was the Sierra Club's only salaried full-time representative in Alaska. Pourchot had invited him as an observer. The news that he was absent at the end of the trip could instantly cause hopes to rise in Alaska, where the Sierra Club has long been considered a netherworld force and Hession the resident Belial. Hession, though, was not going to perish on the Salmon. Pressures from Anchorage had travelled with him, and before long would get the better of him, and in cavalier manner—in this Arctic wilderness— he would bid us goodbye and set out early for home. Meanwhile, in the morning sun, we put together the collapsible kayaks—two single Kleppers and Snake Eyes. Hession's own single was the oldest of the three, and it had thirty-six parts, hardware not included. There were dowels of mountain ash and ribs of laminated Finnish birch, which fitted, one part to another, with hooks and clips until they formed a pair of nearly identical skeletal cones—the internal structures of halves of the boat. The skin was a limp bag made of blue canvas (the deck) and hemp-reinforced vulcanized rubber (the hull). The concept was to insert the skeletal halves into the skin and then figure out how to firm them together. We had trouble doing that. Hession, who ordinarily used rigid boats of fiberglass in his engagements with white water, could not remember how to complete the assembly. Stiff toward the ends and bent in the middle, his kayak had the look of a clip-on tie, and would do about as well in the river. We all crouched around and studied amidships—six men, a hundred miles up a stream, above sixty-seven degrees of latitude, with a limp kayak. No one was shy with suggestions, which were full of ingenuity but entirely failed to work. By trial and error, we finally figured it out. The last step in the assembly involved the center rib, and we set that inside the hull on a tilt and then tapped it with a rock and forced it toward the verti- cal. When the forcing rib reached ninety degrees to the longer axis of the craft, the rib snapped into place, and with that the entire boat became taut and yare. Clever man, Johann Klepper. He had orga- nized his foldboat in the way that the North American Indians had developed the construction of their bark canoes. Over the years, the Klepper company had simplified its process. Our other single kayak, the more recent model, had fewer and larger skeletal parts, and it went together more easily; but it was less streamlined than the first. Snake Eyes, for its part—all eight hundred dollars' worth of Snake Eyes—was new and had an interior of broad wooden slabs, conve- niently hinged. Snake Eyes had the least number of separate parts (only fifteen) and in the way it went together was efficient and simple. Its advanced design had been achieved with a certain loss of grace, however, and this was evident there on the gravel. The boat was lumpy, awkward, bulging—a kayak with elbows.

Toward noon and after an early lunch, we set off on foot for a look around. Pourchot went straight up the hills to the west, alone. Stell Newman and John Kauffmann intended lesser forays, nearer the campsite. I decided I'd go with Bob Fedeler, who, with Jack Hession, had the most ambitious plan. They were going north up the river some miles and then up the ridges to the east. I hoped my legs would hold up. I didn't want to embarrass myself, off somewhere in the hills, by snapping something, but I could not resist going along with Fedeler. After all, he was a habitat biologist, working for the state, and if the ground around here was not habitat then I would never be in country that was. The temperature had come up to seventy. The sky was blue, with moving clouds and intermittent sun. We stuffed our rain gear into day packs and started up the river.

Generally speaking, if I had a choice between hiking and peeling potatoes, I would peel the potatoes. I have always had a predilection for canoes on rivers and have avoided walking wherever possible. My experience, thus, was limited but did exist. My work had led me up the Sierra Nevada and across the North Cascades, and in various eras I had walked parts of the Long Trail, the Appalachian Trail, trails of New Hampshire, the Adirondacks. Here in the Brooks Range, of course, no one had been there clearing the path. A mile, steep or level, could demand a lot of time. You go along with only a general plan, free lance, guessing where the walking will be least difficult, making choices all the way. These are the conditions, and in ten minutes' time they present their story. The country is wild to the limits of the term. It would demean such a world to call it pre-Columbian. It is twenty times older than that, having assumed its present form ten thousand years ago, with the melting of the Wisconsin ice.

For several miles upstream, willow and alder pressed in on the river, backed by spruce and cottonwood, so the easiest path was the river itself. Gravel bars were now on one side, now the other, so we crossed and crossed again, taking off our boots and wading through the fast, cold water. I had rubber-bottomed leather boots (L. L. Bean's, which are much in use all over Alaska). Fedeler was wearing hiking boots, Hession low canvas sneakers. Hession had a floppy sun hat, too. He seemed to see no need to dress like Sir Edmund Hillary, or to leave the marks of waffles by the tracks of wolves. He was a brief, trim, lithe figure, who moved lightly and had seen a lot of such ground. He stopped and opened his jackknife, and stood it by a track in sand at the edge of the river. Other tracks were near. Two wolves running side by side. He took a picture of a track. We passed a deep pool where spring water came into the river, and where algae grew in response to its warmth. Grayling could winter there. Some were in the pool now—bodies stationary, fins in motion, in clear deep water as green as jade. Four mergansers swam up the river. We saw moose pellets in sand beyond the pool. I would not much want to be a moose just there, in a narrow V-shaped valley with scant protection of trees. We came, in fact, to the tree line not long thereafter. The trees simply stopped. We took a few more northward steps and were out of the boreal forest. Farther north, as far as land continued, there would be no more. I don't mean to suggest that we had stepped out of Sequoia National Park and onto an unvegetated plain. The woods behind us were spare in every sense, fingering up the river valley, reaching as far as they could go. Now the tundra, which had before been close behind the trees, came down to the banks of the river. We'd had enough of shoelaces and of bare feet crunching underwater stones, so we climbed up the west bank to walk on the tundra—which from the river had looked as smooth as a golf course. Possibly there is nothing as invitingly deceptive as a tundra-covered hillside. Distances over tundra, even when it is rising steeply, are like distances over water, seeming to be less than they are, defraying the suggestion of effort. The tundra surface, though, consists of many kinds of plants, most of which seem to be stemmed with wire configured to ensnare the foot. For years, my conception of tundra—based, I suppose, on photographs of the Canadian north and the plains of the Alaskan Arctic slope—was of a vast northern flatness, water-flecked, running level to every horizon. Tundra is not topography, however; it is a mat of vegetation, and it runs up the sides of prodigious declivities as well as across the broad plains. There are three varying types—wet tundra, on low flatland with much standing water; moist tundra, on slightly higher ground; and alpine tundra, like carpeted heather, rising on mountains and hills. We moved on, northward, over moist tundra, and the plants were often a foot or so in height. Moving through them was more like wading than walking, except where we followed game trails. Fortunately, these were numerous enough, and comfortably negotiable. They bore signs of everything that lived there. They were highways, share and share alike, for caribou, moose, bears, wolves—whose tracks, antlers, and feces were strewn along the right-of-way like beer cans at the edge of a road. While these game trails were the best thoroughfares in many hundreds of square miles, they were also the only ones, and they had a notable defect. They tended to vanish. The trails would go along, well cut and stamped out through moss campion, reindeer moss, sedge tussocks, crowberries, prostrate willows, dwarf birch, bog blueberries, white mountain avens, low-bush cranberries, lichens, Labrador tea; then, abruptly, and for no apparent reason, the trails would disappear. Their well-worn ruts suggested hundreds of animals, heavy traffic. So where did they go when the trail vanished? Fedeler did not know. I could not think of an explanation. Maybe Noah had got there a little before us.

On the far side of the river was an isolated tree, which had made a brave bid to move north, to extend the reach of its progenitive forest. The Brooks Range, the remotest uplift in North America, was made a little less remote, fifty years ago, by the writing of Robert Marshall, a forester, who described several expeditions to these mountains in a book called *Alaska Wilderness*. Marshall had a theory about the tree line, the boundary of the circumboreal world. He thought that white spruce and other species could live farther north, and that they were inching northward, dropping seeds ahead of them, a dead-slow advance under marginal conditions. Whatever it may have signified, the tree across the river was dead, and out of it now came a sparrow hawk, flying at us, shouting *kee kee kee,* and hovering on rapidly beating wings to study the creatures on the trail. There was not much it could do about us, and it went back to the tree.

The leaves of Labrador tea, crushed in the hand, smelled like a turpentine. The cranberries were early and sourer than they would eventually be. With the arrival of cold, they freeze on the vine, and when they thaw, six months later, they are somehow sweeter and contain more juice. Bears like overwintered berries. Blueberries, too, are sweeter after being frozen on the bush. Fried cranberries will help relieve a sore throat. Attacks in the gall bladder have been defused with boiled cranberries mixed with seal oil. The sedge tussocks were low and not as perilous as tussocks can be. They are grass that grows in bunches, more compact at the bottom than at the top—a mushroom shape that can spill a foot and turn an ankle. They were tiresome, and soon we were ready to move upward, away from the moist tundra and away from the river. Ahead we saw the configurations of the sharp small valleys of three streams meeting, forming there the principal stem of the Salmon. To the east, above the confluence, a tundra-bald hill rose a thousand feet and more. We decided to cross the river and go up the hill. Look around. Choose where to go from there.

The river was so shallow now that there was no need for removing boots. We walked across and began to climb. The going was steep. I asked Jack Hession how long he had been in Alaska, and he said seven years. He had been in Alaska longer than two-thirds of the people in the state. He was from California, and had lived more recently in western Washington, where he had begun to acquire his expertise in boats in white water. Like Fedeler—like me, for that matter—he was in good condition. Hession, though, seemed to float up the incline, while I found it hard, sweaty work. From across the river it had looked as easy as a short flight of stairs. I went up it a trudge at a time—on reindeer moss, heather, lupine. The sun had suddenly departed, and a cool rain began to fall. At the top of the hill, we sat on a rock outcropping and looked back at the river, twelve hundred feet below. Everywhere around us were mountains—steep, treeless, buff where still in the sun. One was bright silver. The rain felt good. We nibbled M&M's. They were even better than the rain. The streams far below, small and fast, came pummelling together and made the river. The land they fell through looked nude. It was all tundra, rising northward toward a pass at the range divide. Looking at so much mountain ground—this immense minute fragment of wilderness Alaska—one could wonder about the choice of words of people who say that it is fragile. "Fragile" just does not appear to be a proper term for a rugged, essentially uninvaded landscape covering tens of thousands of square miles—a place so vast and unpeopled that if anyone could figure out how to steal Italy, Alaska would be a place to hide it. Meanwhile, earnest ecologues write and speak about the "fragile" tundra, this "delicate" ocean of barren land. The words sound effete, but the terrain is nonetheless vulnerable. There is ice under the tundra, mixed with soil as permafrost, in some places two thousand feet deep. The tundra vegetation, living and dead, provides insulation that keeps the summer sun from melting the permafrost. If something pulls away the insulation and melting occurs, the soil will settle and the water may run off. The earth, in such circumstances, does not restore itself. In the nineteen-sixties, a bulldozer working for

Geophysical Service, Inc., an oil-exploration company, wrote the ini-
tials "G.S.I." in Arctic Alaskan tundra. The letters were two hundred
feet from top to bottom, and near them the bulldozer cut an arrow—
an indicator for pilots. Thermokarst (thermal erosion) followed, and
slumpage. The letters and the arrow are now odd-shaped ponds,
about eight feet deep. For many generations that segment of tundra
will say "G.S.I." Tundra is even sensitive to snow machines. They com-
press snow, and cut off much of the air that would otherwise get to the
vegetation. Evidence appears in summer. The snow machines have
left brown trails on ground they never touched.

Both sunlight and rain were falling on us now. We had a topographic map, of the largest scale available but nonetheless of scant
detail—about five miles to half a thumb. Of the three streams that
met below us, the nearest was called Sheep Creek. A rainbow wicketed
its steep valley. The top of the arch was below us. The name Sheep
Creek was vestigial. "Historically, there were Dall sheep in these
mountains," Fedeler said.

"What happened to them?"

"Who knows?" He shrugged. "Things go in cycles. They'll be
back."

Alders had crept into creases in the mountainside across the
Salmon valley. I remarked on the borderline conditions in evidence
everywhere in this spare and beautiful country, and said, "Look at
those alders over there, clinging to life."

Fedeler said, "It's hungry country, that's for sure. Drainage and
exposure make *the* difference."

We ate peanuts and raisins and more M&M's—and, feeling
rested, became ambitious. On a long southward loop back to camp,
we would extend our walk by going around a mountain that was separated from us by what looked to be the fairly steep declivity of a tributary drainage. The terrain sloped away to the southwest toward the
mouth of the tributary. We would go down for a time, and then cross
the tributary and cut back around the mountain.

We passed first through stands of fireweed, and then over ground
that was wine-red with the leaves of bearberries. There were curlew-
berries, too, which put a deep-purple stain on the hand. We kicked
at some wolf scat, old as winter. It was woolly and white and filled
with the hair of a snowshoe hare. Nearby was a rich inventory of caribou pellets and, in increasing quantity as we moved downhill,

blueberries—an outspreading acreage of blueberries. Fedeler stopped walking. He touched my arm. He had in an instant become even more alert than he usually was, and obviously apprehensive. His gaze followed straight on down our intended course. What he saw there I saw now. It appeared to me to be a hill of fur. "Big boar grizzly," Fedeler said in a near-whisper. The bear was about a hundred steps away, in the blueberries, grazing. The head was down, the hump high. The immensity of muscle seemed to vibrate slowly—to expand and contract, with the grazing. Not berries alone but whole bushes were going into the bear. He was big for a Barren Ground grizzly. The brown bears of Arctic Alaska (or grizzlies; they are no longer thought to be different) do not grow to the size they will reach on more ample diets elsewhere. The Barren Ground grizzly will rarely grow larger than six hundred pounds.

"What if he got too close?" I said.

Fedeler said, "We'd be in real trouble."

"You can't outrun them," Hession said.

A grizzly, no slower than a racing horse, is about half again as fast as the fastest human being. Watching the great mound of weight in the blueberries, with a fifty-five-inch waist and a neck more than thirty inches around, I had difficulty imagining that he could move with such speed, but I believed it, and was without impulse to test the proposition. Fortunately, a light southerly wind was coming up the Salmon valley. On its way to us, it passed the bear. The wind was relieving, coming into our faces, for had it been moving the other way the bear would not have been placidly grazing. There is an old adage that when a pine needle drops in the forest the eagle will see it fall; the deer will hear it when it hits the ground; the bear will smell it. If the boar grizzly were to catch our scent, he might stand on his hind legs, the better to try to see. Although he could hear well and had an extraordinary sense of smell, his eyesight was not much better than what was required to see a blueberry inches away. For this reason, a grizzly stands and squints, attempting to bring the middle distance into focus, and the gesture is often misunderstood as a sign of anger and forthcoming attack. If the bear were getting ready to attack, he would be on four feet, head low, ears cocked, the hair above his hump muscle standing on end. As if that message were not clear enough, he would also chop his jaws. His teeth would make a sound that would carry like the ringing of an axe.

One could predict, but not with certainty, what a grizzly would do. Odds were very great that one touch of man scent would cause him to stop his activity, pause in a moment of absorbed and alert curiosity, and then move, at a not undignified pace, in a direction other than the one from which the scent was coming. That is what would happen almost every time, but there was, to be sure, no guarantee. The forest Eskimos fear and revere the grizzly. They know that certain individual bears not only will fail to avoid a person who comes into their country but will approach and even stalk the trespasser. It is potentially inaccurate to extrapolate the behavior of any one bear from the behavior of most, since they are both intelligent and independent and will do what they choose to do according to mood, experience, whim. A grizzly that has ever been wounded by a bullet will not forget it, and will probably know that it was a human being who sent the bullet. At sight of a human, such a bear will be likely to charge. Grizzlies hide food sometimes—a caribou calf, say, under a pile of scraped-up moss—and a person the bear might otherwise ignore might suddenly not be ignored if the person were inadvertently to step into the line between the food cache and the bear. A sow grizzly with cubs, of course, will charge anything that suggests danger to the cubs, even if the cubs are nearly as big as she is. They stay with their mother two and a half years.

None of us had a gun. (None of the six of us had brought a gun on the trip.) Among nonhunters who go into the terrain of the grizzly, there are several schools of thought about guns. The preferred one is: Never go without a sufficient weapon—a high-powered rifle or a shotgun and plenty of slug-loaded shells. The option is not without its own inherent peril. A professional hunter, some years ago, spotted a grizzly from the air and—with a client, who happened to be an Anchorage barber—landed on a lake about a mile from the bear. The stalking that followed was evidently conducted not only by the hunters but by the animal as well. The professional hunter was found dead from a broken neck, and had apparently died instantly, unaware of danger, for the cause of death was a single bite, delivered from behind. The barber, noted as clumsy with a rifle, had emptied his magazine, missing the bear with every shot but one, which struck the grizzly in the foot. The damage the bear did to the barber was enough to kill him several times. After the corpses were found, the bear was tracked and killed. To shoot and merely wound is worse than not to shoot at all. A bear that might have turned and gone away will possibly attack if wounded.

Fatal encounters with bears are as rare as they are memorable. Some people reject the rifle as cumbersome extra baggage, not worth toting, given the minimal risk. And, finally, there are a few people who feel that it is wrong to carry a gun, in part because the risk is low and well worth taking, but most emphatically because they see the gun as an affront to the wild country of which the bear is sign and symbol. This, while strongly felt, is a somewhat novel attitude. When Robert Marshall explored the Brooks Range half a century ago, he and his companions fired at almost every bear they saw, without pausing for philosophical reflection. The reaction was automatic. They were expressing mankind's immemorial fear of this beast—man and rattlesnake, man and bear. Among modern environmentalists, to whom a figure like Marshall is otherwise a hero, fear of the bear has been exceeded by reverence. A notable example, in his own past and present, is Andy Russell, author of a book called *Grizzly Country.* Russell was once a professional hunter, but he gave that up to become a photographer, specializing in grizzlies. He says that he has given up not only shooting bears but even carrying a gun. On rare instances when grizzlies charge toward him, he shouts at them and stands his ground. The worst thing to do, he says, is to run, because anything that runs on open tundra suggests game to a bear. Game does not tend to stand its ground in the presence of grizzlies. Therefore, when the bear comes at you, just stand there. Charging something that does not move, the bear will theoretically stop and reconsider. (Says Russell.) More important, Russell believes that the bear will *know* if you have a gun, even if the gun is concealed:

> Reviewing our experiences, we had become more and more convinced that carrying arms was not only unnecessary in most grizzly country but was certainly no good for the desired atmosphere and proper protocol in obtaining good film records. If we were to obtain such film and fraternize successfully with the big bears, it would be better to go unarmed in most places. The mere fact of having a gun within reach, cached somewhere in a pack or a hidden holster, causes a man to act with unconscious arrogance and thus maybe to smell different or to transmit some kind of signal objectionable to bears. The armed man

does not assume his proper role in association with the wild ones, a fact of which they seem instantly aware at some distance. He, being wilder than they, whether he likes to admit it or not, is instantly under even more suspicion than he would encounter if unarmed.

One must follow the role of an uninvited visitor—an intruder—rather than that of an aggressive hunter, and one should go unarmed to insure this attitude.

Like pictures from pages riffled with a thumb, all of these things went through my mind there on the mountainside above the grazing bear. I will confess that in one instant I asked myself, "What the hell am I doing *here?*" There was nothing more to the question, though, than a hint of panic. I knew why I had come, and therefore what I was doing there. That I was frightened was incidental. I just hoped the fright would not rise beyond a relatively decorous level. I sensed that Fedeler and Hession were somewhat frightened, too. I would have been troubled if they had not been. Meanwhile, the sight of the bear stirred me like nothing else the country could contain. What mattered was not so much the bear himself as what the bear implied. He was the predominant thing in that country, and for him to be in it at all meant that there had to be more country like it in every direction and more of the same kind of country all around that. He implied a world. He was an affirmation to the rest of the earth that his kind of place was extant. There had been a time when his race was everywhere in North America, but it had been hunted down and pushed away in favor of something else. For example, the grizzly bear is the state animal of California, whose country was once his kind of place; and in California now the grizzly is extinct.

The animals I have encountered in my wilderness wanderings have been reluctant to reveal all the things about them I would like to know. The animal that impresses me most, the one I find myself liking more and more, is the grizzly. No sight encountered in the wilds is quite so stirring as those massive, clawed tracks pressed into mud or snow. No sight is quite so impressive as that of the great bear stalking across some mountain slope with the fur of his silvery robe rippling over his mighty muscles. His is a dignity and power matched by no other in the North

American wilderness. To share a mountain with him for a while is a privilege and an adventure like no other.

I have followed his tracks into an alder hell to see what he had been doing and come to the abrupt end of them, when the maker stood up thirty feet away with a sudden snort to face me.

To see a mother grizzly ambling and loafing with her cubs across the broad, hospitable bosom of a flower-spangled mountain meadow is to see life in true wilderness at its best.

If a wolf kills a caribou, and a grizzly comes along while the wolf is feeding on the kill, the wolf puts its tail between its legs and hurries away. A black bear will run from a grizzly, too. Grizzlies sometimes kill and eat black bears. The grizzly takes what he happens upon. He is an opportunistic eater. The predominance of the grizzly in his terrain is challenged by nothing but men and ravens. To frustrate ravens from stealing his food, he will lie down and sleep on top of a carcass, occasionally swatting the birds as if they were big black flies. He prefers a vegetable diet. He can pulp a moosehead with a single blow, but he is not lusting always to kill, and when he moves through his country he can be something munificent, going into copses of willow among unfleeing moose and their calves, touching nothing, letting it all breathe as before. He may, though, get the head of a cow moose between his legs and rake her flanks with the five-inch knives that protrude from the ends of his paws. Opportunistic. He removes and eats her entrails. He likes porcupines, too, and when one turns and presents to him a pygal bouquet of quills, he will leap into the air, land on the other side, chuck the fretful porpentine beneath the chin, flip it over, and, with a swift ventral incision, neatly remove its body from its skin, leaving something like a sea urchin behind him on the ground. He is nothing if not athletic. Before he dens, or just after he emerges, if his mountains are covered with snow he will climb to the brink of some impossible schuss, sit down on his butt, and shove off. Thirty-two, sixty-four, ninety-six feet per second, he plummets down the mountainside, spray snow flying to either side, as he approaches collision with boulders and trees. Just short of catastrophe, still going at bonecrushing speed, he flips to his feet and walks sedately onward as if his ride had not occurred.

His population density is thin on the Arctic barren ground. He needs for his forage at least fifty and perhaps a hundred square miles that are all his own—sixty-four thousand acres, his home range. Within it, he will move, typically, eight miles a summer day, doing his travelling through the twilight hours of the dead of night. To scratch his belly he walks over a tree—where forest exists. The tree bends beneath him as he passes. He forages in the morning, generally; and he rests a great deal, particularly after he eats. He rests fourteen hours a day. If he becomes hot in the sun, he lies down in a pool in the river. He sleeps on the tundra—restlessly tossing and turning, forever changing position. What he could be worrying about I cannot imagine.

His fur blends so well into the tundra colors that sometimes it is hard to see him. Fortunately, we could see well enough the one in front of us, or we would have walked right to him. He caused a considerable revision of our travel plans. Not wholly prepared to follow the advice of Andy Russell, I asked Fedeler what one should do if a bear were to charge. He said, "Take off your pack and throw it into the bear's path, then crawl away, and hope the pack will distract the bear. But there is no good thing to do, really. It's just not a situation to be in."

We made a hundred-and-forty-degree turn from the course we had been following and went up the shoulder of the hill through everthickening brush, putting distance behind us in good position with the wind. For a time, we waded through hip-deep willow, always making our way uphill, and the going may have been difficult, but I didn't notice. There was adrenaline to spare in my bloodstream. I felt that I was floating, climbing with ease, like Hession. I also had expectations now that another bear, in the thick brush, might come rising up from any quarter. We broke out soon into a swale of blueberries. Hession and Fedeler, their nonchalance refreshed, sat down to eat, paused to graze. The berries were sweet and large.

"I can see why he's here," Hession said.

"These berries are so big."

"Southern exposure."

"He may not be the only one."

"They can be anywhere."

"It's amazing to me," Fedeler said. "So large an animal, living up here in this country. It's amazing what keeps that big body alive." Fedeler went on eating the blueberries with no apparent fear of growing fat. The Barren Ground bear digs a lot of roots, he said—the roots of milk vetch, for example, and Eskimo potatoes. The bear, coming out of his den into the snows of May, goes down into the river bottoms, where overwintered berries are first revealed. Wolf kills are down there, too. By the middle of June, his diet is almost wholly vegetable. He eats willow buds, sedges, cotton-grass tussocks. In the cycle of his year, roots and plants are eighty per cent of what he eats, and even when the salmon are running he does not sate himself on them alone but forages much of the time for berries. In the fall, he unearths not only roots but ground squirrels and lemmings. It is indeed remarkable how large he grows on the provender of his yearly cycle, for on this Arctic barren ground he has to work much harder than the brown bears of southern Alaska, which line up along foaming rivers—hip to hip, like fishermen in New Jersey—taking forty-pound king salmon in their jaws as if they were nibbling feed from a barnyard trough. When the caribou are in fall migration, moving down the Salmon valley toward the Kobuk, the bear finishes up his year with one of them. Then, around the first of November, he may find a cave or, more likely, digs out a cavern in a mountainside. If he finds a natural cave, it may be full of porcupines. He kicks them out, and—extending his curious relationship with this animal—will cushion his winter bed with many thousands of their turds. If, on the other hand, he digs his den, he sends earth flying out behind him and makes a shaft that goes upward into the side of the mountain. At the top of the shaft, he excavates a shelf-like cavern. When the outside entrance is plugged with debris, the shaft becomes a column of still air, insulating the upper chamber, trapping the bear's body heat. On a bed of dry vegetation, he lays himself out like a dead pharaoh in a pyramid. But he does not truly hibernate. He just lies there. His mate of the summer, in her den somewhere, will give birth during winter to a cub or two—virtually hairless, blind, weighing about a pound. But the male has nothing to do. His heart rate goes down as low as eight beats a minute. He sleeps and wakes, and sleeps again. He may decide to get up and go out. But that is rare. He may even stay out, which is rarer—to give up denning for that winter and roam his frozen range. If he does this, sooner or later he will find a patch of open water in an otherwise frozen river, and in refreshing himself he will no doubt wet his fur. Then he rolls in the snow, and the fur acquires a thick plate of ice, which is less disturbing to the animal than to the forest Eskimo, who has for ages feared—feared most of all—the "winter bear."

Arrows broke against the armoring ice, and it can be heavy enough to stop a bullet.

We moved on now, in continuing retreat, and approached the steep incline of the tributary valley we'd been skirting when the bear rewrote our plans. We meant to put the valley between us and him and reschedule ourselves on the other side. It was in fact less a valley than an extremely large ravine, which plunged maybe eight hundred feet, and then rose up an even steeper incline some fifteen hundred feet on the other side, toward the top of which the bushy vegetation ceased growing. The walking looked promising on the ridge beyond.

I had hoped we might see a den site, and this might have been the place. It had all the requisites but one. It was a steep hillside with southern exposure, and was upgrown with a hell of alders and willows. Moreover, we were on the south side of the Brooks Range divide, which is where most of the dens are. But we were not high enough. We were at something under two thousand feet, and bears in this part of Alaska like to den much higher than that. They want the very best drainage. One way to become a "winter bear" is to wake up in a flooded den.

The willow-alder growth was so dense and high that as we went down the hillside we could see no farther than a few yards ahead. It was wet in there from the recent rain. We broke our way forward with the help of gravity, crashing noisily, all but trapped in the thicket. It was a patch of jungle, many acres of jungle, with stems a foot apart and as thick as our arms, and canopies more than twelve feet high. This was bear habitat, the sort of place bears like better than people do. Our original choice had been wise—to skirt this ravine-valley—but now we were in it and without choice.

"This is the sort of place to come upon one of them unexpectedly," Hession said.

"And there is no going back," Fedeler said. "You can't walk uphill in this stuff."

"Good point," Hession said.

I might have been a little happier if I had been in an uninstrumented airplane in heavy mountain cloud. We thunked and crashed for fifteen minutes and finally came out at the tributary stream. Our approach flushed a ptarmigan, willow ptarmigan; and grayling—at sight of us—shot around in small, cold pools. The stream was narrow, and alders pressed over it from either side. We drank, and rested, and looked up the slope in front of us, which must have had an incline of fifty degrees. The ridge at the top looked extremely far away. Resting, I became aware of a considerable ache in my legs and a blister on one of my heels. On the way uphill we became separated, Hession angling off to the right, Fedeler and I to the left. We groped for handholds among bushes that protruded from the flaky schist, and pulled ourselves up from ledge to ledge. The adrenaline was gone, and my legs were turning to stone. I was ready to dig a den and get in it. My eyes kept addressing the ridgeline, far above. If eyes were hands they could have pulled me there. Then, suddenly, from far below, I saw Jack Hession lightly ambling along the ridge—in his tennis shoes, in his floppy cotton hat. He was looking around, killing time, waiting up for us.

Things seemed better from the ridge. The going would be level for a time. We sat down and looked back, to the north, across the deep tributary valley, and with my monocular tried to glass the grazing bear. No sight or sign of him. Above us now was a broadly conical summit, and spread around its western flank was a mile, at least, of open alpine tundra. On a contour, we headed south across it—high above, and two miles east of, the river. We saw what appeared to be a cairn on the next summit south, and decided to go to it and stand on it and see if we could guess—in relation to our campsite—where we were. Now the walking felt good again. We passed a large black pile of grizzly scat. "When it's steaming, that's when you start looking around for a tree," Hession said. This particular scat had sent up its last vapors many days before. Imagining myself there at such a time, though, I looked around idly for a tree. The nearest one behind us that was of more than dwarf or thicket stature was somewhere in Lapland. Ahead of us, however, across the broad dome of tundra, was a dark stand of white spruce, an extremity of the North American forest, extending toward us. The trees were eight hundred yards away. Black bears, frightened, sometimes climb trees. Grizzlies almost never climb trees.

At seven in the evening, after wading up a slope of medium to heavy brush, we came out onto more smooth tundra and reached the hilltop of the apparent cairn. It was a rock outcropping, and we sat on it in bright sunshine and looked at the circumvallate mountains. A great many of them had such outcroppings projecting from their ridges, and they much resembled the cairns shepherds build on bald summits in Scotland. For that matter, they suggested the cairns—closer to the Kobuk—that forest Eskimos once used in methodical slaughter of caribou. The cairns were built on the high tundra in a great V, open end to the north, and they served as a funnel for the southbound herd. To the approaching caribou, the cairns were meant to suggest Eskimos, and to reinforce the impression Eskimos spaced themselves between cairns. At the point of the V, as many caribou as were needed were killed and the rest were let through.

Before us now, lying on the tundra that stretched away toward the river we saw numerous caribou antlers. The Arctic herd cyclically chooses various passes and valleys in making its way south across the range, and of late has been favoring, among other places, the Salmon and Hunt River drainages. Bleached white, the antlers protruded from the tundra like the dead branches of buried trees. When the forest Eskimo of old went to stalk the grizzly bear, he carried in his hand a spear, the tip of which was made from bear bone or, more often, from the antler of the caribou. A bearskin was the door of an Eskimo's home if the occupant had ever killed a bear, for it symbolized the extraordinary valor of the hunter within. When the man drew close and the bear stood on its hind legs, the man ran under this eave of flesh and set the shaft of the spear firmly on the ground, then ducked out from under the swinging, explosive paws. The bear lunged forward onto the spear and died.

Eskimo knife handles were also made from caribou antlers, and icepicks to penetrate the surface of the river, and sinkers for the bottoms of willow-bark seines, and wood-splitting wedges, and arrowheads. All caribou, male and female, grow antlers. The horns of sheep, cattle, buffalo consist of extremely dense, compactly matted hair. The antler of the caribou is calcareous. It is hard bone, with the strength of wrought iron. Moving downhill and south across the tundra, we passed through groves of antlers. It was as if the long filing lines of the spring migration had for some reason paused here for shedding to occur. The antlers, like the bear, implied the country. Most were white, gaunt, chalky. I picked up a younger one, though, that was recently shed and was dark, like polished brown marble. It was about four feet along the beam and perfect in form. Hession found one like it. We set them on our shoulders and moved on down the hill, intent to take them home.

We headed for the next of the riverine mountains, where we

planned to descend and—if our calculations were accurate—meet the
river at the campsite. The river, far below us, now and again came into
view as we walked abreast over open tundra. Fedeler, even more alert
than usual, now stopped and, as before, touched my arm. He pointed
toward the river. If a spruce needle had been floating on the water
there, Fedeler would have seen it. We saw in an instant that we had
miscalculated and were heading some miles beyond the campsite and
would have come eventually to the river not knowing—upstream or
downstream—which way to go. Fedeler was pointing toward a gravel
bar, a thin column of smoke, minute human figures near the smoke,
and the podlike whiteness of the metal canoe.

Another two miles, descending, and we were barefoot in the river,
with pink hot feet turning anesthetically cold. We crossed slowly. The
three others were by the campfire. On the grill were grayling and a fil-
leted Arctic char. The air was cool now, nearing fifty, and we ate the
fish, and beef stew, and strawberries, and drank hot chocolate. After a
time, Hession said, "That was a good walk. That was some of the easiest hiking you will ever find in Alaska."

We drew our route on the map and figured the distance at fourteen miles. John Kauffmann, tapping his pipe on a stone, said, "That's
a lot for Alaska."

We sat around the campfire for at least another hour. We talked
of rain and kestrels, oil and antlers, the height and the headwaters of
the river. Neither Hession nor Fedeler once mentioned the bear.

When I got into my sleeping bag, though, and closed my eyes,
there he was, in color, on the side of the hill. The vision was indelible,
but fear was not what put it there. More, it was a sense of sheer luck at
having chosen in the first place to follow Fedeler and Hession up the
river and into the hills—a memento not so much of one moment as of
the entire circuit of the long afternoon. It was a vision of a whole land,
with an animal in it. This was his country, clearly enough. To be there
was to be incorporated, in however small a measure, into its substance—his country, and if you wanted to visit it you had better knock.

His association with other animals is a mixture of enterprising
action, almost magnanimous acceptance, and just plain willingness to ignore. There is great strength and pride combined with
a strong mixture of inquisitive curiosity in the make-up of grizzly character. This curiosity is what makes trouble when men

penetrate into country where they are not known to the bear. The grizzly can be brave and sometimes downright brash. He can be secretive and very retiring. He can be extremely cunning and also powerfully aggressive. Whatever he does, his actions match his surroundings and the circumstances of the moment. No wonder that meeting him on his mountain is a momentous event, imprinted on one's mind for life.

RICHARD NELSON IS A cultural anthropologist and nature
writer who lives on a large island in the Alaskan panhandle. His
several books include *Hunters of the Northern Ice* (1971), *Hunters of
the Northern Forest: Designs for Survival Along the Alaskan Kutchin*
(1977), *Make Prayers to the Raven: A Koyukon View of the Northern
Forest* (1983), and, most recently, *The Island Within* (1990). He is
currently writing a book about the coastal black-tailed deer of
Southeast Alaska, which he has studied intensively for a number
of years. Nelson has devoted his life to nature conservation and to
documenting and preserving traditional Amerindian cultures,
particularly those of the Pacific Northwest and Alaska.

Intimacy with and respect for nature is central to the culture
of the Koyukon Athapaskan Indians, who inhabit a vast region in
the western Interior of Alaska. In this selection from *Make Prayers
to the Raven,* we catch a glimpse of how these Native Americans
view the grizzly: "Koyukon people have great respect for the
unpredictability, aggressiveness, tenacity, and physical power of
brown bears. . . . When a man comes across brown bear tracks on
the fall snow, he is likely to leave the area immediately." Their
dealings with the grizzly are full of taboos: men "avoid talking
about the brown bear around women or children" and are
"extremely circumspect" when planning hunts. It is "especially
bad, perhaps fatally so, to brag about hunting the brown bear." In
the northern forests of the Koyukon Athapaskan, only the
"wolverine has a more powerful spirit."

"Brown Bear," taken from Richard Nelson's Make Prayers to the
Raven: A Koyukon View of the Northern Forest *(University of
Chicago Press, 1983), is reprinted by permission of Richard Nelson.*

*All references to anthropological sources in the Nelson selection can be
found in the bibliography of* Make Prayers to the Raven.

4. BROWN BEAR

RICHARD NELSON

W E COME NOW UPON AN EVEN GREATER POWER, ONE whose physical and spiritual presence moves menacingly through the Koyukon world, whose very name should be spoken with utmost caution, if at all. Nearly everything that is done to respect and placate the black bear is also done for the brown bear; but the acts and emotions are intensified, the danger and fear are greater, the consequences of error more grievous. I noticed that the tone of people's voices often became lower and softer when they talked of this animal. This, as much as the words they spoke, revealed the meaning of the bear in their lives. For nothing else that visibly or invisibly occupies the wildland did I hear this change of voice.

Not surprisingly, Sullivan writes that the Nulato Koyukon invest this animal with the strongest of all spirits (1942:85). But my instructors from the Koyukuk River villages held without exception that the wolverine has a more powerful spirit, though the animal is not physically threatening like the bear. Perhaps it is this difference—the bear is dangerous in two ways and the wolverine in only one—that accounts for the Koyukon people's seemingly unparalleled feeling of awe toward brown bears.

A creature of the open slopes and high mountain tundra, the brown bear is not often encountered in forested river valleys. In former times, older Koyukon people say, its tracks were never seen away from the mountains, but over the past forty years or so it has spread gradually down into the flats. "When I was a kid," a Huslia woman recalled, "we could walk anywhere without a gun. No brown bears or moose around here. But now it's not like that, and we've got to be more careful." Nevertheless, brown bears are not at all common anywhere, and it is unusual to see one.

Biologists have had difficulty with the taxonomy of these animals. Most recently they have preferred brown bear as the English name and *Ursus arctos* as its scientific designation. This lumps the inland and coastal populations together, though common usage in Alaska differentiates them as grizzly bears and brown bears. The coastal bears are larger and often darker. Interior bears range from five hundred to eight hundred pounds (for males); they are brownish, with noticeably humped shoulders and very long claws.

A carefully maintained code of etiquette governs naming of the brown bear in Koyukon. My teachers in Koyukuk villages gave it the basic name *ghonoy tlaaga,* which they translated "bad animal." This word is used only by men, and when women are within hearing they call it simply *ghonoya.* If a woman used these proper names the bear would be angered and offended, and bad luck would come as a result. Instead, she should refer to it obliquely as *dlil ta bahoolaance,* "those who are in the mountains." In English the women usually call it "big animal," again to avoid the familiarity of its true name.

Jetté (n.d.*a.*) mentions a variety of the brown bear reputed to be exceptionally fierce and of lighter color than usual. It is called *tsoltl'deenaalaaya,* a name that translates metaphorically as "that which doesn't have long belly moss." However, to avoid directly naming this animal, people may refer to it as "the one we call the shrew" (*loodolts'iyhdla dozeel'aana*).

I was told about two varieties of the brown bear. One is found in the Kanuti (*Kk'oonootna*) River country and is described as lean-bodied, long-legged, and especially aggressive toward people (I did not learn a special name for this variety). The other is oddly proportioned, with a small body but abnormally large head and feet. It is said to be quick, powerful, and extremely dangerous, and it is fittingly named *bik'ints'itldaadla,* "keep out of its way." In the early days men would never even try to kill one of these creatures, because it was too much for a spear. The late Edwin Simon and his companion once saw one of them in the mountains, and since they had powerful rifles they tried to intercept it. "But it moved so fast, just like a ptarmigan, and there was no way to catch it." This is the most dangerous kind of bear—"If he sees you, I don't think he'll back away from you."

Someone not familiar with its habits might expect the brown bear to be a rapacious predator, but generally it is not. Its omnivorous diet includes a wide assortment of plants and roots, carrion, small animals like ground squirrels, and occasionally large game. Koyukon elders say that a brown bear will sometimes stalk a moose while it is lying down, then jump onto its back and kill it. In October and November, black bears often become prey to their larger relative. Hunters occasionally find a brown bear's track wandering widely over the countryside, investigating every potential den from which a black bear might be pulled. In turn, both brown and black bears are sometimes attacked and killed by wolves, proving again the efficiency of the social predator.

Needless to say, Koyukon people have great respect for the unpredictability, aggressiveness, tenacity, and physical power of brown bears. Unnecessary encounters are strictly avoided, and any approach to them is made with utmost caution, very different from the confidence hunters show in pursuing the milder, more predictable black bear. When a man comes across brown bear tracks on the fall snow, he is likely to leave the area immediately. If he returns to hunt the bear he will probably bring along a group of men. Then if the bear is found it can be killed with a volley of bullets, insuring against anyone's being hurt. People emphasize that this is a very difficult animal to kill, that a man alone could shoot it many times and still be attacked. There are many stories about wounded bears charging hunters, though all of them end without harm being done.

I cannot overstress the caution Koyukon hunters exercise when these creatures are involved. They always carry heavy rifles for fall den hunting, largely in case they meet a brown bear. People apparently do not hunt brown bears in their dens, I suspect because it is considered too dangerous and because such a den is rarely discovered. If hunters find brown bear tracks they avoid moving upwind of them, lest the animal begin stalking their scent. And even a group of men, after locating a bear, will all shoot it at once from a good distance. One man who described several brown bear hunts to me ended each story by saying, "We got rid of that one." It underscored his feeling that these animals are not only a resource but also a menace.

Brown bears seem to keep away from people, but there are occasional exceptions. A few years ago, for example, two men were charged by an unprovoked bear, but the animal was stopped by a lane of open water in the otherwise frozen Koyukuk River. They hurried back to their camp, keeping a close watch for the animal. A short while later it came up the riverbank toward their camp and they killed it. The bear was in very poor condition and was obviously hunting them. The man who told me this story ended with a warning: "When you come across a mean grizzly, either you kill the bear or it kills you." And he added that "mean bears" are often ones that have been wounded earlier and are in poor condition because of it. For this reason a hunter should always do everything possible to track down and kill a bear he has wounded.

Most of the rules and gestures for proper treatment of living brown bears are the same as those I discussed for black bears, but doubly important. For example, if someone is confronted by a threatening brown bear, talking to it will usually soothe the animal and calm it down or else drive it away. People say a brown bear is more likely to respond to this than a black bear.

Men should generally avoid talking about the brown bear around women or children. When they discuss plans to hunt this animal, men are extremely circumspect. A man who has found brown bear tracks may go and ask others to help him hunt it, but he will make no mention of its name: "I came to talk to you, cousin. A big animal has been bothering my trail, and I want to find men to go after it. Be sure that no one talks about it." The man who told me this added, "One year I did this with another guy and we took our two boys along, but we didn't even tell them what we were going to hunt."

It would be especially bad, perhaps fatally so, to brag about hunting the brown bear—to say something like, "I'm going to go out and kill such-and-such animal." One man who did this was later attacked and seriously injured. Similarly, no one should ever lie or exaggerate about brown bears, for example, claiming to have seen one when he had only found tracks. "That animal might come back to you, let you know about it." If a man kills one of these bears he does not announce it immediately when he comes home, but will let people know by making obvious hints some hours afterward. At Huslia I went to see a movie called *Night of the Grizzly,* and in it a boy shouted triumphantly to his mother that he had killed a menacing bear. As we left the movie, a man shook his head and commented to me: "Gee, that was real *hutlaanee* [taboo] there, the way he just shouted that he killed the bear!"

Women should not speak much of brown bears, cannot hunt them, and must look away if one should come within their sight. When two of my Koyukon instructors visited my home in Southeast Alaska, we chanced upon a brown bear:

> Catherine saw the animal before any of us, and even though it was far off she mumbled softly that "a dark thing" was on the far riverbank. When we did not understand, she finally said, "A big animal is over there," without pointing and while looking in the opposite direction. Our boat drifted toward the animal. It showed little fear, and as we approached Catherine remained silent, her eyes averted and her back partly toward it, her entire countenance almost morose. Everything about her expressed the danger of a woman coming so close to a creature of such spiritual power. I do not believe I ever saw her more serious than during those minutes before the great bear finally turned and ambled into the brush. [Journal, July 1978]

Men who do not precisely follow the rules for respect toward brown bears will have difficulty finding them. They might pass one right by and not see it, though they may notice its tracks after it is gone. The bear is simply not giving itself to them, though it may come easily to someone else. Sometimes a man tries to shoot a brown bear from good range, but nothing happens even though the bullets "couldn't miss." This means more than just bad luck with the animal—it is a sign that the hunter or someone in his family will encounter misfortune, perhaps illness or death.

When a brown bear has been killed, none of its meat should be brought into the village for some days or weeks; it is too fresh and potent with easily affronted spiritual energy. During earlier years, in fact, it was left in a cache at the kill site until the midwinter potlatch

memorializing people who had died in the previous year. The meat
was finally brought in just before it was cooked. Nowadays it is left
"out there someplace" at least until it is frozen. Doing this ensures
that the meat is fully dead before it comes near the dangerous presence of women. And it eliminates all chances of getting the animal's
blood on the sled, canvas cover, or anything a woman might later
touch or step over.

Each brown bear that is taken receives a ritual feast, just as is done
for a black bear (I have not attended one, but I was not told of any dif-
ferences). The meat is also used for village potlatches, after being
cooked in a bachelor's house where no woman will come near it.
Women must take care never to breathe the steam from the cooking
brown bear meat, or even to smell it. And the meat or any part of this
animal is strictly tabooed for women, except perhaps the very old.
When it is present at a potlatch an older man sees that it is set well
apart from everything else, and when it is passed out he makes sure
that each recipient is told what it is—this way no woman will acciden-
tally eat or handle it. Violating these taboos would make a woman
mean, insane, or physically ill.

Aside from the complete taboo against women eating brown bear,
I learned only one further restriction that applies to men. Nothing
from the animal's head should be eaten by young men—in fact, it is
best avoided by anyone—because it can cause meanness and quick
temper. The brain should always be removed and burned; and one
elder advised hanging the skull in a tree somewhere near a regularly
used trail, where it can be seen but not approached too closely. "That
way people can see that one of those bears has been killed."

Brown bears are less tasty than their smaller counterparts, and
their quality is unpredictable. Even fat ones may not be very desirable:
If the fat is white like a black bear's the meat will be good, but a
brownish color indicates that it is poor. Incidentally, the Koyukon
people always try to freeze or dry all bear meat immediately, because
they say it spoils very fast. Once it has spoiled a bit they consider it
inedible, unlike meat from other animals.

The brown bear's hide is rarely used today, and hunters prefer to
leave it in the wilds to ensure that no woman comes near it. In earlier
times the hide was stretched and dried, then kept in a secure place for
several years before it could be used. It was mainly used as a door on
the traditional winter house, perhaps also to cover things; but never

was it placed where someone might step over it. Since the hide would be touched by women it had to be well aged to ensure that no more life remained in it. The spiritual potency of this animal's hide was perhaps greater, or at least more dangerous, than that of any other object a woman might regularly touch.

Some old-timers—Chief John, Old Thomas, Big John—told me this a long time ago: Every hair on the brown bear's hide has a life of its own. Every hair moves, vibrates, by itself when something surprises the bear; so it can't keep still; it can't keep its temper. It takes a few years for all that life to be gone from a brown bear's hide. That's the kind of power it has.

JOHN HAINES CAME TO ALASKA in the early 1950s and eventually built a homestead near Delta Junction on the Tanana River. From 1954 to 1969 he led a largely subsistence existence—hunting, fishing, trapping, and growing vegetables near his cabin. More recently, Haines has served as a visiting professor, writer-in-residence, and guest lecturer at universities that include the University of Montana, Missoula, and Ohio University at Athens. John Haines is known primarily as a poet, and his seven volumes of poetry include *Stories We Listened To* (1986), *News from the Glacier: Selected Poems 1960–1980* (1982), and *Winter News* (1983). Nature writer and novelist Edward Abbey called *News from the Glacier* the finest book of poetry to come from Alaska. Haines has also published two essay collections, *Living Off the Country: Essays on Poetry and Place* (1981) and *The Snow, The Stars, The Fire* (1989). Haines's long apprenticeship as a painter at Hans Hofmann's school of art in New York after World War II is evident in the intensely visual quality of both his poetry and his prose.

John Haines provides a view of the grizzly that is different from others in this collection. For Haines, as for many residents of Alaska and the Yukon, the grizzly is not an exotic animal preserved in some distant national park but is, rather, a familiar resident of the local neighborhood. While Haines is out hiking in early July—intent on reaching his distant hunting cabin to get ready for the August hunting season—he surprises a grizzly in a brushy creek bottom. When the grizzly runs toward Haines and his dog, and shows no sign of slowing down, Haines is left with no choice and shoots the bear in self-defense. Remarkably, the bear seems to survive the encounter, as Haines later finds signs that "the bear was still around, alive and well."

"Out of the Shadows" is taken from The Snow, The Stars, The Fire *by John Haines, published by Graywolf Press, 1989. Reprinted by permission of John Haines and Graywolf Press.*

5. OUT OF THE SHADOWS

JOHN HAINES

IT WAS EARLY IN JULY. I WAS ON MY WAY TO CABIN Creek, eight miles distant by trail in the Redmond drainage. I intended to make a quick overnight trip to secure our hunting cabin for the season and to see what the prospects might be for blueberries later that summer.

For company I had brought with me our youngest dog, a female husky named Moppet. She was nearly two years old, a quiet, alert and intelligent animal. Glad to be along, to have been chosen, she trotted ahead of me on the trail, the thick grey and white plume of her tail swinging from side to side.

I was carrying my big pack basket containing a small axe, some food, and an old sweater to wear in the evening. I was also carrying one of the two rifles I owned, an ancient 8mm Mannlicher carbine I had inherited from an old resident in the country. It had once been a fighting weapon of the German Army in World War I. It had a scarred stock and a worn barrel, but was compact and light and easy to carry.

We had left home early to take advantage of the morning cool-ness. Now, five miles out, with the sun high at our backs on the open, sloping bench above Redmond Creek, the midmorning was clear and warm. As always here, the trail was wet underfoot, the moss and the dark sod still soaking from the spring runoff. Mosquitoes and small gnats rose out of the moss; a continual and shifting cloud of them swarmed about us.

As we walked along, skirting one dark pool of melt-water after another, I was thinking of many things: of the summer before me, of the fishing about to begin, the hoped-for success of the summer garden, and not too far ahead another hunting season. I took casual note of the places where in the winter just past I had set my traps: a shelter of twigs and sticks fallen together, and every so often under the lower boughs of a spruce tree standing near the trail a rusty marten trap was hanging, wired to its toggle stick.

It was a typical summer day in the subarctic backcountry. I was alone with a dog in a country that with its creeks, ridges and divides, and with the high, brown slope of Banner Dome visible to the north, was as familiar to me as any suburban backyard. On the changing features of the landscape I seemed to see written my own signature of use.

We rounded the steep spruce-clad prow of the hill above Glacier Creek and stopped briefly at a cache I kept there below the point of hill. Here, three years before and late in the fall, we had camped in a tent while hunting moose. The ground poles of our tent were lying where we had left them under the trees. It was not hard for me to visu-alize things as they had been then: the grey slope of the canvas tent, smoke from the stovepipe and snow in the wind. For a few weeks that tent had been home. Moppet was not yet born. Now I looked up at the narrow platform of the cache fixed solidly in the three spruces above me. A half dozen traps were hanging from a spike in one of the supports. The ridge pole of the tent and the rest of its framework were pitched together and standing upright against the cache to keep them dry. I saw that everything was as I had left it when I stopped here with the dogs and sled on the last snow of the season.

We left the cache and went on down the trail toward the creek. The brush was thick, of dense, small-statured black spruce inter-spersed with thickets of alders. The trail wound about so that at no time could I see more than thirty feet ahead of me. Moppet was now out of sight somewhere ahead and probably waiting for me at the crossing.

As I came out of the woods and onto the open bench above the creek, I saw Moppet sitting at the edge of the steep slide down which the trail led to the creek bottom. Her ears were pricked sharply forward, and she was staring intently at something in the creek.

When I came up to her, I saw what she was watching. Down in the creek and less than twenty yards away, the shoulders and back of a large brown animal showed above the heavy summer grass and clumps of ice-cropped willows. It was moving slowly downstream at the far edge of an island that divided the creek.

At first I thought the animal was a young moose feeding on the fresh grass or on some waterplants in the shallow streamcourse. And yet there was something about its size and bulk and the way that it was moving that was not quite familiar. And then the creature's head came into partial view, and I saw how the brown hump of its shoulders rippled as it moved. It was a bear, larger than any bear I had yet seen in that country. One look at that heavy square head and the shoulder hump, and I knew we had met a grizzly.

No more than a minute passed as I stood there with Moppet at my feet, watching the big bear in the grass below us. I was glad now that I had not brought one of our other dogs, who would have immediately rushed barking into the creek after the bear. I was grateful for this quiet and obedient animal sitting at my feet with her hair stiffened on her shoulders and her nose twitching.

Where I stood at that moment I had an easy shot broadside into the bear's chest or shoulders. I could perhaps have killed it then and there. But I did not want to leave a dead bear to rot in the creek, and we were too far from home to pack out more than a small portion of the meat.

In the brief time that we stood there, I quickly went over my choices. We could not proceed down into the creek and follow the trail across to the opposite bank; the bear was by now directly in our path. We could stay where we were and let the bear go on downstream if that was its intention. But would Moppet remain quiet long enough?

I thought of easing away from the scene, of moving upstream far enough to cross without disturbing the bear. It would have to be done quickly and quietly. At any moment the bear might discover us, or the noise of our retreat might alarm it. In an emergency there were no trees large enough to climb, and there was no hope of outrunning an aroused bear in that wet and spongy ground. My one advantage lay in the fact that we were above the bear and that it had not yet discovered us.

But the bear soon left me no choice. Something in our unseen presence on the bank above the creek, some sound, some prickling sense that it was not alone, seemed to change the bear's intentions. It stopped feeding. Its head came up, and it began to move more rapidly through the grass. As it did so, it turned in our direction. It was now in full view, no more than fifty feet away, and closing the distance between us.

In my sudden alarm that grizzly loomed larger and more of a threat than any black bear or bull moose I had ever met with. I was ready to fire, but in those swift moments I thought I might be able to frighten the bear, and by some noise or movement scare it back into the woods. Still holding my rifle, I raised my arms over my head. In what seems now to have been a ridiculous gesture, I waved my arms and did a small dance on the moss; I yelled and hooted and hoped. But the sudden noise, coming out of the stillness, seemed only to panic the animal. It broke into a loping run, heading directly toward us, and had already reached the bottom of the bank below us. I had no choice now. I put the rifle to my shoulder, took hurried aim at the heavy chest of hair below that big head, and fired.

At the sound of the gunshot the bear abruptly stopped a few feet below. It rose on its hind legs and stood at full height in front of us. In a rush of images I saw the stocky, upright length of its body, a patch of pale fur on its underthroat, the forepaws raised in a defensive gesture; I saw the blunt muzzle and the suddenly opened jaws. The bear growled loudly, swung its head to one side, and tried to bite at its chest. I was ready to fire again, and at that moment I might have put a shot squarely into its thick neck or broad upper chest. But for some reason in those tense seconds I again held my fire.

The bear dropped back to the ground. It turned away from us and ran back through the grass and brush in a tremendous, lunging gallop, scattering leaves and splashing water. I watched it climb the bank on the opposite side of the creek and disappear. A heavy crashing came from the dry alders on the far side, and then all was still.

I stood at the top of the bank with my rifle half-raised, listening.

Over everything in that sudden stillness I was aware of my heart as a loud pounding above the calm trickle of water in the creek below. I heard a low whine, and glanced down. All this time Moppet had remained crouched and quiet at my feet. But now she rose with her hair bristling, searching the air with her nose, trying to catch some scent of that enormous creature so suddenly discovered and now vanished.

I moved away from the trail and walked a short distance upstream to where a bulky, crooked spruce grew at the edge of the bank. It was as large as any tree in the vicinity, and for some reason I felt more comfortable standing close to it. I removed my pack and set it on the ground beside me. I placed my rifle against the tree while I searched in my shirt pocket for tobacco and papers. In those days I was an occasional smoker. With trembling hands I rolled a cigarette, lit it, and smoked in silence.

It had all happened so quickly. Perhaps no more than three minutes had elapsed since I had first seen the bear. Now that I had some space in which to think, I realized that I had been extremely lucky. Had the bear not stopped, a second shot might have killed it, but if not there would have been no way I could have escaped at least a severe mauling.

Somehow in that blur of excitement and indecision, I knew that I would not turn and run. Out of whatever stubborn sense of my own right to be there, or simply from an obscure pride, I would stand my ground, fire my shot, and from then on fend off the wounded bear as best I could, using my rifle for a club. In that event I would most likely have been killed, or I would have been so badly maimed that I could never have made it home without help, and there was no help anywhere near. Days might have passed before anyone came looking for me.

I stood there and smoked, gradually coming to some calm in myself. I could hear nothing from the woods on the far side of the creek. There was not the slightest movement to be seen in the brush growing upon that low bank, nothing at all in the grass below. From time to time I gazed up or down the creek as far as I could see above the willows and alders. Nothing.

I did not know how badly hit that bear was. Perhaps it was now lying dead over there. Or it might only be wounded, lying in the brush near the trail, gathering its strength and waiting for me to pass. At such times events and probabilities seem magnified; fear has a thousand faces.

I finished my cigarette, and picked up my pack and my rifle. I knew that I would have to go down into the creek and search the sand and grass for blood. Whatever I found, I would follow the bear's path across the creek and into the woods. I wanted above all to be on my way to the cabin and out of any further trouble. But first I had to be sure of that bear.

I waited another few minutes. Then, with Moppet at my heels, I returned to the trail, and we began our descent into the creek.

At the bottom of the bank I easily found the place where the bear had stood up after I fired at him. His big tracks were pressed deeply into the wet sand, the long toenails and the pad marks clearly outlined at the edge of the small channel.

Slowly and quietly I began to trace the bear's path through the grass. Stopping frequently to look around me over the grass and through the brush, I followed as well as I could the paw marks in the sand and the muddy sod. Where I could not see his tracks, I guided myself by the bent and broken grasses in the deep trough of the bear's passage. As I walked, half-crouched, searching the ground, I examined with care every blade of grass and every leaf on the willows. But I found no sign of blood.

We went on through the grass and brush. Across the far channel we found the trail, climbed the shallow bank and entered the woods. Moppet remained at my heels, at times pressing closely against my leg. Though I tried quietly to coax her, she would not go ahead but stayed close behind. The hair on her shoulders and neck was stiffened, and as she looked from side to side into the woods a muted and anxious throaty sound came from her, half growl and half whine.

Once up the bank and into the woods, we stopped. It was spooky as hell under that shadowy, sun-broken canopy of leaves. I searched the woods around me for the slightest movement and listened for any sound: wounded breathing, a growl, anything. Nowhere in all that wilderness could I hear a sound above the muted purling of water in the creek behind me, and the song of a fox sparrow somewhere in the watercourse.

We walked on, following the trail where it skirted the edge of a narrow ravine holding a wayward tributary of the creek. To cross the ravine I had built a rough bridge out of spruce poles. On the far side the trail turned upstream and continued through a swamp toward Cabin Creek.

When Moppet and I had crossed the bridge, I stopped again. Here an old game trail, deeply cut into the moss, intersected our sled trail and took its narrow, twisting way downstream. I hesitated. Nothing I had seen so far convinced me that the bear was at all wounded, but I was still not satisfied. I stepped into the game trail and began a careful circuit of the downstream woods into which I had seen the bear vanish. As quiet as it was, as eerily still, I felt that somewhere in that dim tangle of alders, willows and dwarf birch the bear must be lying and listening to our movements. As in an episode of warfare, a pervasive uneasiness seemed to divide the shadows and the sunlight. I had that acute sense of being watched and listened to by an invisible foe. Each twig-snap and wave of a bough seemed a potential signal.

After about twenty minutes of what I considered to be a reasonably careful search, I returned to the trail. I now felt, from the lack of any bloodsign or other evidence, that the bear had not been badly hit. I decided not to pursue the search any further. With Moppet following me, I went on through the swamp, climbing steadily toward the saddle that divided Glacier from Cabin Creek. We went carefully, every so often stopping to look back down the trail behind us. We were well away from the creek before Moppet would put aside her fear and go ahead of me.

It seemed to me now that I had merely grazed the underside of the bear's chest. I had fired downhill at a running target, and had aimed low. Moreover, the front sight of the old carbine had been damaged years ago and repaired with solder in a makeshift fashion. The gunsight was uncertain at best.

So obviously I had fired too low, and the bear had suffered no more than a nasty sting from the heavy 230 grain bullet I was using. Had the bear been solidly hit, there would surely have been blood somewhere, and there would by now be a dead or dying bear in the woods. As we came down off the hill on the last half mile stretch to the cabin I began to feel a great deal easier, satisfied that I had not left a badly wounded animal behind me, and glad too that we had gotten off from the encounter ourselves with no more trouble.

WE SPENT THE NIGHT at the cabin. I fed Moppet and cut some fire-wood. In the late afternoon I did a few needed chores about the cabin. On going to the creek for a bucket of water, I found a few unripe blueberries among the bushes overhanging the deep, wet moss hummocks beside the creek. The berries were scattered, and it did not seem to me that they would be worth a trip later to pick them. As the evening light deepened over the hills and the air grew cooler, a thrush sent up its spiraling song from the aspens on the hillside across the creek. Mosquitoes whined at the screen door. Otherwise, things were very quiet there on the hill above Cabin Creek.

The following morning I secured the cabin for the remainder of the summer. I set a strong barricade over the door, and closed and nailed heavy shutters over the two windows. In the late morning Moppet and I set out for home.

As we came down through the swamp near Glacier, Moppet once more dropped behind me and refused to go ahead. I walked quietly with the rifle safety off and my hand half-closed on the trigger. Again I watched the brush and listened to either side of the trail for the slight-est sound. There was nothing but the quiet sunlit air of a summer day.

We crossed the creek, striding the small channels and pushing aside the grass, and on the far side we climbed the bank again. When we came to the top, I looked down. There, squarely in the trail and almost exactly where I had stood the day before when I fired at the bear, was a fresh mound of bear dropping. Nearby lay the spent shell from my rifle.

I looked closely at the dropping. It contained a few unripe blue-berries, seeds and other matter. It was still wet, though not warm. Moppet sniffed at it, and the grizzled hair once more rose on her neck and shoulders. For a moment my uneasiness returned, that vague, shivery sense of being watched and followed. The bear was still around, alive and well. Dangerous? I had no way of knowing.

The bear had probably not run far on the previous day, but had found a place in which to lie and lick its wound, baffled as to the source of its sudden hurt. It had heard us pass on the trail, had heard every sound of my passage in the brush, had followed every detail of my search. Perhaps much later in the evening it came out of its hiding place, out of the late cool shadows, and returned to the trail. It had stood where we were standing now, with its great, shaggy head down, sniffing the moss, the wet, black sod, trying to place in its dim sense of things an identity it would carry with it for the rest of its life.

I looked back down into the grass and brush of the creek from which we had just come. I turned and looked ahead of me to where the stubby black spruce wood closed in around the trail. If the bear was still somewhere in that dense green cover, nursing its hurt and its temper, waiting for revenge, it would have its chance.

But nothing vengeful and bloody came out of the woods to meet us as we went on up the trail. The walk home by Redmond, the long uphill climb to the homestead ridge passed without further incident. We came down off the hill as on many another occasion, to the sunlit vista of the river and the highway, to the sound of the dogs' furious barking. I had a good story to tell, and Moppet was petted and praised for her wise behavior.

In many subsequent hikes over the trail to Cabin Creek, in hunting forays along the benches above Glacier, we never saw that bear again. Now and then in later summer and early fall a blue mound of dropping in the trail gave evidence of a bear in the country, and that was all.

Never before or since have I been so rattled on meeting an animal in the woods. Years later, when I began to think of writing these pages, I rehearsed for myself another outcome to the adventure. I described in detail how the bear, badly hit in its lungs, had waited in the brush on the far side of the creek. When Moppet and I went by on the trail, the bear suddenly lunged from its hiding place with a terrible, bubbling roar and struck me down.

In that instant of confusion and shock I was joined to the hot blood and rank fur at last. All my boyhood dreams of life in the woods, of courage and adventure, had come to this final and terrifying intimacy.

Following the initial shock, as I lay sprawled by the trail with the bear standing hot and wounded above me, I managed to regain a grip on my rifle. Though stunned and, as it seemed, half blinded, I raised the short muzzle of that ancient weapon and got off one last shot into the bear's throat. And with the sound of that shot in my ears, I lost consciousness.

In what may have been an hour or only minutes, I returned to a dazed sense of myself. I sat up, struggling to free myself of the things that seemed to hold me: my pack harness, torn clothing, and bits of broken brush. I seemed to look at myself and my surroundings from a great distance through a sun-dazzled semi-darkness. I was still alive, though in the numbed, head-ringing silence I knew I was hurt, badly cut and bitten about my face and body. Moppet was gone. A short distance away from me the bear lay dead.

Somehow, maimed, stiffened and bleeding, using a dry stick for a crutch, I found my way home. Patched and scarred, I wore my changed face as an emblem of combat, and walked in my damaged body to the end of my days, survivor of a meeting terrible and true.

RICK McINTRYE GREW UP in the mountains of New England
and was educated at the University of Massachusetts, where he
received a degree in forestry. For the past fifteen years he has
worked as a seasonal ranger for the National Park Service,
dividing his time equally between Denali National Park and
Preserve in the summer and Joshua Tree National Monument in
the Mojave Desert in the winter. During his many years at Denali,
where he has been stationed over sixty miles from the nearest
paved road, Rick McIntyre has had the opportunity to learn much
about grizzlies, both generally and individually. In the process of
his studies—he now knows the resident grizzlies probably as well
as Jane Goodall knows the chimpanzees of Tanzania's Gombe
Sanctuary—McIntyre has taken over 5,000 photographs,
documenting the bears' ecology and behavior.

Based on these experiences, McIntyre wrote *Grizzly Cub*
(1990) about one bear he knew particularly well, Stony, named
for the Stony Hill area in which the bear was born and reared.
Like so many bears, Stony found it difficult to adjust to people.
Photographers, always anxious to "fill the frame," got too close to
him; backpackers failed to obey regulations regarding safe
behavior in bear country. Conflicts inevitably occurred.

Bear management policies in Denali, as McIntyre emphasizes
in his book, have generally been very successful. Despite the fact
that there are more than 600,000 visitors each year—and that
figure is steadily growing—there has never been a fatal bear attack
on a person within the park boundaries.

The excerpts from Grizzly Cub *by Rick McIntyre (Alaska Northwest
Books, 1990) are reprinted by permission of Rick McIntyre.*

6. GRIZZLY CUB

RICK McINTYRE

Year Five

THE NEXT SUMMER, MY FIRST SIGHTING OF STONY occurred in early June. He still had his radio collar and ear tags, but his fur had turned brown. I had been watching a mother bear with twin cubs when Stony came on the scene. The sow stood up, looked at him, then fled with her cubs. Stony followed them for a distance, but when he crossed the road, he was distracted by some vehicles. After investigating the cars, he fed near the road. As he did, the sow and cubs watched from about three hundred yards away. The cubs were nervous and only calmed down when allowed to nurse.

About ten minutes later, Stony walked toward them. Both cubs ran behind their mother for protection. The sow then went into action; she charged Stony, who immediately turned and ran off. After chasing him for a few minutes, she trotted back to her cubs. As soon as she reversed directions, Stony turned back and again approached the family. The mother bear charged again and drove him away. This routine repeated itself two more times, and each time the sow seemed to get angrier. Once Stony had been chased off for the fourth time, he lost interest in the family and wandered off. The mother joined her cubs, who were frantic.

After the incident was over, I wondered about his intentions. Had he approached the family so that he could kill one of the cubs or was this just another aspect of his playful, curious nature? The mother and cubs certainly believed he was a threat and acted accordingly.

For a while during his fifth summer, Stony's life seemed to be going well. He stayed away from garbage cans and hikers. His diet consisted of the things "good" bears should eat: roots, grass, and ground squirrels. In midsummer, he found a ewe that had died of natural causes and made several meals from its carcass.

Around that time, he made another lucky discovery. A pack of wolves had killed a caribou on Stony Hill. After stuffing themselves as full as they could, they walked off a few hundred yards, and lay down to nap. An hour later Stony wandered by and noticed the wolves. He charged into the pack and sent them running. The wolves ran off, but were too full to go far. They soon stopped and looked back at Stony. By then he was sniffing the air with a great deal of interest. Turning to the west, he trotted off and followed the scent directly to the carcass. Within a few hours, he finished it off. The wolf pack watched him, but didn't do anything to drive him away.

By the middle of August, Stony had left his usual domain around Stony Hill and had begun to head west. On August 20, he was seen about twenty-five miles away, just south of Wonder Lake. He was tranquilized again and had his radio collar replaced. The rangers who handled him estimated his weight at 280 pounds, a good-sized bear by local standards.

I saw him feeding on berries near the Wonder Lake campground a few weeks later. That year the berry crop was poor, but the area around Wonder Lake had produced a decent number of blueberries. Perhaps Stony had drifted out of his normal range looking for better berry patches and ended up there.

After I left the area to return to Eielson, Stony headed toward the north end of the lake. That route took him near the Wonder Lake ranger station, an old house used as a residence and office. Behind the station were several small cabins that housed additional employees. Rorie Hammel was doing some chores in one of the cabins; her husband, Rob, the local Park Service grader operator, was out working. Their children, three-year-old Raina and nine-month-old Ryan, were outside playing. Rorie went out to check on the kids, and just as she reached them she saw Stony approaching the station.

They rushed back to their cabin. Once safely inside, they watched the bear through a window. Stony sniffed around the ranger station and then continued on, passing within a few feet of their window. He paused on the north side of the cabin and went up to Raina's little plastic swimming pool. In Raina's own words:

"We heard a big 'whoomph' and I asked Mom, 'What happened, what happened?' I climbed up on the bed, looked outside and saw the bear by my swimming pool. The air was going out, the bear had bit it! I looked again and saw him inside the pool, playing and rolling around in the water. Then he wandered off and went toward the mountain. We went outside and looked at the pool. The pool looked like it had exploded, it was flat on the ground. There were many tiny pieces of plastic all over."

After he was done playing with the pool, Stony walked over to the road and continued north, past Wonder Lake and on into Kantishna, an old gold-mining district that was added to the park in 1980. Several miles up the road, he paused at the entrance to Camp Denali and scratched himself on a post. Once finished, he went back to the road and walked on. A short time later, he came to the Kantishna Roadhouse. This was a new tourist resort built on a piece of property that had been the center of Kantishna back in the early 1900s, when the area was at the peak of a gold rush.

As Stony walked into the area, he sniffed the air and made a bee-line for the Roadhouse garbage dump. He rooted around and found more than enough to make a good meal.

The Roadhouse employees told the Wonder Lake rangers about the bear and they passed the word on to Dave Albert and Joe Van Horn, two rangers who specialized in bear management. Dave was the first to arrive on the scene. By then, Stony was sniffing the air around the Roadhouse kitchen. Dave shot two cracker rounds at Stony, which frightened him enough to move a short distance out of the camp. The bear was reluctant to leave and circled the area. A short time later, he was seen sniffing around the dump again. This time he was hit with a rubber bullet, which caused him to move over to the opposite side of a nearby creek.

For the rest of the day, Stony continually tried to get back to the dump. Dave used rubber bullets and cracker shells to scare him off, but they were becoming increasingly ineffective. A heavier projectile called a "bear thumper" was tried, but it also had little effect. Stony was determined to get back in the dump one way or another.

The next day he found a pickup truck that had several bags of dog food in its bed. Stony climbed into the truck and ate part of the dog food. After being scared off, he circled the area and found a nearby trailer. He smashed through the front door, trashed the inside of the trailer, and then exited by crashing through a kitchen window and leaping to the ground. He returned to the Roadhouse, where he sneaked back to the pickup and tried to eat more dog food. Dave found him there at 11 P.M. and drove him away. The Roadhouse dogs barked all night, indicating that Stony was close by.

The following day, September 14, Stony was first seen at 6 A.M., tearing apart some empty dog-food bags. All morning he stayed near the dump. Joe Van Horn came out to the area and he and Dave Albert did everything they could think of to drive off Stony. They were running out of options.

I'd heard about Stony's adventure over the CB, and since it was my day off, I went out to Kantishna. Joe filled me in on Stony's actions of the past two days. At that point he was nowhere in sight, so Joe turned on the radio receiver and picked up the signal from Stony's collar. It looked like he was resting in the woods to the south of the dump. Since things were quiet, I walked over to the trailer Stony had broken into. The owner gave me permission to go inside. It looked like vandals had torn apart everything in the living room. The gaping hole in the front door was matched by a bear-sized hole in the kitchen window.

Things looked bleak for Stony. He had gone on a rampage and still hadn't left the area. Breaking into the trailer was a serious offense. Also, he was getting used to the rubber bullets and cracker shells, and their effectiveness was now minimal.

When I got back to Joe, he told me that Stony was still off in the brush and things were quiet. He was going to wait near the dump to see if the bear came back. If Stony did, he said they might decide to drug him and try relocating him to a distant section of the park.

Relocating problem grizzlies has been a common management practice in many national parks. A relocation is an attempt to give a bear another chance in a new area, far removed from garbage and other temptations. Unfortunately, most relocations fail because the bears return home. Once a garbage-addicted bear knows where a good source of food lies, it will quickly return to it once the drugs wear off.

This would most likely be the case with Stony. He had enjoyed some great meals from the Roadhouse dump and from the bags of dog food. He wouldn't let a few days of travel deter him from going back for more. If he came back, there wouldn't be much that could be done. In Alaska, it is legal to shoot a grizzly in defense of life and property. After Stony broke into the trailer, anyone in Kantishna was within his rights to shoot Stony if he approached his property.

The last thing I wanted was to have Stony die from being shot while digging up garbage, but at the moment it looked like that might be his fate. I thought about the possibility of offering him to a zoo. At least it would be a fate better than to be shot in a garbage dump.

Stony was tranquilized later that day and loaded into a helicopter. He was dropped off near the Foraker River, in the western end of the park. All of us who knew Stony waited to see if he would stay there or come back to Kantishna.

The next day, the park plane passed over the relocation area and picked up Stony's radio signal. It seemed to be coming from the exact spot where he had been dropped off. When the crew passed over the area, they saw him lying on the ground, apparently still unconscious from the drug. He should have revived by now. Something was wrong.

Epilogue

THE PLANE COULDN'T LAND and the helicopter was unavailable. A week later, the copter returned and Joe Van Horn was flown out to investigate. Stony had been dead for a week and had been partially eaten by another grizzly. Since the drug dosage he'd received was in the normal range for a bear of his weight, it seemed unlikely that the cause of death was an overdose. Joe concluded that Stony may have regurgitated while unconscious and choked to death.

News of Stony's fate quickly spread throughout the park. Initially, I was angry over his death but gradually came to realize that it may have been the lesser of two evils. Had he revived, he almost certainly would have gone straight back to Kantishna.

At least Stony died in wild grizzly country, without pain and with some dignity. The fact that another bear ate part of his carcass may sound distasteful, but it means part of him lives on in the Denali ecosystem.

Stony's life is an apt illustration of the basic conflict built into the mission of the National Park Service. When the agency was created in 1916, Congress stated that its purpose in managing national parks was "to conserve the scenery and the natural and historic objects and the wildlife therein and to provide for the enjoyment of the same in such manner and by such means as will leave them unimpaired for the enjoyment of future generations."

Conflict arises over the relationship between conserving wildlife and other natural features and managing the ways people enjoy those resources. That relationship must be balanced in such a way that the animals and natural resources are preserved for the future. It's not an easy task.

Denali National Park was created to protect the wide array of large mammals that live in the area. To help visitors see and enjoy the wildlife, the eighty-five-mile park road was built in the thirties. The road makes the grizzlies and other animals far more accessible to people. On an average summer day, thousands of tourists get to see bears, often within a few feet of their bus. Without the road, only a few backpackers would be able to get a close look at the park's wildlife.

But the road and other developments, which are intended to help people enjoy the wildlife, can be detrimental to the very animals that the park was created to protect. In Stony's case, the traffic on the road and the bridge construction project were sources of temptation that eventually led him astray.

Stony's personality made him curious about human-related objects, particularly food. If Denali had been established solely as a wildlife sanctuary and had no mandate to provide access to the animals, there would have been no road, no construction site, no resorts. Under those circumstances, Stony would have lived in an environment that offered few temptations and he might still be alive today.

But the Park Service mission in Denali is to provide for reasonable access to the park as well as to protect the animals. The trick is to manage the developments that enable access in such a way that the wildlife is left as unimpaired as possible. For the most part, things work in Denali. Unfortunately, Stony's life is an example of how things can go wrong.

No one ever intentionally did anything to harm him, but the

chain of events that started with an unsecured trash can, continued with the incident involving the hiker, and ended with a garbage dump, shows how the system could not protect this particular bear.

BIG STONY IS STILL AROUND and doing well. She mated again and gave birth to a pair of female cubs. These half-sisters of Little Stony are now two years old. Both of the new cubs are more wary than he was of people and their things. Also, they have each other to play with, a factor that seemingly has helped them develop into well-adjusted young bears. They have so much fun playing together that their mother often comes over and joins them. Big Stony has become a more attentive and involved mother.

This coming year the family will split up. The cubs, like Little Stony, will probably stay near their mother's home range. If you visit Denali, watch for grizzlies in the Stony Hill area. When you see one, there is a good chance it will be Little Stony's mother or one of his sisters. The sight of one of his close relatives will be an event tens of thousands of people will experience in the coming years. While one bear may have been lost, the rest of the Denali grizzly population is thriving. May those bears continue to live their lives in a truly wild manner.

PART II

THE NORTHERN ROCKIES

"As the sky broke light over the peaks of Glacier [National Park], I found myself deeply moved by the view from our elevation, off west the lights of Montana, Hungry Horse, and Columbia Falls, and farmsteads along the northern edge of Flathead Lake, and back in the direction of sunrise the soft and misted valleys of the parklands, not an electric light showing: little enough to preserve for the wanderings of a great and sacred animal who can teach us, if nothing else, by his power and his dilemma, a little common humility."

—William Kittredge
"Grizzly," *Owning It All*
1987

THE NORTHERN ROCKIES' GRIZZLY BEAR ECOSYSTEM, which includes about 9,600 square miles of occupied habitat, is the last secure refuge in the Lower 48 states for the North American grizzly. An indication of the health of bear populations in this vast region is the fact that state and federal wildlife managers currently permit a small number of grizzlies to be hunted each year, a management policy that reportedly poses no threat to the sizable population and that was upheld in court in April 1991. This ecosystem includes Glacier National Park, parts of the Flathead and Blackfeet Indian reservations, parts of five national forests (Flathead, Helena, Kootenai, Lewis and Clark, and Lolo), and various other Bureau of Land Management, state, and private lands. Scientists estimate that there are around 200 grizzly bears in Glacier National Park and from 440 to 680 grizzlies in the ecosystem as a whole. Grizzly bears from British Columbia and Alberta replenish this and other border bear populations as they move freely back and forth over the international boundary. The Nature Conservancy's Pine Butte Swamp Grizzly Bear Preserve is located in the ecosystem near Choteau, Montana, on the East Front of the Rocky Mountains.

Because the mountainous regions surrounding the northern Continental Divide are heavily forested, opportunities to observe the grizzly bear in the wild are rare. Nevertheless, backcountry visitors—backpackers, fishermen, and hunters—do occasionally report seeing the silvertips. Although grizzlies at this latitude and in this region are often more active at night, they still can be spotted in the morning and evening as they feed on vegetation in open meadows, along avalanche runs, and beside streams and lakes. Most often, people encounter grizzly bear sign, which includes trails, tracks, scat piles, large dig sites, rubbing areas, daybeds, and excavated dens. Probably the greatest benefit of hiking though this rugged Northern Rocky wilderness is just knowing that the grizzlies are out there, living much as they did when Lewis and Clark first ascended the Missouri River in 1805.

EDWARD ABBEY, AUTHOR of two dozen works of fiction and nonfiction, thoroughly dominated the American environmental and literary scene for well over twenty years. His second novel, *The Brave Cowboy* (1956), was made into the critically acclaimed film *Lonely Are the Brave,* with actor Kirk Douglas. His later works of fiction include *The Monkey-Wrench Gang* (1974), *The Fool's Progress* (1989), and the posthumous *Hayduke Lives!* (1990). Perhaps Abbey's most famous work—there are now over half a million copies in print—is *Desert Solitaire* (1968), which chronicles a season he spent as a ranger in Arches National Monument, Utah. Abbey's works of nonfiction include *Abbey's Road* (1974), *The Journey Home* (1977), and *Beyond the Wall* (1984). The "Thoreau of the Modern West," as Larry McMurtry called him, died in March 1989. There is already a movement to establish a desert wilderness area in his name. In this selection from *The Journey Home,* Abbey provides a look at grizzly country in Glacier National Park, Montana, where he worked as a seasonal fire lookout.

"Fire Lookout: Numa Ridge," taken from Edward Abbey's The Journey Home *(1977), is reprinted by permission of Clarke Abbey.*

7. FIRE LOOKOUT: NUMA RIDGE

EDWARD ABBEY

July 12, Glacier National Park

WE'VE BEEN HERE TEN DAYS BEFORE I OVER-
come initial inertia sufficient to begin this
record. And keeping a record is one of the things the Park Service is
paying us to do up here. The other, of course, is to keep our eyeballs
peeled, alert for smoke. We are being paid a generous wage (about
$3.25 an hour) to stay awake for at least eight hours a day. Some
people might think that sounds like a pretty easy job. And they're
right, it is an easy job, for some people. But not for all. When I mentioned to one young fellow down at park headquarters, a couple of
weeks ago, that I was spending the summer on this fire lookout he
shuddered with horror. "I'd go nuts in a place like that," he said,
thinking of solitary confinement. I didn't tell him I was cheating,
taking my wife along. But that can be risky too; many a good marriage
has been shattered on the rock of isolation.

Renée and I walked up here on July 2, packs on our backs, two
hours ahead of the packer with his string of mules. The mules carried
the heavier gear, such as our bedrolls, enough food and water for the

first two weeks, seven volumes of Marcel Proust, and Robert Burton's *Anatomy of Melancholy*. Light summer reading. Renée had never worked a fire lookout before, but I had, and I knew that if I was ever going to get through the classics of world lit it could only be on a mountain top, far above the trashy plains of *Rolling Stone, Playboy, The New York Times*, and *Mizz* magazine.

The trail is about six miles long from Bowman Lake and climbs 3,000 feet. We made good time, much better time than we wished because we were hustled along, all the way, by hordes of bloodthirsty mosquitoes. We had prepared ourselves, of course, with a heavy treatment of government-issue insect repellent on our faces, necks, arms, but that did not prevent the mosquitoes from whining in our ears and hovering close to eye, nostril, and mouth.

We also had the grizzly on our mind. Fresh bear scat on the trail, unpleasant crashing noises back in the dark of the woods and brush, reminded us that we were intruding, uninvited, into the territory of *Ursus horribilis*, known locally as G-bear or simply (always in caps) as GRIZ. It was in Glacier, of course, only a few years ago, that two young women had been killed on the same night by grizzlies. We clattered our tin cups now and then, as advised, to warn the bears we were coming. I was naturally eager to see a GRIZ in the wild, something I'd never done, but not while climbing up a mountain with a pack on my back, tired, sweaty, and bedeviled by bugs. Such an encounter, in such condition, could only mean a good-natured surrender on my part; I wasn't *about* to climb a tree.

Bear stories. My friend Doug Peacock was soaking one time in a hot spring in Yellowstone's back country. Surprised by a grizzly sow and her two cubs, he scrambled naked as a newt up the nearest pine; the bear kept him there, freezing in the breeze, for two hours. Another: Riley McClelland, former park naturalist at Glacier, and a friend were treed by a GRIZ. Remembering that he had an opened sardine can in his pack, Riley watched with sinking heart as the bear sniffed at it. Disdaining the sardine lure, however, the bear tore up the other man's pack to get at a pair of old tennis shoes.

Sacrifice, that may be the key to coexistence with the GRIZ. If we surprise one on the trail, I'll offer up first my sweat-soaked hat. If that won't do, then cheese and salami out of the pack. And if that's not enough, well, then nothing else to do, I guess, but push my wife his way. *Droit du seigneur à la montagne,* etc.

We reach the lookout without fulfilling any fantasies. The lookout is a two-room, two-story wood frame cabin at timberline, 7,000 feet above sea level. On the north, east, and southeast stand great peaks—Reuter, Kintla, Numa, Chapman, Rainbow, Vulture. Northwest we can see a bit of the Canadian Rockies. West and southwest lie the North Fork of the Flathead River, a vast expanse of Flathead National Forest, and on the horizon the Whitefish Range. Nice view: 360 degrees of snow-capped scenic splendor, lakes, forest, river, fearsome peaks, and sheltering sky.

We remove the wooden shutters from the lookout windows, shovel snow from the stairway, unlock the doors. The pack string arrives. The packer and I unload the mules, the packer departs, Renée and I unpack our goods and move in. Except for a golden-mantled ground squirrel watching us from the rocks, a few Clark's nutcrackers in the subalpine firs, we seem to be absolutely alone.

July 17

STILL NO REAL FIRES, aside from a few trivial lightning-storm flare-ups in the forest across the river, soon drowned by rain. But we are ready. Perhaps I should describe the equipment and operations of a lookout.

We live and work in the second story of the cabin. The ground-floor room, dark and dank, is used only for storage. Our room is light, airy, and bright, with windows running the length of all four walls. Closable louvred vents above each window admit fresh air while keeping out rain. In the center of this twelve-foot by twelve-foot room, oriented squarely with the four directions, stands the chest-high fire finder. The Osborne Fire Finder consists essentially of a rotating metal ring about two feet in diameter with a handle to turn it by and a pair of sights, analogous to the front and rear sights of a rifle, mounted upright on opposite sides. When the lookout spots a fire, he aims this device at the base and center of the smoke (or flame, if discovered at night) and obtains an azimuth reading from the fixed base of the fire finder, which is marked off into 360 degrees. By use of the vernier scale attached to the rotating ring, the lookout can get a reading not only in degrees but precisely to the nearest minute, or one-sixtieth of a degree.

Having determined the compass direction of the fire from his own location, the lookout must still establish the location of the fire. To do that he must be able to recognize and identify the place where the fire is burning and to report its distance from his lookout station. A metal tape stretched between front and rear sights of the fire finder, across a circular map inside the rotating ring, gives the distance in kilometers. Another aid is the sliding peep sight on the rear sight, by means of which the lookout can obtain a vertical angle on his fire. Through a bit of basic trigonometry the vertical angle can be translated into distance. Or if another lookout, at a different station, can see the same fire, the line of his azimuth reading extended across a map of the area intersects the line of the first lookout's reading to give the exact point of the fire. Assuming both lookouts are awake, fairly competent, and on duty at the same time.

If these procedures sound complicated, that is an illusion. The technical aspects of a lookout's job can be mastered by any literate anthropoid with an IQ of not less than seventy in about two hours. It's the attitude that's difficult: Unless you have an indolent, melancholy nature, as I do, you will not be happy as an official United States government fire lookout.

Anyway, having determined the location of his fire, and being reasonably certain it is a fire and not a smoking garbage dump, a controlled slash burn, a busy campground, floating vapors, or traffic dust rising from a dirt road, the lookout picks up his radio microphone or telephone and reports his discovery to fire-control headquarters. After that his main task becomes one of assisting the smoke-chasers in finding the fire, relaying messages, looking for new and better fires.

July 20

BEAR CLAW SCRATCHES on the wooden walls of the ground-floor storage room. Last thing before retiring each night I set the bear barrier in place on the stairway leading to our quarters. The bear barrier is a wooden panel with many nails driven through it, the points all sticking out. Supposed to discourage *Ursus stairiensis* from climbing up to our catwalk balcony. In a previous lookout's log we had read this entry:

Woke up this morning to see a big black bear staring at me thru window, about six inches from my face. Chased him off with a Pulaski.

The Pulaski is a fire-fighting tool, a combination ax and pickax. I keep one handy too, right under the bed where I can reach it easy. I'd keep it under the pillow if my old lady would let me.

Thinking about GRIZ. Almost every day, on the park or forest radio, we hear some ranger report a bear sighting, sometimes of grizzly. Campers molested, packs destroyed by hungry and questing bears. Somebody was recently attacked and mauled by a GRIZ north of the line, in Waterton Lakes. Bear jams on the park highway, though not so common here as they used to be in Yellowstone, before so many of Yellowstone's bears mysteriously disappeared, do occur in Glacier from time to time.

No doubt about it, the presence of bear, especially grizzly bear, adds a spicy titillation to a stroll in the woods. My bear-loving friend Peacock goes so far as to define wilderness as a place and only a place where one enjoys the opportunity of being attacked by a dangerous wild animal. Any place that lacks GRIZ, or lions or tigers, or a rhino or two, is not, in his opinion, worthy of the name "wilderness." A good definition, worthy of serious consideration. A wild place without dangers is an absurdity, although I realize that danger creates administrative problems for park and forest managers. But we must not allow our national parks and national forests to be degraded to the status of mere public playgrounds. Open to all, yes of course. But—*enter at your own risk.*

Enter Glacier National Park and you enter the homeland of the grizzly bear. We are uninvited guests here, intruders, the bear our reluctant host. If he chooses, now and then, to chase somebody up a tree, or all the way to the hospital, that is the bear's prerogative. Those who prefer, quite reasonably, not to take such chances should stick to Disneyland in all its many forms and guises.

WILLIAM KITTREDGE WAS raised on and later managed his
family's cattle ranch in eastern Oregon. He is currently professor
of creative writing and director of the Master of Fine Arts
program in creative writing at the University of Montana,
Missoula. His fiction and nonfiction have appeared in *The Atlantic,
Harper's, Rolling Stone, Outside, Rocky Mountain Magazine,* and
Triquarterly. Kittredge's books include a collection of short stories,
We Are Not In This Together (1984), and *Owning It All* (1987), a
collection of personal essays about his life in the West. Kittredge
is widely regarded as one of the deans of contemporary writing in
the American West.

In this essay from *Owning It All,* William Kittredge describes
an encounter with the legendary Doug Peacock in a fire lookout
tower deep inside Glacier National Park. After listening to the
latter's poignant defense of the bears, Kittredge wanders out on
the porch and wonders if Peacock is right, if "wilderness must
indeed, by definition, be inhabited by some power greater than
ourselves." Despite the fact that one of Kittredge's friends was
killed by a grizzly, his sojourn in the wilderness convinces him
that the bears are necessary because they "can teach us, if nothing
else, . . . a little common humility."

"Grizzly" is taken from William Kittredge's Owning It All *(Graywolf
Press, 1987) and is reprinted by permission of William Kittredge.*

8. GRIZZLY

WILLIAM KITTREDGE

STARLIGHT IS BEGINNING TO SHOW off the lake water. In this mountaintop land we are absolutely isolated, except for the fire burning near the rocky shoreline, the flitterings of light touching at our bright tent. Occasionally a trout rises and splashes, and the rings undulate away on the perfect stained-glass stillness of the water.

Someone claims to have heard the distant crackling of branches, but this is wilderness and now the only sounds are the faint humming of the earth and the snapping of the pineknot fire. Under the clean, smoky odor we rebuild the fire and finally drift to sleep. Then you feel a hand clutching at yours, and you come slowly awake into awareness that this is not a dream.

There is a snuffling sound outside the tent, and the grunting of some animal; it comes twice, and then the fabric is ripped away, and the vast dark animal is there in the faint glow of the fire, silent and intent as someone prepares to scream, and then there is

the screaming, the quick scuffling movements, and the quiet after the
screaming, which stopped so abruptly.

A FRIEND OF MINE, Mary Pat Mahoney, was killed by a grizzly in
1976, over in the Many Glaciers Campground of Glacier National
Park, about a hundred and fifty yards from the Ranger Station.
Contemplation of her death led me to that dream, a waking night-
mare I learned to articulate at home in my bed the nights after she
was dragged from her tent. It thinned any mountain man resolve I
might ever have possessed to spend a pleasant campfire evening in the
vicinity.

Up here on this night, however, we are barricaded from whatever
might be out there, and we have been speculating about loss of reverence for that which is majestic and legitimately awesome, and about
the usefulness of all creatures, particularly the fearful usefulness of
the great *Ursus arctos horribilis,* the grizzly.

We have been talking habitat and viable populations, and carnivorous predator-prey relationships. And outside, a frog is eating the
moon. That's an old Native American legend about a phenomenon
we know as lunar eclipse.

We are in the midst of the best grizzly country left below the
Canadian border, high up on the lookout tower atop Huckleberry
Ridge, the peaks of Glacier National Park looming eastward in the silvery light, and we are talking sociobiology and primitive religion,
primate social behavior, and the notion that reason springs from
humility.

The full moon of this mid-July night is more than half gone
behind the earth's shadows. We are talking confrontations, and reasons for courting fear.

Our host on the mountain, Doug Peacock, when he is not out on
the veranda cranking away at the eclipse with his old spring-wound
16mm Bolex movie camera, is sipping at our bottle of Glenlivet
whiskey and imitating the ways the grizzlies conduct themselves when
interacting with their own kind and when facing down humans.

In his jam-packed 15-by-15-foot room atop the lookout tower,
Peacock is standing tall on his toes and eyeing us like we are invaders
of his most prime ripe berry patch, then dropping and hunching
his back and growling and circling at us with a kind of quartering

half-drunk and rough-handed playfulness.

"Yeah, for damned sure," he says, and his eyes are gleaming. "You got to come back when the bears are around, and hear them sons-a-bitches when they are coming at one another."

"Sure," I say, and I think, *Most certainly*. No.

Peacock jams the cork into the scotch bottle.

"You think about it," he says. "It'll do you more good than anything. That roaring will chill your piss. On a warm night."

I'm thinking about being out there alone with God and the grizzly bear, on some tangled hillside right after sunset, and those bears coming at one another. . . . Sure.

LISTENING TO PEACOCK, I find myself drawn to his forthright love of the animal and the wilderness untamed by even so much as back-packer paths, and yet . . . how about that implacable denizen of the bad dreams, the killer in the night?

Such a tangle of feelings toward the grizzly is nothing new. On October 20, 1804, near what is now the border between the Dakotas, along the Missouri River, the Lewis and Clark party ". . . wounded a white bear, and saw some tracks of those animals which are twice as large as the tracks of a man."

So the first recorded wounding came with the first recorded contact by our first scientific foray into the Far West, the beginnings of the cataloguing and grid survey, the naming of parts. The expedition wintered at Fort Mandan, and it was the following spring, April 29, 1805, just upstream from the place where the Yellowstone empties into the Missouri, near the border between Montana and the Dakotas, that the next substantial and legendary encounter took place.

> He attacks rather than avoids a man, and such is the terror he inspires, that the Indians who go in quest of him paint themselves and perform all the superstitious rites customary when they make war on a neighboring nation.
>
> Hitherto those we had seen did not seem desirous of encountering us, but although to a skillful rifleman the danger is very much diminished, yet the white bear is a terrible animal. On approaching these two, both Captain Lewis and the hunter fired, and each wounded a bear. One of them made his escape.

The other turned on Captain Lewis and pursued him seventy or
eighty yards, but being badly wounded he could not run so fast
as to prevent him from reloading his piece . . . and a third shot
from the hunter brought him to the ground. He was a male not
quite full grown and weighed about 300 pounds. Its legs were
somewhat longer than those of a black bear, and the talons and
tusks were much larger and stronger. . . . Add to that, it is a
more furious animal, and remarkable for the wounds it will
bear without dying.

*A neighboring nation . . . remarkable for the wounds it will bear without
dying.*

The Lewis and Clark expedition traveled 7,689 miles between May
of 1804 and September of 1806. On the way they discovered 122
animal species or sub-species. The only one deemed truly dangerous
was the grizzly.

By 1890, the last grizzly was killed on the plains. In California,
which once had the greatest population of grizzlies, the mighty
golden bear was killed out by 1922. They were gone from Utah by
1923, from Arizona by 1930, and from New Mexico by 1931. A female
was killed in the San Juan Mountains of southern Colorado in 1979,
the first sighted that far south in 30 years. No trace of others has been
found.

It was in 1832, up the Missouri at Fort Union, painting the
Mandan Indians—who were to be killed out by smallpox within ten
years—that George Catlin saw what was happening. He imagined
saving some of it, ". . . a beautiful and thrilling specimen. . . . A
Nation's Park, containing man and beast, in all the wild and freshness
of their nature's beauty."

On March 1, 1872, Yellowstone Park, 2,221,773 acres, was established by Congress as a public "pleasuring-ground" for "the
preservation, from injury or spoilage, of all timber, mineral deposits,
natural curiosities, or wonders within . . . and their retention in their
natural condition." Glacier National Park was established on May 11,
1910, with essentially the same mandate. Some of our great wild country has been saved. And some of our grizzlies. Today the grizzly
occupies only one percent of its original habitat below the Canadian
border.

Probably, even by 1916, when Congress established the

National Park Service, nobody sensed in any clear way the knife of contradiction implicit in the establishment of these parks, the mutually exclusive purposes implied by the words "pleasuring-ground" and "preservation." The parks were eternally caught in some conceptual no-man's-land between zoo and sanctuary. This dichotomy lies at the heart of the sad controversy that exists today over the National Park Service's grizzly policy. The bears cannot be scrutinized in their wilderness without danger.

Doug Peacock knows this to be true. A man of tangled complexity, bearded and thick-shouldered and animated by obsessive fascination with wild country and the grizzly, Peacock operates outside the scientific wildlife-management community, without proper credentials beyond his years of experience with the animals and his driven hatred of anyone who threatens them.

At the same time Peacock is one of the legendary celebrities of antidevelopment politics. It started when Ed Abbey based his famous character George Hayduke, in *The Monkey-Wrench Gang*, on his friend Peacock. Such renown, while it can open doors, is also a burden. Doug would like to be seen as more than George Hayduke; he would like to be taken more seriously. He wants people to listen when he says the grizzlies must be given their own country to run.

Coming from a childhood colored by what he calls the "saintliness" of his father, a Boy Scout executive, and weeklong solitary trips into the Big Two-Hearted Country of the Upper Peninsula, Doug found himself an SDS radical at the University of Michigan, and then a Green Beret medic in Vietnam. He came home wounded in the soul from a bloody ordeal of healing Vietnamese, and for two years, he says, he was pure crazy, unable to talk in any sort of openly responsive way with anyone.

His cure came while he was living in a tent in the outback country of northwestern Wyoming, where he encountered his first grizzly, a great black alpha-dominant male. The indifferent, dignified otherness of the animal touched Peacock in a way that forced his craziness and anger out into the open, where he could see it as something other than a natural condition of life. Peacock focused his energy on the firm idea of helping to save the grizzly, and he began making a film that would reveal the bear as more than the spook-in-the-night killer inhabiting so many of our worst dreams.

Now Peacock is coming from a decade of trailing the bear

through Yellowstone in the snow-drifted spring, and Glacier in the berry-feeding season of summer, bushwhacking out alone into their country with his cameras. As he stalks about the lookout room where he has lived with his wife, Lisa, these last six summers, shouting when he gets excited, I think back to the lovely footage he showed us in the afternoon: a sow and her cubs at play in a tiny shallow tarn high in these mountains, batting at one another and blowing bubbles and breaking them in their fun, undisturbed in what we may without senti-mentality call a necessary wildness—necessary if we are to continue knowing ourselves as more than extensions of our machines.

"Yeah, that's a nice idea," Peacock says when I tell him where my thoughts are running. "But don't get sappy. With the grizzly you're always taking chances. Some old sow may eat me out from the asshole up. But they got a right. It's their country."

In one sequence, filmed in Yellowstone a couple of years ago, a huge yellow bear comes quietly on Peacock, taking him from the blind side, and just stares him down from close up. At least that was what the animal seemed to be doing in the beginning, jaws chomping softly as if contemplating action—but then the bear lowered its eyes and began pawing at clumps of sedge and pretending to eat, looking up full into the camera and then away again, as if willing to consider the possibility of not being the dominant animal in that scenario, maybe forced into a nervous behavior resembling the play-acting indifference of junior-high children at a dress-up party staged by adults. That is what Peacock calls displacement behavior: something to do while you back down gracefully.

If that's what it was, backing down. There is no knowing what a bear might be thinking, but it is obvious they are capable of coming to decisions of real complexity. I keep recalling those stone-hard bar-fighter eyes, and then the flickerings of softness, and wondering if the animal *was* backing down. Maybe it was just taking pity.

"How close was that bear?"

"Right there. I was had. I had to step back to focus." Peacock pulls the cork on our bottle of Glenlivet again. "There was nothing to do but keep the camera running."

Peacock stares down into the neck of the bottle, then looks up grinning. "It was the camera," he says. "He was trying to stare down the camera."

PEACOCK SAYS HE'S been charged maybe 40 times, and so far never touched. From what he tells me, and judging from his film, the bears react to people somewhat as they react to one another, always evaluating social and predator-prey signals and relationships—if you give them a little time and some space.

There is a "critical attack distance," about 50 yards in open country, within which the bear will feel threatened and, by automatic response, attack rather than retreat. Peacock's advice is to let them know you are coming. Otherwise, up close and surprised—big quick trouble.

Out in the backlands, Peacock says, move slowly through the brush, as any animal does. Stop every few yards and listen, like a deer. The grizzlies are threatened by no one but man and usually make a great deal of noise, feeding and crashing about in their self-assured way. When you hear them, give them room. Move slowly once they are aware of you. What Peacock does is talk to them, slowly, in a deep voice. Stand tall, do not panic, and if they charge give them time to stop.

If they don't know you are around, climb a tree. Once they spot you, it is too late. They are too close. If they go at you, drop to a fetal position, and do not resist. They'll generally chew at you a little, and give up. You hope.

Most of all, Peacock says, do not strike out and run blindly. Grizzly country is a dumb place to go jogging. You will resemble prey trying to escape, and they will come after you at an impressive rate of speed in rough country—300 yards in 20 seconds, faster than a quarter horse.

A sow with cubs will often come and look you over, primarily because grizzlies suffer poor vision and can't make out a man for what he is at more than a couple of hundred yards. But then, if you don't get between her and her babies, she'll usually back off.

Sometimes they are just cranky, he says, like the sows when they are weaning their young. Often you can get in trouble with young subadults, maybe three or four years old, who have been driven from their mothers but have not yet found their place in the world. They suffer stress and adolescent bewilderment and are about as unpredictable as bears get. And in the fall, when most of the berries are gone and the grizzlies are trying to put on a layer of fat for the oncoming winter, when the competition for forage is most intense, the mature bear can be edgily dangerous.

You can feel it, Peacock says. He and Lisa were ten miles away the night Mary Pat Mahoney was killed in the Many Glaciers Campground. You could smell danger in the air, Peacock says.

"Ask Lisa," he says.

So I ask Lisa.

"Yeah," she says. "It's true. Craziness."

It was the same in late September of 1980, Peacock says, when Laurence Gordon was killed while camped in the middle of a feeding ground at Elizabeth Lake. Peacock and Lisa were a couple of drainages away. Many of the animals, Peacock says, were nervous that afternoon, quick on the draw. From what I can make of the story, in the various tellings I have heard, that bear, unlike almost all grizzlies, was intent on killing. Maybe it was just quick anger at the intrusion, or the simple prospect of animal protein for dinner, or one individual's vengeance for endless insult to the species—if you believe, as some do, that some bears have the wit to hate us. Whatever the reason, Laurence Gordon was a dead man from the time he set up his tent.

With the Glenlivet in hand, I step out on the veranda porch and watch the eclipse proceed, and wonder whether we all share a taste for such secondhand dangers, something inherited from childhood—boogeymen in the bedroom—and whether that yearning for darkness doesn't contaminate much of our response to the grizzly. And I wonder if we cannot, as Peacock claims, have a true North American wilderness without the great and dangerous and emblematic bear out there feeding on bulbs of blue camas and tubers of yampa, on biscuit-root, pine nuts, and stinking dead-overwinter carrion. I wonder if wilderness must indeed, by definition, be inhabited by some power greater than ourselves.

The wind blows heavily as we settle toward sleep. The Glenlivet is gone and the eclipse wanes. For this night the frog has given up on eating the moon.

IF YOU UNDERSTAND science as I have been taught it, as measurement and data and hypotheses and verifiable conclusions, grizzly studies look pretty shaky—with good reason. Belling a grizzly is not exactly like studying the genetics of fruit-fly populations. To study the bear you've got to get your ass out there in the deepest backwoods and take the risk that your object of scrutiny may come rearing from the next berry patch with a pissed-off look in its eye.

There was no remotely sensible way of getting in close and scientific with the grizzly until 1959, when effective tranquilizers and dart guns came on the scene together. Twenty-some years is not much time in the evolution of science, and so far hard data is in short supply. Too many decisions seem to be made on the basis of personal guesswork, informed opinion, but nevertheless, opinion.

In 1959 John and Frank Craighead, brothers, began their work with the grizzly in Yellowstone, trapping and immobilizing and examining more than 600 bears, radio-collaring and monitoring the activities of a few, collecting what is still the largest bank of data on movements, home ranges, food habits, social and denning behavior, age-sex ratios, mortality rates, and other population factors, generally working toward some understanding of the complex relationships between men and bears. By the late 1960's the Craigheads felt they had identified about 75 percent of the grizzlies in the Yellowstone ecosystem, estimating the total in 1967 to be 245 bears.

That was the year the big trouble began. In separate incidents on the night of August 13, 1967, two 19-year-old women, Michele Koons and Julie Helgesen, suffered horror-movie deaths by grizzly attack. The killings were vividly detailed in a book called *Night of the Grizzly*. One of those women, it is thought, was killed by a bear that had been feeding at an open garbage dump near Granite Park Chalet in Glacier. The dump was closed. For reasons that in retrospect seem to have been results of bureaucratic panic, officials at Yellowstone decided to close their own dumps, where grizzlies had been feeding for generations.

The Craigheads, who had done most of their trapping near those dumps, recommended that they be closed gradually. They warned that with sudden closure garbage-habituated bears would likely move out into campgrounds, drastically increasing the chances of human-bear confrontation. Yellowstone officials disagreed and suggested the Craigheads mind their own business. By 1971, the same year the last dumps were shut down, the Craigheads were gone from Yellowstone.

The next year, a grizzly in Yellowstone killed a young camper named Harry Walker. Walker's parents sued the National Park Service in U.S. District Court in California. Despite Park Service claims that Walker had been illegally camped and careless with his garbage, Judge

A. Andrew Hauk found for the plaintiffs in 1975 and sharply rebuked the Park Service for ignoring the Craighead predictions. Harry Walker's heirs were awarded $87,417.67 in damages. The judgment was later reversed on courtroom technicalities. Along the way a lot of battle lines were drawn, and grizzly science became inextricably embroiled in politics.

CONFLICTS OVER SCIENTIFIC grizzly studies—and the numbers such studies produce—are politically loaded. For instance, population studies: nobody seems to know how many bears we have in the various ecosystems, or whether these populations are on the upswing or decline, or even how many bears it takes to keep a population alive. Answers depend on whom you ask—and to some degree, on why they are guessing.

Clearly it is in the interest of hunters and state fish and game officials, who sell highly valued permits to kill the grizzly, for population estimates to run high. The more bears we have, the more we have for hunters to "harvest." Conservationists and biologists would like to keep population estimates on the low side. An endangered species, after all, tends to generate grant money—more studies, employing more biologists, more bureaucrats. But without an accurate population count your guess is as good as anybody's.

Through all this scientific uncertainty, the National Park Service must concern itself with a very real conflict: how to preserve the bear, host millions of visitors a year, and keep dangerous confrontations minimal. Meanwhile the troubles get worse.

From 1910, when Glacier was created, through 1955, only one person was injured by a grizzly. As park use accelerated and backpackers replaced horsepackers, the situation changed drastically. Ten persons were injured between 1956 and 1966. Then, in 1967, the dark "night of the grizzly," the deaths of Michele Koons and Julie Helgesen, and, in 1972, Harry Walker, and my friend Mary Pat Mahoney in 1976.

On July 24, 1980, Kim Eberly and Jane Ammerman were killed while camping near the eastern boundary of Glacier, and on September 28, 1980, Laurence Gordon was killed at Elizabeth Lake. Some bears were relocated, others shot.

The park grizzlies clearly have lost what they may never have had, their so-called "shyness"—fear of man. There is vague talk of weeding out the troublemakers, selecting for shyness—which sounds like genetic nonsense—or just plain teaching them some respect. The bears in the Bob Marshall Wilderness, people say, are hunted each fall, and they don't cause all that trouble. Of course, they haven't been crowded by people, either.

There is talk of shooting the bear with rubber bullets, rock salt, and number-nine bird shot, all kinds of "aversive conditioning." The operative concept is pain, and the bottom line, from what I can gather listening to experts, is that nothing really works, consistently. Different bears react in different ways. A hide full of bird shot may cause some to run for cover, but others may come seeking revenge. The only real deterrent seems to be luck and common sense, and, when all else fails, a .44 magnum pistol.

The solution that looks most promising is the management of people: closing areas and trails and keeping the public and bears away from one another. One thing is sure. If we don't take some pains, there are going to be no more grizzlies in our wilderness.

> The whole shitaree. Gone, by God, and naught to care savin'
> some who seen her new. . . .   —*The Big Sky*

Bud Guthrie lives alongside the Teton River in central Montana, near where he grew up, and dead center in the country he celebrates in the novel. "I wrote that book," he says, "to show the way people kill the things they most love. Like a child with a kitten, they squeeze it to death."

From Bud's kitchen window you can see close-up the fancy mountains of the Rockies' front, the eastern edge of the Bob Marshall ecosystem, some 3,500,000 acres of wilderness, if you include Glacier Park. And all of it is overthrust country. Already, out on the plains around Bud's house, the seismic testing is pretty much completed. And there continues to be talk of oil and natural gas exploration in the Bob Marshall Wilderness itself. Just a couple of miles south from Bud's house lies the Pine Butte Swamp, most of which is owned by The Nature Conservancy, a private foundation dedicated to the preservation of vital wildlife habitat, in this case territory where the last grizzlies dare to come down from their mountain hideout and onto the plains.

But . . . there is talk that we ought to hire professional hunters and wipe the bears out, slick and clean, and have done with all the wilderness management problems they create. It wouldn't be a matter of their extinction from the earth. There are thousands in Canada and Alaska.

Our major problem is grizzly habitat. The bears need huge spaces to roam, maybe a hundred square miles for males (Peacock says more), preferably without roads or trails or backpackers with orange tents, or industrial activity. The bears seem to react to overcrowding as we do: they lose all sense of themselves and drift into a wild aggressiveness, which is beyond doubt one reason for maulings and blood killings in the National Parks. The grizzly, like us, can find the rewards of civilization to be too much of a good thing.

Up there on Huckleberry Mountain, I couldn't sleep after our night with the eclipse and the Glenlivet—call it informational and emotional overload, not to speak of a narrow bed. As the sky broke light over the peaks of Glacier, I found myself deeply moved by the view from our elevation, off west the lights of Montana, Hungry Horse, and Columbia Falls, and farmsteads along the northern edge of Flathead Lake, and back in the direction of sunrise the soft and misted valleys of the parklands, not an electric light showing: little enough to preserve for the wanderings of a great and sacred animal who can teach us, if nothing else, by his power and his dilemma, a little common humility.

A. B. GUTHRIE WAS RAISED near Choteau, Montana, where his father was a high-school principal. After graduating from the University of Montana in 1923, he worked for *The Lexington Leader* in Kentucky for twenty-one years as a newspaper reporter, city editor, and editorial writer. While studying at Harvard under a Nieman Fellowship in 1944, Guthrie wrote his second novel, *The Big Sky*, which related the adventures of a trio of mountain men on the Upper Missouri River in the early nineteenth century. The novel was made into a Howard Hawks film in 1952, starring Kirk Douglas. Guthrie's third novel, *The Way West* (1952), was awarded the Pulitzer Prize for fiction and was made into a highly successful film. In the early 1950s, Guthrie worked in Hollywood as a screenwriter and was nominated for an Academy Award in 1953 for his script for *Shane*. Guthrie was an ardent environmentalist; he worked for the preservation of wild lands and wildlife before those causes were as popular as they are today.

In this selection from his collected essays, *Big Sky, Fair Land: The Environmental Essays of A. B. Guthrie, Jr.* (1988), edited by Dave Petersen, A. B. Guthrie writes about the grizzlies of the Rocky Mountain Front east of Glacier National Park in Montana. The Nature Conservancy's Pine Butte Swamp Grizzly Bear Preserve is only a short drive from the Guthrie ranch. Guthrie knows from experience that, although the bears are dangerous, they are also intelligent animals and will go out of their way to avoid people: "I know they've been near, but I don't see them, for these are unspoiled mountain bears. They travel by dark or in the cover of draws, wanting no trouble." Guthrie deplores the "extremists" and "rumor-mongers" who wildly exaggerate the dangers posed by grizzlies, and argues eloquently here on behalf of his beloved Montana grizzlies.

"The Rocky Mountain Front" is taken from A. B. Guthrie's Big Sky, Fair Land: The Environmental Essays of A. B. Guthrie, Jr., edited by David Petersen, copyright © 1988 by A. B. Guthrie, Jr., and David Petersen, published by Northland Publishing. The piece was originally published in Montana magazine. It is reprinted by permission of A. B. Guthrie.

9. THE ROCKY MOUNTAIN FRONT

A. B. GUTHRIE, JR.

I AM A RESIDENT, YOU MIGHT ALMOST SAY A PRODUCT, OF the Rocky Mountain Front, "the Front," as we have come to call it. It is a strip of land just east of the Continental Divide and includes an edge of the plains, the higher benchlands, the foothills and then the great, jagged wall of the mountains. It starts just east of Glacier Park and includes on its outer rim the towns of Browning, Dupuyer, Bynum, Augusta, and Helena. The crow-flight distance is about 160 miles.

When we speak of the Front we are thinking not of the towns and the plains but of the western rises, the benches, the hills and the mountains that seem to stand guard over creature and land.

I know the Front well, particularly that section west of Choteau, where the Muddy and the Teton and Deep Creek flow, for I spent my young life in the town. I live now 25 miles to the west of it. Just four miles from our home rears my vision site of Ear Mountain. I use the term by extension. It was to the mountain that young Indian boys came, staying on top of it without food or water until, feverish and fanciful, they found their talismans, or medicine, in the form of bird or animal, thereafter held sacred. Don't think of them as foolishly superstitious. Superstition, as a philosopher remarked, is the other fellow's religion. I find my medicine just by looking.

Again to the west of us, three miles or less, runs the Old North Trail, which, it is surmised, travelers from Siberia followed after crossing the Bering land bridge to Alaska. One theory is that they merged with or became our American Indians. Well, maybe. Another is that they continued on to South America. Maybe again. The truth lies centuries beyond the backward reach of history. But there is no question that man came down the Front.

The trail is just one evidence of prehistory to be found on the Front. In late years 10 miles from our place, paleontologists have uncovered thousands of fossils of duck-billed dinosaurs—those of adults, infants, nests and eggs, all vestiges of the life of 70 million years ago. It perished, that life, seemingly all at once. Scientists incline to the belief that a great asteroid struck the earth and that the animals died from the dust and debris and especially from the cold that came with the blotting out of the sun. They wonder, too, about the classification of dinosaurs. They are commonly called reptiles, but the evidence suggests they were warm-blooded creatures that cared for their young, as reptiles are not and do not.

After the dinosaur came the mammal, notably the buffalo that included the Front in its range. If it weren't for obstacles in the way of sight, I could see a buffalo jump from our home. The bottom of that jump, where Indians butchered the dead and dying, has been mined and screened for arrowheads and mined and screened again, for it has been a rich source.

At the age of 86, living on the Front, I have come to feel a part of what has gone before, kin to dinosaur and buffalo and departed Indians that lived here. When I step out of doors and hear a small crunch underfoot I sometimes suspect I may be treading on the dusted bones of duckbill or bison or red man killed in the hunt.

But as I am part and brother of what went before, so am I related to the living creatures that inhabit the Front. They exist in great variety. That fact struck me again this past July when my wife, Carol, and I were returning from a meeting up the Teton canyon. It was night, but the long light of summer held on, and there in the middle of the road, magical, a mountain lion paused, then glided across into the bushes. A mountain lion! A creature so shy of man, so elusive, as to be rarely seen. Sometime travelers in the mountains hereabouts have never spotted one.

To find mountain lions you need dogs, and one day, I fear, hunters' dogs will find the scent of this one and tree it after a chase, and the hunters, following, will shoot it down and get their proud pictures in the paper along with their trophy.

I count out animals in my mind—bears, black and grizzly, deer, coyotes, badgers, beavers, raccoons, otters, minks, skunks, ground squirrels, three kinds of rabbit, sometimes an elk, rarely a wolf, maybe a moose, more rarely a mountain lion. An experienced guide once told me that the Front, at least part of the time, was home to virtually every Rocky Mountain creature.

Of these, bears get the most attention, particularly grizzly bears. The black bear is quite common and almost always harmless, and so people accept it, more or less. In our 12 years here, two have nosed around the house, hoping for garbage that we don't leave outside. The grizzly is a different proposition. Alarmed suddenly, chased or in the presence of imagined danger to its cubs, it is a fearsome animal.

Some people have criticized me for defending the grizzly. How wrong-headed was I to overlook the danger and discount the losses? All right. The passions of the moment pass and don't count in the long run. I stand by my convictions while tending to forget and forgive.

But while thinking of that great bear, the most memorable creature alive on this continent, this part of our lore and our heritage, I don't want it to disappear. Let him live.

Our visitors, in addition to the two black bears, include a badger. It ambles around the house, intent on some business of its own, and, unafraid, takes its flowing body down the bank to the river and is lost to sight. Deer are frequent presences in our backyard. Coyotes often sing at night. Once Carol spotted a wolf.

We are hosts now to five cottontails, a mixed blessing since they eat the plants in our ground-level flower boxes. We threaten to shoot them, but don't. Our impulses are contradictory. Last winter we heard a cry, that seldom-uttered, plaintive cry of the desperate, and we hurried to the back window to see. A cottontail was jumping, jumping to dislodge a little white death that swung from its neck. But no jumps could loosen that throat hold. The rabbit fell down and quivered and died, and the little white death fed on its blood. And our sympathies were with the pesky rabbit, not with the weasel.

The Bob Marshall Wilderness just west of the Front is great and needs no justification other than its being wilderness. Horseback riders and backpackers penetrate the miles of it to their great enjoyment. But what far more visitors see and appreciate is the Front. They come to it to picnic, to fish and to hunt and perhaps just to breathe the breath of free space. They can reach it easily, for there are roads to many spots. Men and women, residents of the Front towns and of the bigger ones farther east, come in numbers.

The situation may change. Some of the Front is privately owned. Far more is under the control of the Bureau of Land Management and the Forest Service. Much hinges on their decisions, for oil men and miners and timber cutters keep filing for permission to drill and blast and cut. In one instance I know of, drillers didn't wait for clearance. Activities like these frighten wild animals away, deface the land and in the case of timber felling give rise to floods.

Officials of counties like my own tend to line up with the despoilers, not without immediate reason, for counties are hard put these days, suffering from two years of dry weather and low prices for cattle and grains. Anything at all promising in the way of cash and jobs exerts its appeal. I believe, if reluctantly, that the officials are reflecting the convictions of the constituents.

They forget. They forget. As one man said of the Forest Service, they have no memory function. Without remembrance of the past, they are compelled to repeat it, as the philosopher Santayana said of history and civilizations. Few remember when the Teton River ran full, season to season. That was before clear-cutting and overgrazing and cultivation made a spring flood of it and a dry creek bed later.

Real estate developers threaten us, too. They regard every open space that may yield profit as an invitation to hammer and saw. Given opportunity and customers they would develop all the miles of the Front. That would be the end of it, of course.

We who live near the mountains tend to be protective of our environment. When it was proposed to sell cabin sites on about 150 acres along the south fork of the Teton, we filed suit. By we I mean ourselves, the Kenneth Gleasons, and the Wilderness Society. A few contributors helped us. The cabin sites, 37 of them, lay at an important entrance to the Bob Marshall Wilderness.

We proved in court that the contour of the acreage prevented effective septic disposal. We proved that the likelihood of finding water was remote. We proved that the State Board of Health, one of the defendants, had hardly investigated at all before giving the development approval.

Unaccountably, the judge, after accepting our contentions, found for the defendants.

We prepared to appeal and went so far as to have a transcript made. We didn't win the case then, so much as wear it out. Facing an appeal, the developers gave up, so advised, I would bet, by their attorneys, who felt that a reversal was sure.

It may sound as if I oppose every would-be cabin builder, as if, given the power, I would close the Front to all cabin seekers. That is not my position and not, I am sure, the position of other dwellers here. What's a cabin here and there, reasonably insulated by space? But 37 cabins on limited acreage! One building to about every four acres! Suburban cluster in our foothills!

I have fished most of the streams of the Front. I have hunted its covers for rabbits and grouse. From its beaver basins and lakes I have flushed mallards and bluebills, three kinds of teal and other waterfowl I made sure to identify. I have picnicked with family and friends. I have known all its weathers—the caress of spring, the frying heat of summer and the bite of cold when sundogs dog the sun. I can't say, with the naturalist John Burroughs, that always have goodness and joy waited on my comings and goings. It's enough that I have come out ahead.

I suppose people not of the Front think it odd of us, or at least eccentric, to live where we do, away from cities and the offerings of cities, away even from a small town where we could have close neighbors and take part in community activities. Maybe we are a bit strange, but I look to the north and the south, where foothills rise, east to the great roll of the high plains and west to the mountains and my vision site of Ear Mountain, and good medicine lies all around.

DOUG PEACOCK, ON WHOM Edward Abbey based the
character of George Hayduke in *The Monkey-Wrench Gang*, is one
of the most outspoken and visible defenders of the grizzly bear in
America today. Since returning from the Vietnam War in the late
1960s—a tour that included frontline duty as a Green Beret
medic—Peacock has sought out and studied the grizzlies of both
Yellowstone National Park and Glacier National Park. Peacock's
personal memoir of his life with bears, *Grizzly Years* (1990), was
published to immediate critical acclaim; the entire first edition
sold out within a month. Peacock is a tireless, impassioned, and
uncompromising defender of the grizzly. He has been the subject
of essays written by authors of the stature of Peter Matthiessen
and William Kittredge (see the Kittredge selection, "Grizzly"). In
this essay from *Grizzly Years,* Peacock describes a difficult cross-
country excursion over the Continental Divide in northern
Montana. Peacock is famous for such adventures, which take him
far from maintained trails but deep into the heartland of the
mountain grizzly.

"Across the Divide" is taken from Doug Peacock's Grizzly Years *(Henry
Holt, 1990) and is reprinted by permission of Doug Peacock and Henry
Holt Company, Inc.*

10. ACROSS THE DIVIDE

DOUG PEACOCK

AT DAWN, I WALKED BACK UP THE SNOWY BASIN AND watched the morning light creep into the valley. The snow-filled amphitheater seemed less ominous. We had to find a route over the divide, and we hoped Bob's bear would show us the way. I saw the paw prints on the snow and picked up the line of bear tracks above the timber, traversing the white ledges and climbing up to the blanket of snow covering the upper drainage of Morning Eagle. He was traveling alone; there was no sign of the smaller bear with whom he crossed the divide. His trail crossed the creek and climbed steeply south and east out of the U-shaped valley. We would be following his spoor.

We broke camp in silence. Bob packed away his equipment after trying to monitor the bear. I shook the dew off the tent, rolled it into a sloppy cylinder, and stuffed it into my backpack. Passing the last big trees in the valley, I picked a route over a series of snowy ledges, roughly following the tracks of the grizzly, contouring up and out of the upper basin. We walked as much as possible on the snow, which was still deep enough to cover the alder. We crossed the bear tracks, which led west, and continued climbing south along the ledges.

All of a sudden we found ourselves staring up at a vertical section of rock and brush—not exactly a technical climb but an awkward and arduous one considering our sixty-pound packs. Stupidly I had wandered too far south, beyond the cascade of gradual ledges leading down from the divide. I should have stayed on the track of the grizzly, who knew where he was going.

I relaxed a bit. My mood lightened as I concentrated on the mountain. Lisa, who was already an accomplished technical climber when I met her, would have welcomed a challenge like this. For years now I had gone up the easy sides of mountain peaks. Too stubborn to turn around, we decided to keep climbing up the steplike cliffs. The rock was mixed with a jumble of glacial moraine, partially weathered into thin soil, making the trip up to the ridge miserable and filthy. We paused on a slick, muddy ledge and looked up at five-needle evergreens, whitebark, or limber pine, indicating that we were approaching the ridgetop. It could not be more than a couple of hundred feet above us.

We climbed over the lip of the last rotten cliff into the shade of the deep green trees. Breathing and sweating heavily, I sat on the three feet of snow lingering under the timber and cooled off. This was as wild as the country gets in the lower forty-eight. All that is necessary to control human impact on a place like this is to leave the mountain valleys without constructed foot trails. It's cheap and democratic. I wonder why the park and forest services have not figured out that if you leave every other backcountry drainage without trails, you create entire regions to which animals like grizzlies can escape during the peak months of human travel.

There are precious few drainages, mesas, or playas within our so-called wilderness areas in the lower forty-eight that are not crisscrossed by an extensive network of foot trails. The valleys and passes through which we had just traveled were hardly remote; they simply did not have developed trail systems. They received just the right amount of human visitation without the imposition of management: the animals had a sanctuary, a place to which even the shiest ones, like grizzlies, could retreat and be left undisturbed. Man has been a member of grizzly bear biotic communities for at least the last twelve thousand years—so it's quite natural to have a few *Homo sapiens* pass through.

The pines thinned out as we scrambled over the moguls of crusted snow onto the open ridge. We found a short, steep pitch of packed snow where Bob practiced an ice axe arrest—a technique for stopping yourself if you fall and start sliding down a steep slope of snow. It's a good tool when crossing the Great Divide in early June, and a new one to Bob. I had some earlier practice, having once done three unsuccessful ice axe arrests on a fall down a frozen eight-hundred-foot snow gully: the fourth one bit in and held a hundred feet from the bottom, where the chute dropped into a boulder field. That was one of two climbing records I held in the North Cascades. The other was when I fell into a crevasse on a glacier while traveling alone. Luckily I landed on a snow bridge twelve feet down and was able to claw myself out without embarrassment, since no one was watching. I blamed my horoscope, which said I was accident-prone. I was sure such mountaineering ignominy happened all the time, though no one else advertised. I neglected to fill Lisa in on this, as I was putting the move on her and had my image to protect.

The ridge climbed out to a huge sloping slab of snow and ice, dotted by a few clumps of dwarf alpine trees. We hurried into the nearest timber, a patch of stunted fir trees, as a storm squall swept across the whiteness, blowing stinging hail into our faces. It appeared these little storms would continue throughout the day, so we waited this one out. Above us were a string of small snow-covered glaciers, below which I planned on passing. Above the snowfields stretched the divide itself, undulating and gently sloping to the east, but dropping off abruptly to the west into the hidden recesses of Silenos Cirque three thousand feet below. Finding a route in there would normally have been our biggest problem on this trip. Instead, I was trusting the trail of the young bear to lead us safely to the bottom.

We waited out another snow squall, which restricted our visibility. The grizzly trail led south over the snow, around the foot of towering snowfields, and climbed toward a low pass between two peaks. We passed two tiny azure tarns beginning to melt in the weak spring sunlight filtering through the breaks in the clouds. This pass was the route Bob's bear and his consort had taken the week before. Snow covered the old spoor; only the previous day's tracks remained. He was going down into Silenos by himself.

About midday, the snow began to melt and we wallowed, breaking through the crust to our knees. We had only about a mile to go to the pass. We kicked steps up a moderate incline, walked out onto a small flat, and looked out into space. We were there: the Continental Divide, the high point of our trip.

A forest of windswept stunted pine trees clung to a partially melted-out ridge on the southwestern exposures. Before us the country dropped off into a large glacial valley thousands of feet below, which ran off twenty miles into the gray distance of the North Fork of the Flathead River. I could have stayed there forever, but bad weather was on the way in from the west. We sat on a mat of heather with our feet dangling down toward Silenos.

The shallow valley bottom of the North Fork and its mosaic of low meadows stretched toward Canada. Bob had studied the vegetation of these meadowlands, some of which are fallow fields from early homesteads, and said there was more grizzly food in those old farmlands than any other place he had studied in Glacier National Park. Other meadows lay over old alluvial channels of the river and were rich in cow parsnip in the spring and sweetvetch in the fall. This complex of open areas along the North Fork is the most important spring habitat for grizzlies down here, especially in April and May, when higher areas are under show. By June, grizzlies begin to disperse, drawn by spring green-up and the dynamics of the mating season.

I owned an acre of land somewhere down there. I bought it from another whacko–Nam vet whose trust I won by bailing him out of the slammer after he got busted on an old deer-poaching rap. I had no plans for improvement or development; I bought the place only so no one else would. The whole idea of owning the land was still alien to me. I bought it for Lisa and my dog during a period when I was not particularly happy, to hedge my bets against mortality and cut the inevitable losses. I knew that the land would last.

We lingered between storms, enjoying this enchanted swale where the snowfields began. I wandered off looking for the trail of the bear. On a cornice of snow overhanging a dizzying abyss, I found a set of tracks five inches long with the clawed thumbprint registering in the soft snow: a wolverine shared the snowy pass with Bob's bear. That part of Montana around Glacier National Park is the last place left in the contiguous states where all the Rocky Mountain megafauna that was here when the white man showed up on the East Coast can still be found: the wolf, the wolverine, the woodland caribou, and the grizzly.

We started down off the pass into the huge cirque, the head of

which was hidden behind sheer cliffs. The bottom reportedly contained the most impenetrable jumble of downfalls in the region,
having been overprotected from wildfires, which would otherwise
burn through it every thirty years or so and keep the timber open.
The steep slopes of Silenos provided some of the best late spring and
early summer habitat for grizzlies. Dropping rapidly, we slipped and
slid a thousand feet down the gulch, then contoured north at the foot
of the cliffs above the awful mix of brush and downed timber.

Slowly we made our way below the steep cliffs and edged down
toward the trees, where Bob wanted to check out a bedding spot on
which he had located his bear from the air the previous week. He
stopped and dug out his radio gear while I glassed the wild basin. A
black bear was grazing beneath the far cliffs despite my expecting to
see nothing but grizzlies up there. Bob rotated his antenna and heard
a faint signal from somewhere far off in a distant corner of the cirque.
The transmission bounced off the cliffs and bedrock, so that he could
not pinpoint the young grizzly.

Following the animal path we made the best time we had made in
five days. The sun dropped behind low clouds in the western sky. It
must have been past midafternoon. Bob took out his topographic
maps and located a radio fix where his bear had bedded the week
before. The spot lay directly below us, in an angle of timber a thousand feet below. As much as we hated to leave this facilitating game
trail for the agonies of bushwhacking, our job was to do ground investigations of all the sites Bob had marked.

We entered the trees and almost immediately ran into a vertical
jungle of downfalls stacked twenty feet in the air. We spent half an
hour looking for the specific bed site. It could have been anywhere in
that maze. We dropped down to the bottom of the small creek hoping
for easier going. Instead, we found the labyrinth of windfalls piled
high with uprooted trees and the debris of countless avalanches
coming off the opposite slope. It began to rain. We tottered along the
spines of slippery deadfalls, leaning on our ice axes for stability as we
leapt down to the next tier of dead wood. By evening we had not
come much more than a mile. We were tired, frustrated, and irritable.
I told Bob that he was heading in the wrong direction.

"Fuck you, all you want to do is go up to that lake and go fishing."

"Go die alone, asshole," I said. "I'm not going into that valley
bottom."

We decided to take the shortest route to the creek, since we needed to find water and make camp. We launched ourselves into another vertical stack of downed timber, slipping on the treacherous sections of wet, naked logs. We fell a dozen times apiece but were too loose and inebriated by fatigue to injure ourselves. The rain continued. Just at dark we hit the creek and forded the knee-deep water. I found a soggy campsite within a few feet of the glacial stream, which I hoped would not rise during the night. I pitched the tent in a puddle of water and we crawled into our wet sleeping bags. We shared a canteen-cupful of murky protein powder, which ended our bickering.

I felt for a hip-shaped depression in the sump over which we had put up the tent. I was too weary to sleep deeply. My stomach growled and I conjured up a vision of leg of lamb stuffed with many cloves of garlic, basted with oil and rosemary, and roasted over mesquite coals. Of course I try to boycott lamb because the sheep industry has the habit of poisoning or shooting every bear, coyote, or eagle in rifle range. Running sheep is incompatible with grizzly habitat. A grizzly will wade through a herd of woollies tossing the mangled carcasses left and right. The whining and bleating and endless run of excreta seem to trigger something in the bear's predatory wiring to make him attack solely out of irritation.

The next morning found us sore and bruised but in better spirits. The rain had stopped, and, despite the fact that we had covered only a mile and a half in six hours the previous day, we were on our way out. The bushwhack down the side of the big lake in the valley would, we thought, take only two or three days. Meanwhile, as a result of my unceasing lobbying, we started upstream to visit Silenos Lake.

We scaled the last latticework of branches and trunks and stepped into a meadow of false hellebore and cow parsnip. Three minutes later we gazed across the cerulean waters of Silenos Lake and the half dozen waterfalls pouring off the ice and rock into this great hole. The lake was free of ice, though large snowfields lingered at the northern end. Bob caught movement high up the eastern wall, just below the snow line. A brown grizzly sow, with one of the smallest cubs I had ever seen, moved directly across a snow patch into avalanche brush and disappeared. She was too far away to notice us. The cub was what I call a spring cub, a guess on my part that the tiny bear might have been born a few weeks after the normal birthing time of late January and February.

We returned to the lake shore and cut long willow poles. I tied on ten feet of fly line attached to another eight feet of nylon leader and let a small, orange-bellied streamer drift out at the mouth of one of the feeder creeks. I always carry line, leader, and a few flies. Once, in Alaska, I lived for seven days on the grayling I caught on a dwarfed willow pole. This time the willow fly pole did not pan out.

We gave it up and walked along the shore. The openness of the alpine cirque, the turquoise water, and the sky beyond were salve to our soggy souls. The clouds, brush, and dark forests had worn us down. I savored these moments in the heart of our journey, this wild basin from which a river of ice flowed.

Stepping up on a slab of baked claystone, I surveyed the far corner of the lake. On the fan of snow alongside the lake below the glacier were patterns of tracks and networks of patterns. Even at that distance there was no mistaking the sign of adult bears. We moved in for a closer look. Long, large, sliding tracks—like those on Bullshoe trail—streaked down a slope. Sets of tracks ran together in at least two distinctive gaits. The front track of a smaller grizzly disappeared, and at one point the tracks of a large running grizzly were etched on the snow—claws digging and rear pads straining forward. There was much more than I could read. What I did not understand I imagined.

THE SOW WAS YOUNG, four and a half or five and a half years old. Although she had mated before, the breeding had not been success-ful. She had returned to this cirque, where she had spent much time as a cub and yearling, from the wet meadows twenty miles west, where, throughout the spring, she had fed on grass and forbs along the ripar-ian zone of the major river. She had been aware of the boar browsing upwind for some time, but she grazed on unconcerned.

The male grizzly was fully mature and fairly large—about 450 pounds. By the time the big bear noticed the female, they fed only a hundred yards apart. Without hesitation he approached directly with his stiff-legged swagger, his neck arched and his head held low. She stood motionless until he came close; she lowered her head and shoulders, pointing her nose in the air. They stood side by side like this for a long time. The boar sniffed along the side of her head and rubbed his flanks against her. She moved off a few feet and pretended to graze. He nuzzled her and tried to herd her away from her feeding, but she persisted. They spent several hours nibbling the fresh green leaves of *Heracleum;* the female did most of the feeding while he attended her. They bedded close together in the slide alder during the middle of the day.

The shadows fell over the great amphitheater of Silenos and the pair rose and moved. They loped and romped over the open areas, sometimes side by side, sometimes with the female in the lead. Within minutes they reached the snowfield at the head of the lake below the glacier. She broke into a short run. He followed, his swaggering gait greatly exaggerated now. The boar appeared to lick the female's ears. She turned back with her jaws open like a cowering, playful shepherd dog. He mounted her, grasping her flanks with his front legs. They remained motionless for a while. He leaned forward and nibbled at her neck. He was salivating and his rear legs were wet with urine. She turned back toward him and they exchanged bites. She knelt at one point, then got up and shuffled forward on the snow. The copulation went on for twenty minutes. Afterward they stood quietly.

Suddenly the boar bowed his neck and lowered his head. He snorted, arched his neck, and took long, stiff-legged strides on the snow, swinging his large head violently from side to side.

I REREAD THE SCENE with my binoculars one more time from about 120 yards away. That was the closest we should be. This white flat was the arena below the great amphitheater of Silenos, the wild stage on which the grizzlies danced for no one; this was a mating area.

Distinctive breeding grounds for grizzlies have not been identified, but that doesn't mean they do not exist. They were perhaps like elephant burial grounds, sacred ground, at least for me: I wanted my reverence to buy me an ounce of grace. I buried the orange streamer at the edge of the lake as a token offering.

We packed up and crawled back down the creek into the tangle of brush and dead trees. By midday we passed the previous night's camp and picked up our stashed equipment. Straining under full packs, we struggled up and over the piles of ancient timber. We told ourselves what we had been saying each successive day: This was the worst bushwhacking we had ever seen.

By late afternoon we reached the head of a long, narrow lake filling a glacial trough. We picked up a game trail along the north shore of the lake and made good time until dusk. A cascading creek ran off the mountain, depositing a small alluvial delta at the edge of the lake. We stepped out on the spit and watched the sun set over the distant shore.

The dawn was a flat gray over the calm waters. We pushed out early, knowing that we were only a long day's travel to the nearest trail and that it was going to rain. With some luck and steady humping, we would be out by dark. We climbed above steep rocky cliffs that plunged into the lake, struggling upward on the dry southeast-facing slope until we reached a mixed forest of pine and fir. Animal trails traced the contour of the ridge. Our game trail faded out and we scrambled higher on the hill looking for another. Climbing too high on the ridge we found ourselves lost in a sea of little gullies undulating endlessly across the breast of the mountainside. We rolled up and down the convoluted landscape for an hour, then found a rock promontory from which we could survey the area.

We sat on the rock studying the country. The route we should have taken lay below us a few hundred feet. The rest of the way out would be easy. We looked back at the divide, at the wild snowy pass we came through two days earlier. The odds were that neither of us would ever come this way again.

PART III

YELLOWSTONE NATIONAL PARK

"Alive, the grizzly is a symbol of freedom and understanding —a sign that man can learn to conserve what is left of the earth. Extinct, it will be another fading testimony to things man should have learned more about but was too preoccupied with himself to notice. In its beleaguered condition, it is above all a symbol of what man is doing to the entire planet. If we can learn from these experiences, and learn rationally, both the grizzly and man may have a chance to survive."

—Frank C. Craighead, Jr.
Track of the Grizzly
1979

NO PARK HAS BEEN WRITTEN ABOUT MORE THAN Yellowstone, and perhaps no issue related to the park has been the subject of greater debate than the management of its grizzly bears. Yellowstone was formed in 1872—the world's first national park—and currently is home to around 200 grizzly bears. These bears move freely across the park borders and occupy an area of around 9,500 square miles, primarily in northwestern Wyoming but also including parts of Montana and Idaho. The bears are found in Yellowstone National Park as well as Grand Teton National Park, parts of six national forests (Shoshone, Bridger-Teton, Targhee, Gallatin, Beaverhead, and Custer), and on various other state and private lands.

The key to the health of this population—which was decimated in the early 1970s through various government control measures following the dump closures—is the number of breeding females. Almost all of the scientific debate about the future of the bears centers around this critical fact, because unless natality exceeds mortality the species is doomed in Yellowstone. Supporters of current management policy believe there is a sufficiently high number of breeding females and that the species is on the road to recovery and eventual delisting as a threatened or endangered animal. Critics, on the other hand, assert that the number of breeding females is dangerously low and that the bears will become extinct in Yellowstone. Discussion also invariably focuses upon Grant Village and Fishing Bridge, two controversial tourist developments that happen to be located in what almost all scientific authorities agree is critical grizzly bear habitat.

Yellowstone is not the best bear habitat in the world—certainly not as rich an environment as the Northern Rockies in Montana or the Southern Rockies in southwestern Colorado. The park contains a high and relatively dry mountain plateau that was—until the forest fires of 1988—heavily forested and was also suffering from the effects of burgeoning elk populations formerly held in check by the native wolves, their natural predators. The forest fires opened up previously timbered country for the secondary growth—particularly berry bushes—so prized by grizzly bears. That will definitely help in the 1990s. Also, it now appears the Park Service and U.S. Fish and Wildlife Service will proceed with wolf restoration, which will introduce at least ten breeding pairs of wolves into the park. The wolves will control the elk, which have destroyed much of the habitat, particularly the aspen groves on which the beaver depend to build their all-important ponds. These pond systems create the valuable wet acreage essential to the survival of the grizzly in this ecosystem. Finally, the wolves will occasionally have to relinquish carcasses to grizzlies, which are inefficient hunters of big game and which will benefit from the additional source of protein.

Grizzlies are almost impossible to see in Yellowstone these days. Rangers sometimes work in Yellowstone for two or three seasons before spotting their first bear. Some say this is good, while others disagree. Only time will tell. For those who are interested in perhaps seeing a grizzly in the wild, one of the better places is Hayden Valley—which is wide open country affording excellent views in all directions. One of the best times of year to look for bears in Hayden Valley is in the spring, particularly the early spring when grizzlies come out of the forest to scavenge winter-killed bison, elk, deer, and moose. When the wolves are reintroduced, this will also be a superb location for observing the wolf packs in organized hunts and to listen to the wolves howling. Hopefully the grizzly population will recover in the Yellowstone ecosystem and children yet unborn will still be able to hike across Hayden Valley and place their hands inside one of the great front paw prints of Old Bruin.

IN 1959, BIOLOGIST BROTHERS John and Frank Craighead began a now-historic twelve-year study of the grizzly bear in Yellowstone National Park. The length and depth of their investigations, as well as the innovative methods employed, have made the study legendary. The Craigheads developed such techniques as radio-tracking collars, biotelemetry, and satellite telemetry. Their work in the park concluded abruptly in 1971 when they had a disagreement with the park superintendent over management policy. Whole books, essays, and articles have been devoted to the dispute, which involved some of the most fundamental issues of science and government, freedom and censorship. The whole affair began as the Park Service was preparing for the Yellowstone Centennial of 1972. The park superintendent, among other things, ordered that the park dumps, where grizzlies had fed for most of the century, be immediately closed. The Craighead research team suggested the dumps be phased out over time to diminish the shock to the bears as they sought alternative food sources. A series of sharp exchanges and escalating tensions ensued, and the brothers finally left the park. As a result of the sudden dump closure, there were many serious problems with the grizzly bears. Nearly 100 grizzly bear deaths in the Yellowstone population can be documented in the early 1970s, many as a direct result of the sudden dump closure. The Craigheads estimated there were around 200 bears in the system at that time. The grizzly population is still recovering.

Frank Craighead's *Track of the Grizzly* (1979), which is a personal memoir of his years in Yellowstone, is now considered a classic of the genre. In this essay, Craighead writes about his favorite grizzly, a mature female named "Marian" by the research team. Based on her mild temperament and willingness to adapt to humankind, the scientists found guarded hope for the future.

11. THE BEAR MARIAN

FRANK C. CRAIGHEAD, JR.

SUMMER HAD LEFT THE HIGH COUNTRY of Yellowstone National Park; bison, elk, and mule deer were on the move. Under the sleek coats of the grizzlies were thick layers of fat stored for winter use. The gray-streaked skies belching snow flurries behind 10,240-foot Mount Washburn emphasized the change in seasons. From our vantage point overlooking Hayden Valley we could hear the howling of coyotes and the challenging bugle of bull elk. Canada geese honked upriver, and the distinctive calls of sandhill cranes and ravens carried across the valley.

Normally we would have been attuned to these wildland voices, but on September 22, 1961, my brother John, Maurice Hornocker, and I were listening instead for a sophisticated manmade sound, a high-pitched, pulsing signal. Beep, beep, beep, full of portent and meaning, the repetitive metallic pulse came in loud and clear on the crisp fall air. The sound had nothing of wildness about it. No deep primitive instinct of the chase stirred in us at the sound, nor did it evoke a feeling of oneness with nature. Yet this beeping coming to us in the vastness of Hayden Valley thrilled us as few sounds ever had. The vibrant pulsing signal, though new to the Yellowstone wilderness, told us that we were in communication with the grizzly we identified as bear Number 40, just as surely as the distant honking told us that the Canada geese were on the wing. But the beep was more specific than the honk of the goose or the gutteral caw of the raven, for it emanated from one particular grizzly bear somewhere within the three thousand square miles of the park. Hearing this sound meant that we were monitoring the first free-roaming grizzly sow to be tracked by radio.

Number 40's debut as a free-roaming electronic instrument of science took place that day. We had captured her on the previous night, and then the next morning, September 22, we immobilized her. The drug, succinylcholine chloride (sucostrin), that Maurice measured out in a syringe and John administered kept her inert for about fifteen minutes. But putting a radio on her—our first attempt on a bear—required nearly an hour.

"I think she's coming out of it," Maurice said.

"O.K., the anesthesia is ready," said John, who then knelt over Number 40 and injected the drug. The grizzly coughed, and in ten minutes was fully anesthetized.

We quickly began the systematic procedures we had used since 1959 on all the bears we immobilized. Number 40 was first weighed while suspended in a nylon rope net. She tipped the scales at 300 pounds, having gained 125 pounds since the first time she was captured, in 1960. Next we checked the colored ear markers and numbered ear tags that we had placed on her on that earlier occasion, noting that the left ear marker was missing. We recorded other general information: total length sixty-five inches, neck circumference twenty-eight inches, general condition excellent, age three and a half years, never borne cubs. Harry Reynolds and Mike Stephens helped to take dental casts and a blood sample.

The previous night we had worked late to finish assembling the radio collar. The battery pack had been dipped in silastic rubber to waterproof it. The two-ounce transmitter, the fourteen-ounce, seven-cell battery pack, and a section of the loop antenna had been wrapped in fiberglass cloth and coated with resin. The battery terminal had been soldered and then coated with orthodontic acrylic. The entire assembly was then sanded and wrapped with colored tape. The brightly colored collar that John handed me as I knelt by grizzly Number 40 weighed about two pounds and was as waterproof, shock-proof, and bearproof as we could make it. Still, Harry voiced the skepticism we all felt: "Do you really think a grizzly will keep that thing on?" We had gambled time, money, and two years of work on the premise that this powerful carnivore would tolerate a collar. An initial experiment with a rope collar had proved successful, but a bear's tolerance for a fully rigged radio collar was yet to be tested.

In the course of our radio-tracking research, from 1961 to 1969, we were to place radios on forty-eight grizzlies, twenty-four of them different individuals (some were instrumented a number of times). Gradually, one instrumentation procedure blended with another so that recall of individual events is difficult. However, the memories of that first instrumenting are still crystal clear. There were a few tense moments when we thought it was a failure. I had pulled the antenna loop over Number 40's head and saw that it fitted snugly. Mike Stephens carried the receiver up the valley to test the strength of the radio signal. We checked all our procedures. Mike called in by walkie-talkie to say that the signal was very weak, so we rechecked the acrylic sealing, the connection of the loop antenna, and the tuning of the transmitter. Number 40 raised her head slightly. Her respiration rate had more than doubled, signalling that she would soon come out from under the effects of the anesthesia. We had been working for a long time, oblivious to the weather, but our hands were cold and blowing snow was turning the ground white. The bear would soon be up and away, but would our radio transmitter work? Mike called in, "It's colder than hell out here. . . . What's holding things up?" I ignored the query and asked if the signal was any stronger. "No good," came in loud and clear. Number 40 again raised her head, this time a little higher. "We'll have to give it up," John said, for we all knew the signs of the rousing grizzly and had experienced our share of close calls already. As we withdrew, our subject rose unsteadily to her feet. What had gone wrong? Dejectedly we watched our experimental bear head south for the nearest timber. And then Mike's voice boomed in on the walkie-talkie. "We've got it now! The signal's great!" While lying on her side, the grizzly's body had partially shielded the signal, but when she was up and moving, increasing the elevation of the transmitter, the signal strength improved. We had already learned one lesson of many that only experience could teach.

Now, as we listened to the steady beep, we had the answer to the question that had haunted us. The signal started as an invisible, soundless radio wave that spread in all directions from the tiny transistorized transmitter embedded in the newly affixed collar. The radio frequency was transformed into an audible frequency in the receiver beside me. This pulsed beeping, spilling into the afternoon air at seventy beeps per minute, could lead us across the sage-grass valley and through heavy lodgepole timber to grizzly sow Number 40 some miles distant, and could inform us of the exact location of the bear at any moment, day or night, for ninety days or more.

As the signal came in, I slowly rotated the loop antenna of the receiver to obtain first the strongest signal, then the weakest, or null. The position of the loop antenna indicated the direction of the signal source and thus the bear. "She's nearly due west," commented John, "but can we home in on her?" "It's a good start just being able to hear her." Indeed it was, for everything now depended on our keeping this signal. The next step in our experiment was to actually track down the bear by following the signal. From now on we intended not just to cross paths with a grizzly bear but to confront a particular grizzly at a specific time and place, the meeting to be determined by how fast and accurately our electronic equipment would lead us to her.

We climbed a long, sloping hill in the indicated direction, checking the receiver as we went. John and Maurice followed closely behind, carrying cameras, binoculars, and a telescope. Following the contour of the hill, we passed through the lodgepole pines into open parkland, then ascended another hill, and yet another, in a beeline course. Before we topped the last rise the strength of the signal increased. Was the grizzly still some distance away? It was not just an academic question. For the first time in our study of the grizzly, we had the advantage of surprise on our side, especially when we were moving into the wind. Grizzlies are short-sighted and cannot readily discern a man beyond a hundred yards or so, but their sense of smell is extremely keen. Though we carried a firearm, we had yet to use it for defense and hoped we never would. But our purpose was not to avoid the grizzlies; the point was to get close and observe them without being detected. It had been and would be dangerous, for if jumped or startled at close range a grizzly might charge as readily as run. Thus we felt relief along with excitement when we cautiously peered over the hill and saw Number 40, head lowered, plodding along the valley floor unaware of our presence.

"There she is," we exclaimed in unison. John said that he could see the colored collar, and Maurice confirmed his observation as he followed the bear's movements with the scope.

All through the evening of September 22 the beep from our portable receiver told us where Number 40 was in the swirling snow-storm. From then on through the next month it kept us informed as to her whereabouts. We located her feeding on an elk carcass, fol-lowed her on a short foraging trip after pine nuts, and watched her associating with other bears. We tracked her from a daybed to the Trout Creek dump, where she foraged for scraps left over from tourists' tables. At that early point in our study the maximum distance at which we were able to pick up the bear's signal was about a mile, but later we modified and greatly improved the capability of our wildlife telemetry system. However, the system's early limitations in no way detracted from that first thrill when we followed the signal to the crest of the hill and saw the collared grizzly plodding along com-pletely unaware of our presence. At that moment we proved that we had acquired the capability of arranging a meeting between bear and man at times and places of our own choosing. Also, we now had the means to obtain information on free-roaming animals continuously and from afar with a minimum of time, effort, and manpower. Inherent in this prototype system was the potential of gathering physi-ological information simultaneously with ecological data.

Regardless of what fate had in store for Number 40, she had made history as the first grizzly bear to be instrumented and tracked by radio. We felt she deserved a name. Dick Davies of Philco Corporation had designed this first small transmitter, and he and his wife had visited us in Yellowstone to help test the equipment. We thought it appropriate to name the bear after Dick's wife, so with her consent, Number 40 became the bear Marian.

FOR TWO YEARS BEFORE the time Marian and the radio collar came on the scene, we had been at work gathering data. Our study began in 1959, and on June 26 of that year, through the peephole of a culvert trap, we had our first close-up look at a wild grizzly. As my eyes adjusted from the bright sunlight outside to the darkness within the trap, I saw an angry face lunging toward me, and I reared back just in time to avoid the long, lethal claws that flashed through the tiny opening. "Wow," I said, "he looks pretty big." Maurice Hornocker and John agreed, though we soon discovered that, as grizzlies go, this bear was not particularly large. By weighing trap and bear at once, we found that he tipped the scale at two hundred pounds.

On the basis of his weight we computed the amount of sucostrin that would immobilize without harming him. With a graduated syringe John measured out 1 milligram of the drug for every 3.5 pounds of body weight, or a total of about 57 milligrams. (We subsequently learned that we had used a larger dose than was needed; 1 milligram to each 5 pounds of body weight turned out to be sufficient.) He carefully squeezed the sucostrin from the syringe into a hollow projectile dart along with some sterile water, then placed the dart in the chamber of a CO_2 gun set at low compression. Poking the gun through an opening in the trap, I pulled the trigger, aiming the hollow needle at the base of the bear's neck. Within eight minutes the drug had begun to take effect, starting with a slackness in jaws and neck, followed by the relaxation of shoulder, limbs, abdomen, rib muscles, and finally the diaphragm. After the grizzly failed to bite a stick placed in his mouth, we opened the trapdoor, pulled him out, and got to work on the routine that would become so familiar in time. First we attached markers to the ears. Next we recorded the number 1 on the form we had prepared, and set down the measurements of foot, claw, neck, and total body length. Grizzly Number 1 turned out to be a typical animal. He had the silver-tipped guard hairs from which the species derives one of its common names, was of moderate size, and showed no peculiarities worthy of comment. But trapping and marking our first grizzly was no less momentous for that. Our long-range ecological project was now truly under way.

During that first year of study, 1959, we captured and marked with ear tags thirty grizzlies, some in culvert traps and others by immobilizing them with drug-filled syringe darts fired from a gun. Most of these animals were trapped in Hayden Valley, but dispersed widely in fall. The following spring many of the marked bears reappeared, along with others. By the fall of 1960 an additional thirty-seven bears were sporting markers, bringing the total of tagged bears to sixty-seven. By observing both marked bears and a few others readily recognized due to specific physical traits, we were learning to identify a growing number of the grizzlies that constituted the Yellowstone community. Some bears, both marked and unmarked, became old acquaintances. To those with unusual physical and character traits we naturally gave names as well as numbers in order to differentiate them more readily from the less distinctive animals.

One of the bears marked in 1960 was Marian, whom we first trapped on July 1. At this time she was a young bear, two and a half years old and weighing 175 pounds. She was a small female and not particularly aggressive. At the time that we fitted Marian with her radio, she undoubtedly recognized most of the bears within this population, but her means of identification were different from ours. Scent alone probably played an important role.

The grizzlies that Marian foraged with at night or joined in secluded timbered retreats for rest were gradually taking shape as individuals in our minds. Number 76 was Pegleg, who had a stiff walk and was eventually destined to be tracked by radio. Also conspicuous were Scarface, with this battle scars, and Cutlip, with his lower lip hanging permanently askew, a scar from a battle with another large bear. Number 26 was named the Fifty-pound Cub (to distinguish him from another cub trapped about the same time that weighed ninety pounds), and could only be identified by his ear markers or through association with his mother. She was unnumbered, but we called her G.I. because of the strictness with which she disciplined her cubs. Bigfoot was another of Marian's companions, as was the Sucostrin Kid, a yearling who for some inexplicable reason required far more than the normal dosage of sucostrin to immobilize him. Then there were the prominent Rip-nose Sow and Number 88 with his white claws. The latter was named Loverboy and was recognizable without his markers from his cropped left ear and the scar below his right eye. Bruno, Number 14, was later to lead us over the mountainous country of eastern Yellowstone, while we followed his beeping radio signal.

Another particularly conspicuous bear was the Owl-faced Sow, whose facial disc reminded us of a short-eared owl. She was one of the first mothers we observed to adopt the cubs of another sow. Shorty, Notch-ear, and Old Short-ears were unnumbered grizzlies whose names described the characteristics that enabled us to identify them, at least throughout one season. And the Grizzled Sow, Number 65, was a large, powerful female who had confidence to match her size. She produced a litter of four cubs in 1962, and one of her later offspring, Number 202, when fitted with a radio, taught us about the relationship of a yearling's home range to that of its mother.

In 1961, Marian became well acquainted with another young bear, Number 37, since both often sought daytime retreats in the same wooded area of upper Trout Creek. Number 37, later named Beep, was also a pioneer in our radio-tracking research but had even more seniority than Marian. Throughout 1960 and part of 1961 he wore an adjustable rope collar, thereby assuring us that a grizzly would tolerate a collar—the best method, we thought, of attaching a radio to a bear. Number 37 also had the distinction of becoming the second grizzly to be instrumented with a radio, hence his nickname.

Our acquaintance with Beep and his family began in 1960, when we trapped his mother and one yearling and immobilized another with a drug-filled dart. This latter yearling became Number 37. His littermate was Number 38, and his mother, a very aggressive bear, Number 39. Thus in a single day we had added a complete family to a growing list of marked bears. The family as a whole bore the unlucky number 13. It lived up to the superstition, for it was short-lived but nevertheless interesting and scientifically informative.

On July 3, 1960, Number 39 weaned her yearlings and thereafter they were on their own. This was an early weaning; mother and yearlings usually travel, forage, and sleep together throughout the second summer, but Number 37 and his brother were not to know so secure a family life. After their mother weaned them, she left them to fend for themselves. However, they had each other and remained inseparable during 1960, relying on one another for companionship and mutual protection.

When initially captured in late June, the yearlings weighed within five pounds of one another: 145 and 140 pounds, respectively. When Number 37 was retrapped late in August of the same summer, he had gained exactly 100 pounds in a period of almost two months. This was a 69 percent increase over his June 29 weight. It was at this time that we put a self-adjusting braided rope collar containing a mock-up radio transmitter around his neck. The purpose of this experiment was to see if a collar might prove suitable for eventually attaching a radio to a grizzly bear. The answer came about a year later when we retrapped Number 37, still wearing the collar, which was in good condition. Apparently he had made no serious effort to remove it.

In the meantime, both he and his brother were providing us with some interesting information as they grew and developed. As a fall yearling, Beep weighed 245 pounds, but he lost weight during the spring months, as most bears do. However, in less than three summer months he had recovered his loss and increased to 315 pounds. A year later, as a three-year-old, he tipped the scales at 440 pounds, about 150 pounds more than the average fall weight we had so far determined for male three-year-olds. Though Beep and his brother, Number 38, weighed the same as yearlings, there was a difference of 100 pounds between them as fall two-year-olds, illustrating the tremendous variability in growth rate that can occur in young bears.

When we retrapped Number 38 as a two-year-old, we transported him across Yellowstone Lake, leaving him on Promontory Point. Three days later he was back at Pelican Creek, having taken a circuitous shoreline route covering a minimum of thirty-one miles. Number 38 was revealing to us the homing instinct in grizzlies. Late in the fall of 1961, we captured his littermate near a construction camp south of West Thumb and released him forty airline miles to the north near Crystal Creek, in the hope that he would adjust to his new environment and remain away from campgrounds or developed areas. The next spring he was back near West Thumb and from there he wandered over to Old Faithful. In learning to fend for themselves after weaning, Numbers 37 and 38 were developing traits that indicated that they would be troublesome adult grizzlies—approaching too close to humans and even entering campgrounds. We hoped that by putting a radio on Number 37, we might learn more about the activities of problem bears. We also hoped we could help prevent his being killed by a bullet, which was bound to happen if he continued to cause trouble.

There was a light covering of snow on the ground, and the wind was cold and gusty on the day we adjusted the radio around the neck of Number 37, our second radioed bear. The rays of the wintry sun, gold behind black clouds, were disappearing, and it was dark before he ambled off. After a few days we lost his radio signal, but soon we relocated him a considerable distance away at West Thumb. Here he attempted to enter a trailer belonging to construction workers. He was retrapped—when his collar was seen to be missing—transported to the northwestern portion of the park, and released. When he was again fitted with a radio in 1962, he led us up over the Trout Creek divide, down the Nez Percé drainage, and over to the developed region of Old Faithful, thus increasing his chances of getting into trouble.

Had we learned nothing else from Number 37, I would still remember him because of one particular incident. One night I was waiting inside the closed culvert trap, hoping to take pictures of this radio-instrumented grizzly lured from a distance to a bait. It was drizzling slightly when John and Maurice lowered the steel door, effectively sealing me in and the bears out. I had my sleeping bag, flashlight, directional receiver, walkie-talkie, camera, chocolate bars, and a box of crackers, and was armed with a .357 revolver just in case of trouble. I planned to photograph out of an open window cut in the metal side of the trap. The window was large enough for my camera when fitted with long focal lenses, which meant that it could readily accommodate a bear's head as well.

The steady rain, now bordering on snow, increased after I entered the blind, and an early darkness soon enveloped me. Without a light I could see nothing, not even the trees nearby. After I had pulled on a heavy parka, removed my boots, and slipped my feet into a warm sleeping bag, I checked for Number 37 by holding the directional receiver out the window. (This was necessary because the surrounding metal attenuated the signals.) A loud and clear beeping indicated that the grizzly was moving in fast. We had left bait for him the night before, and now he was accustomed to it and heading for it purposefully. He came into view and for some time I observed him, the silvery gleam of raindrops on his guard hairs shining jewel-like in the beam of the flashlight. Although this momentary flashing of my light at first frightened him, he gradually became accustomed to it.

One by one, a few other bears silently joined in the feast, and I decided to attempt a few flash pictures. Very, very slowly I eased the camera and flash rig out the open window, having previously set the exposure and estimated the distance. When growls and muffled noises told me that grizzly was tugging at the staked-down meat close to the trap, I pushed the shutter release. Instead of the instantaneous, white flash I anticipated, I was blinded by a rapid succession of all-engulfing bursts of light. A flood of intense illumination bounced back and forth off the shiny steel walls of the culvert trap. It was as though I were looking at the sun through binoculars. My eyes soon adjusted somewhat, but a pulsating golden glow still so blinded me that I was unable to see the nearby window or even the camera in my hand.

Startled, confused, and temporarily blinded, I felt completely helpless. I could imagine a grizzly flailing with his long claws through the open window, even though I knew it was unlikely. The accumulating water from the steady rain must have shorted out my equipment; I groped for the flash battery case, trying to turn off the power. I felt the wire leading to the camera and ripped it loose. The flashing stopped but instead of being clothed in darkness, I was still enveloped in a golden aftervision, a result of the intense light my eyes had been exposed to. When I could make out the shape of objects in the light of my flashlight, I was able to relocate the window and release the prop that held the hinged door open. Gradually my sight returned to normal and my heart rate dropped. With the aid of the flashlight I dried off my flash equipment, reassembled it, and crawled into my sleeping bag. With the sound of the rain splattering on the metal trap I slept until 2 A.M., when I was awakened by a growl. Again I cautiously opened the window, and during the next half hour took several flash pictures of Number 37, along with another, unidentified grizzly, tearing and tugging at the bait. Satisfied that I had a few good pictures, I dozed restlessly until morning, when John and Maurice arrived to release me from my metal cage.

THROUGHOUT OUR YEARS of study, there were numerous times when we found ourselves in close proximity to free-roaming grizzlies without a radio to pinpoint their locations or a trap for protection, and these occasions provided many of the more dramatic moments in our work. The first time we were charged by a grizzly in the course of our work—an inevitable occurrence that each of us privately imagined many times—the bear did not make contact, but this in no way detracted from the excitement of the event. Naturally we had wondered how we would react to the bear, and the bear to us, upon meeting suddenly and at close quarters.

The pattern of such face-on confrontations was revealed early in our research. One day in September 1959, the lookout on Mount Washburn called our lab by phone to tell me that through his scope he was watching a grizzly feeding on an elk carcass. I drove to the lookout, verified the sighting during lulls between snow flurries, and plotted the bear's position on my map. Deciding to investigate, I asked Bob Howe, a subdistrict ranger, if he would like to accompany me. We hiked through the lodgepole forest, keeping downwind and just uphill of the grizzly. As we arrived near the spot where I thought we might see the bear, a large bull elk arose, walked ahead into a meadow, and trotted off. His course to the south was directly in line with the grizzly, which I could now see at the far end of the meadow.

The bear's front paws were resting protectively atop an elk carcass. From that distance he was unable to see us and the wind was toward us, so he wouldn't scent us, at least for the time being. Though we were concerned that the running elk might alert him, we began a cautious stalk, using terrain and trees to keep out of sight. Leaving the unbroken timber, we crawled out to scattered trees in the open. As yet the grizzly gave no sign of alarm. From a distance I snapped a few pictures of him. He may have caught the light reflecting from my moving camera, for he became restless and began to investigate, moving toward the timber in a circling maneuver, sniffing and trying to pick up a scent. It was our turn to become nervous. We were unable to see the bear after he entered the timber, through which he would be able to approach us quite closely. We debated whether to climb a tree where we were, but decided to sprint back across the open space to a spot where we could still climb trees if necessary, but where the grizzly could not approach us unseen.

During this brief sighting we had observed the grizzly protecting his kill from ravens and several coyotes, and had seen a smaller grizzly approach. The latter appeared to be intimidated by the obviously more dominant bear and had not yet tested to see if he could feed peacefully with the larger animal. Now this second grizzly was also nearby and out of sight. I was observing one of our first grizzly "kills," and I was not at all certain how the bears might react to each other, let alone to human intruders.

From our new refuge, Bob and I observed the larger grizzly's return from his reconnaissance. Apparently satisfied that all was well, he once more spread himself over his kill protectively, and we approached closer while he dozed. Our vision was obscured due to a rise in the ground, and the sun was in our eyes, so we moved back and tried a circuitous stalk, this time getting close enough to see that the bear did not have ear markers and thus was not one with which we were familiar. The bear was now alerted to our presence and moved toward us. We were again in the predicament of having the grizzly nearby and moving toward us through dense timber, so we quickly chose a lodgepole with low limbs and climbed it, waiting in our uncomfortable perches to see what might happen next. As the grizzly neither returned to the carcass nor appeared close by, we concluded that he had picked up our scent and left. Cautiously, we dropped out of the tree and approached the dead elk in the middle of the meadow. The grizzly had buried all but the head and antlers with dirt and grass; we wondered why but were not to find out until later. The elk, a huge one, must have weighed eight hundred pounds, perhaps more, and its antlers measured fifty-two inches from the skull to the tip of the far tine and forty inches across from tip to tip. We tried to roll the dead animal to see if he had been gored by another elk during a mating season fight, but our utmost efforts were inadequate. The animal's size, weight, and apparent good condition made me suspect that it had first been injured by another bull elk, then finished off by the grizzly.

Struggling to turn the elk, I looked up and saw the grizzly jogging out of the shadows to our west. "Bob!" I shouted. "The grizzly—he's coming!" I started backing in the opposite direction, abandoning my lens, tripod, and pack. I slung my camera over my shoulder, readied my .38, and yelled to Bob to throw a shell in the chamber of the rifle he was carrying, just in case. I glanced quickly at the nearest tree a quarter-mile away. The grizzly was still moving rapidly toward us, occasionally stopping to rise up on his hind legs in an attempt to scent or see us. He would then drop on all fours, charge closer, and again rear up only to rush on. Was he attacking? What else? I thought as we continued to back off. As the distance between us dwindled, the grizzly rose and dropped to the ground once more, then increased his speed in a final attack—or was it a rush to the elk? We didn't stop to ponder the question but turned and ran in desperation, though even as we sprinted for the trees I knew we couldn't reach and climb one before the grizzly was upon us. I turned to face him just as he reached the elk carcass, where he picked up our scent, apparently for the first time.

Only now did he identify us as humans, and only now was I sure that he had not been attacking. He paused for a microsecond in surprise before making a rippling, rhythmic turn and running for the far timber. Still running, he disappeared. We were more than surprised; we were scared. But fortunately we had been saved from an encounter, perhaps a disaster, by the grizzly's natural inclination to avoid man. It was not the last time that our human scent would send a large, aggressive grizzly running. We were not misled; the grizzlies did not fear us, but if given an option usually chose to avoid us, even to the extent of temporarily abandoning food.

OUR INITIAL SUCCESS in tracking Marian with a radio collar left us with high hopes for this particular research technique, and we worked continually to improve the dependability and capabilities of our radio-tracking system. With the help of Joel Varney, a very talented and enthusiastic electronics engineer, we developed and tested tracking receivers weighing only two and one-half pounds. Joel miniaturized our fully transistorized transmitters to 1.8 ounces. Our laboratory at Canyon become our base station, equipped with receivers that could quickly be connected to a five-element directional antenna. From the laboratory we monitored the instrumented grizzlies day and night, regularly picking up their signals from ten, twelve, and even twenty miles away under favorable conditions. Supplementing this system was a three-element antenna at our field station, located on a treeless hill eight miles to the south. We used two radio-equipped vehicles to locate and follow grizzlies that wandered to distant parts of the park. From a high point such as Mount Washburn we could readily monitor a thousand square miles of territory and determine whether or not our radio-tagged grizzlies were present. When our bears wandered out of our range, we occasionally resorted to taping our loop antennas to the strut of a fixed-wing plane. The additional altitude permitted us to readily pick up wandering bears from a distance. After locating them by air, we would then take off on foot with our portable directional receivers and follow the pulsed signals to their transmitter source, where we would either sight or jump the bears, usually at a distance of less than a hundred yards. The water- and shock-proof transmitters sent out differently pulsed signals, and these rhythms served to iden-tify each instrumented grizzly. With improved equipment and techniques the inevitable day arrived when we first monitored the sig-nals from a number of instrumented grizzlies simultaneously. We were receiving signals from Marian, at seventy-four beeps per minute; Pegleg, a roaming boar, at ninety-four pulses per minute; Number 75, a belligerent sow, at sixty-two per minute; and Number 7, the Sour Creek Sow, at the slower rate of fifty per minute. In this situation we were receiving more information than we could assimilate.

Telemetry allowed us to gather general information by inference on the location, behavior, and movement of the animals from a distance. A signal that periodically varied in loudness or strength indicated that a grizzly was active and moving about. One of constant loudness, especially during the daylight hours, often meant that the transmitting bear was resting or sleeping. An intermittent signal usually denoted that a grizzly was active, perhaps traveling—the signal varying when a ridge, a hill, or dense timber came between the bear and our receiver, or when the bear changed directions. In this way we learned that Marian's daily eating and sleeping habits were quite regular. After determining the basic pattern of her day's activities by radio-tracking, corroborated by visual observation, we could infer certain activities from the character of the signals we received. At times Number 40 slept in a foot-deep excavation in a low swale among the lodgepole pines nine miles from the base. It was her practice to curl up in bed with her entire body below ground level. When she rested in this manner, the signal emanating from her collar antenna only came in loud and clear on our base receiver when she raised her head. When she lowered it, the shielding effect of the ground at this distance was sufficient to prevent or greatly reduce signal reception. Thus, in the course of the day we heard or lost Marian's signal, depending on whether she slept with her head low, raised it to look around, or stood up to move about.

This type of monitoring also helped us determine when it might be informative to move in and observe. We learned early that, since the signal grew louder the closer we approached to a bear, the receiver volume had to be turned down to prevent alerting the bear to our presence. With practice we became quite expert at estimating our distance from a grizzly merely by observing the position of the volume control knob. However, situations arose when the signal fooled us. On one such occasion Joel Varney and Hoke Franciscus, our electronics collaborators, along with Maurice and me, were closing in on Marian when the rather loud signal began to fade. We assumed that she had arisen from her daybed and was moving away, so we continued to follow the weak signal rapidly. Suddenly the signal boomed out loud and clear even after I turned the volume down, an indication that the bear was dangerously close. At this instant, when we were almost on top of her, Marian suddenly rose up from her daybed and glared at us from only forty feet away. A larger, more aggressive grizzly would almost surely have charged us if we had jumped it in this manner. Marian appeared to be even more surprised than we were. She sprinted away, and then stopped to turn her head and look menacingly back—or was that merely a glance of curiosity? We stood motionless and tense while she assessed the situation, perhaps even deciding whether to return to defend her daytime retreat. When her dark rippling form disappeared into the still darker timber, we broke the silence of the Yellowstone wilderness with a sigh of relief.

While our adrenaline-stimulated hearts returned to normal, we figured out what had caused the near catastrophe. Marian had dug her bed at the base of a fallen tree whose earth-cluttered roots shielded the radio signals as we approached from the east. From the greatly attenuated signals we assumed that the bear was much farther away than she actually was. As we moved past the earth barrier, the signal again loudly boomed in on our receiver. At this moment the startled grizzly had bolted from her bed while we stood petrified.

This incident served to intensify our fondness for Marian. We realized that there were undoubtedly two studies under way: she was learning about us just as we were discovering things about her. Apparently Marian had decided that these human beings that persistently appeared in unexpected and out-of-the-way places were not going to harm her. A relationship of mutual trust, and perhaps respect, was developing. At the very least she was showing a tolerance of our strange actions.

Already our studies were revealing that the grizzly did not fear man but preferred to avoid him when possible and, as other bear-man confrontations showed, to combat him if necessary. Constant experience in handling trapped and drugged bears and in observing others at close range demonstrated the tremendous power, speed, and ferociousness of an enraged grizzly bear, and we took precautions accordingly. But we also had ample opportunity to observe its intelligence and its essentially gentle and inquisitive nature. Although we carried firearms, we were never to use them in the course of a decade of intimate association with the grizzly in its own habitat.

PAUL SCHULLERY HAS WORKED in Yellowstone National Park in a variety of capacities—ranger, naturalist, historian, special assistant—over the years. These jobs, which have involved work with the public, the park archives, and the permanent administrative staff, have given him a unique vantage on the modern history of Yellowstone. Schullery is the author or editor of over a dozen books on the parks, conservation, and trout fishing. One of his most highly regarded books is *Mountain Time* (1984), which is a memoir of his early years in Yellowstone.

"The Bear Doesn't Know," from *Mountain Time,* is an excellent single-essay study of the Yellowstone grizzly. Schullery begins with a personal anecdote about encountering a grizzly in the remote backcountry of the park. Not surprisingly, the bear chooses to go in the opposite direction. Schullery points out an interesting fact: of the seventy million visitors since the park opened in 1872, only four have been killed by grizzlies. The odds are, then, about one in seventeen million. Statistics help to put the threat of bears—often wildly exaggerated—into correct proportion. The essay concludes with another personal anecdote, as Schullery describes what it is like to come face to face with a grizzly caged in a culvert trap.

"The Bear Doesn't Know" is taken from Paul Schullery's Mountain Time *(Nick Lyons, 1984) and is reprinted by permission of Paul*

12. THE BEAR DOESN'T KNOW

PAUL SCHULLERY

THERE IS NO TRAIL TO THE POND. IT LIES, unnamed as far as I know, in a flat alpine saddle between Gray and Little Quadrant peaks, a perfect mountain meadow. There are a few whitebark pine trees, and the whole little plain, a few acres, is quite level. The pond is toward the north end; it may be a spring, or it may get its water during spring melt from the surrounding mountain walls. The elevation is near 9,000 feet. I doubt that the place is as warmly hospitable most of the year as we found it that day in early September.

We'd been told that we could leave the Fawn Pass Trail, to the south, and ride over the saddle by following animal trails and meadows. It's not possible to get lost, with the surrounding mountains serving as such unmistakable landmarks, but I was still a little edgy about such an extended bushwhack. Horses need a lot more space than hikers, and this was steep country.

The pond has a tiny overflow on its east end. The trickle goes a few yards and turns northward, dropping into a forested ravine. The ravine was our recommended avenue north, but it was mostly trailless. We soon were hopping back and forth over the stream, seeking the easiest course for the horses. Too often to suit us, we could only travel in the little streambed itself; steep banks and deadfall kept us pinned there, and the horses slipped and lurched along the wet, rocky streambed.

We didn't notice tributaries, but they were there. Within a mile of the pond the rivulet was a genuine creek, tumbling and twisting over logs and rocks and making passage even more difficult for the horses.

Once, seeking safer trails for the horses, we climbed the east slope of the ravine for some distance above the stream, so far that its noise was inaudible. While moving through fairly open timber on a gentler slope, we heard a large animal crashing through the brush and deadfall ahead of us. My companion, riding ahead of me, got a glimpse of the animal. "I think we scared up a bear."

I was skeptical. We'd been jumping elk for two days, and one large animal can sound pretty much like another when it's running frightened.

Traditional wisdom has it that a surprised bear will often flee until it locates a good spot from which to check out what frightened it. About 150 yards farther along my companion pointed up the slope to our right. "There's the bear."

She stopped her horse, and as I caught up I saw an adequately large grizzly, about fifty yards off, standing on his hind legs. He was watching us from the edge of a tight stand of lodgepole pines.

My companion asked, "Should we take his picture?" just as the bear seemed to decide something; he came down on all fours and took a step down the hill toward us.

"No, the horses haven't seen him yet and I think we'd better just keep going."

We rode quickly out of his sight, but within a few minutes we were rimrocked by a sharp side ravine off the main creek, and we had to retrace our steps back to the bear. He was gone, and we moved on down to the stream and continued north.

The horses amazed us that way. On this trip they plodded past any number of elk and coyotes, and one moose we encountered at about thirty feet, without any sign of noticing. We heard but did not see bighorn sheep; their tenor baaing at least got Midget to perk up his ears. On several occasions, bull elk, getting in voice for later recreations, bugled hoarsely from the slopes above us. The horses plodded on.

But of all that trip—the echoes of elk bugles ringing across the stone walls, the stark lawnlike alpine meadows, the midnight mountains half lost in starshadow, a golden eagle soaring off the point of Gray Peak, and all the rest—that moment near the bear lingers most persistently in my memory. I've relived that encounter hundreds of times, chasing it around in my mind, picking at it for detail or depth and often finding them; running those frames through the projector, editing, enhancing, and embellishing them without wanting or needing to. The bear came down on all fours. He (we both made him male in our minds) watched us until he knew we saw him. He decided something. He came down on all fours and took a step forward. He decided something, he came down on all fours and took a step forward down the hill and into my soul.

That, I had often been told, is the way to see your grizzly—a chance meeting on his doorstep. Whether in a moment's glance or through a morning of distant observations, you must see him at home. The time it takes to see a grizzly, the waiting involved, makes it an event long before it happens. Anticipation and romance crowd into your consciousness so that you may worry, while you're "getting ready," that the bear will somehow disappoint (which isn't possible), or that you will somehow be inadequate and will fail to enjoy, or comprehend, or be adequately enriched by the encounter. That is probably not possible either, if only because once you have realized just how special the event is, your subconscious will take care of making the experience memorable. Like your first kiss or shaking hands with the President, it is memorable even if it went wrong.

And, appropriately, the bear doesn't know; it all means so much to you, but the bear forgets it almost right away.

Since the 1890s, until recently, you could see your grizzly a lot more easily, and a lot less appropriately, at a garbage dump. In the 1960s those few people who knew somebody who could get them into the Trout Creek dump (not near public roads, and off limits except to researchers and park officials) were likely to see anywhere from twenty to a hundred grizzlies at once, a visual overload I have trouble imagining, and am just as glad I can't share, because these dozens of bears were all up to their appetites in garbage.

Feeding Yellowstone's grizzlies at dumps was just as much an institution as feeding the black bears along the roads, and feeding the black bears was the most desired of all visitor experiences for millions of people. I remember the black bears myself. In the early 1960s my parents brought me to Yellowstone and a small black bear tried to eat my sister's camera (or my sister; we never were sure). What I've seen in Yellowstone has convinced me that feeding wild bears, in dumps or along roads, is a stupid, ugly, typically human thing to do. What bothers me most is not so much the people who get hurt but what it does to the bears. Hundreds of people were clawed or scratched in those days (the black bears did some mean work on a few, but most were just scratched and scared; four people have been killed by bears in Yellowstone since 1872, out of seventy million visitors), but look what they were doing: ignoring all sorts of warnings; smearing jelly on a child's face so they could photograph the bear licking the child; placing children on the bear's back for a picture; feeding bears film wrappers, cigarette butts, ice cubes, cherry bombs, and even food; running over an occasional cub . . . in short, doing everything to test the forbearance of an incredibly patient providence. Providence frequently took the form of a mama black bear who finally had had too much and took a swat at the hundredth citizen of Poughkeepsie to make a grab at her cubs that day. Then the rangers would be called to destroy the "dangerous bear." The rangers, who were in on the problem and yet preferred the company of bears most of the time, ended up destroying dozens of bears. Life is not simple, even for idyllic types like rangers and bears.

The rangers knew the bears shouldn't be fed. It had been illegal since 1902. The people did, too; a survey conducted in 1953, when the great Yellowstone "bear-jams" were beginning to reach their mile-long boiling-radiator peak, revealed that 95 percent of the people knew they were breaking the law when they fed bears. Only the bears didn't know. Being bears, extraordinarily adaptive omnivores, they were simply cashing in on an obvious good thing. The Rocky Mountain Free Lunch. Dill pickles, twinkies, ham on rye . . . the wilderness was never like *this*.

The only difference at the dumps was that servers and served were more select groups. Park employees, researchers, and a chosen few dignitary-gawkers were privy audience to lunchtime for one of North America's most spectacular evolutionary achievements, the grizzly bear. But, I am happy to say, this culinary camelot was doomed.

In the early 1970s Yellowstone officials cut off the gravy train. They stopped roadside feeding and they closed the open-pit garbage dumps. The dumps had been frequented by grizzlies for more than eighty years, and their closing (with the bears thus deprived of trash food) caused a monstrous national controversy, with political influence, scientific careers, outrageous egos, and, perhaps, the bears' welfare all at stake. By 1977 only one garbage dump remained open, a small scar near the north entrance, used by the town of Gardiner. Through a long-standing agreement between the park service and the town, this dump was a part of the community's way of life. For all the usual political and practical reasons, it was more difficult to close this dump, which serviced a private community, than it was to close the others, which serviced only park facilities. In every case, something else had to be done with the garbage, and it was harder to convince a small border town to spend the extra money than it was to organize better garbage disposal in the park.

Everyone knew the dump would have to be closed eventually. Not only was it unnaturally influencing the movements of the neighborhood bears, not only was it a flagrant violation of E.P.A. standards, it was a fabulously disgusting sight, even as dumps go.

Someone in the park decided that it would be useful, both scientifically and politically, to know more about the bears who used this dump. It was common knowledge that on most nights there were a few grizzlies at the dump, only a mile or so from town. Kids shot at them with .22's. Grown-ups (ha!) drove around the locked gate at the main road and went down the old service road to the dump so they could sit in their cars and watch the bears. But nobody could say how many bears there were, or how many of them were grizzlies, or if any had radio collars or ear tags from the Interagency Grizzly Study Team. Bears move pretty far sometimes, and knowing how many use what areas is important information when figuring out population levels and such.

A few rangers began taking turns monitoring the dump. Some time after 10:00 P.M., they'd unlock the gate, drive in, lock it behind them and drive the dirt road to where it passed behind a rise and ended at the dump. They'd sit there an hour or so, trying to identify individuals by their size, colors, markings, and other features (bears are as individual as people in appearance, but very few people get to see them enough to get to know what to look for; I never got any good at it).

I'd only been to the dump once before, in daylight, so I didn't have a very good fix on the setting. The Gallatin Mountains, specifically Sepulchre and Electric, slope quickly into the Yellowstone River valley on the park boundary. Between the river and the mountains is a narrow shelf, actually a rolling flat, mostly bare of trees, about half a mile wide. In a hollow, between a low ridge and the base of the mountains, sat the dump. Well, it didn't really sit; it sort of festered. It was perfectly accessible to the grizzlies who roamed the extremely rough country in the north Gallatins.

That evening, as we rounded the rise and bounced along into the dump, Les played the spotlight across the footslopes of the mountain to our left, locking onto four or five brown bear bottoms as they galloped over the ridge into a gulch.

"The engine scares them away. They come back in twenty minutes or so."

We parked at the very end of the road, engine and lights off, with garbage dump on three sides and a small hill immediately to our right. The car sat on a little earth ramp that pointed out over the portion of the dump then in use, but off to our left and behind us stretched several acres of American Fantasia: washing machines and couches, cellophane and freezer wrapper, detergent boxes and tin cans—the broken, the rusty, and the disposable.

"They usually come in through that draw." Les pointed straight ahead to the far side of the clutter, where the hillside split into two humps with a gap between them. "Sometimes they come right over that hill," he continued, pointing to my right, "and right past your side of the car." I voted for the draw.

Fifteen minutes later, our eyes now fully accustomed to the weak moonlight and our ears searching the night for sounds (a rat scrambling over a pile of tin cans sounds a lot like a bear when you're expecting a bear), Les pointed at the draw. "There's one."

Later, I had time to realize that my brief daytime visit to the dump had left me with a poor notion of its size. In the flat moonlight my eyes had misplaced the draw about twice as far away as it really was. So, laboring under this significant misimpression, I saw a bear twice as large as a bear should be. "God, lookit how big!" Eloquence under pressure is natural to the experienced woodsman.

Les didn't answer. I assumed he was as agog as I was, but when I looked over he wasn't even watching. He was calmly taking notes—his clipboard resting on the steering wheel—about the bear's arrival. I squirmed and gaped. The bear lumbered silently down the draw toward the dump (and us), casting a moonshadow like the Astrodome. This bear wasn't large; this bear was *vast*.

Before long, he placed himself in a helpful context. He wandered past an old ice box and didn't dwarf it quite as much as I would have expected. I then realized that I'd been seeing wrong, and that he was a reasonable grizzly bear after all, maybe 300 or 350 pounds. A boar, a little lean, a little ratty; he looked as if he'd slept in his clothes.

Most of the others we saw, on that and subsequent nights, were sleek and fat. Strictly speaking, it isn't true that a partial diet of garbage makes bears sick, but it may increase the risk of natural sickness as essentially solitary animals get together in big groups where diseases that might normally be restricted to one can be transmitted to many.

Before long the boar was joined by a few others, a family group of sow with two young of the year. A coyote skirted the place nervously, almost seeming to need the company more than the food.

I'm sure that the scientists who spent years studying the dump bears in the 1960s got to the point where every moment of watching wasn't a thrill, but I didn't spend years at it, and the excitement didn't wear off. Even after an hour or so of watching them, there was always a gut-tightening surge of adrenaline when a new one wandered close, or when a giant head suddenly loomed up directly in front of the car (one ranger who made his first trip with me later couldn't get over the size of the heads; whenever I'd pick up the clipboard he'd tell me to "make sure you say that they have really large heads").

And watching them, just sitting there watching them feed, was enchanting. Sorting through the junk (one imagines the bear casually pitching a refrigerator over his shoulder, but most of the sorting was of a more delicate type), poking a claw through some wet paper (did I miss any lettuce here last night?), or strolling along swaying that big head back and forth, the bear is just like any other open-minded shopper. Is this detergent good in cold water? Are the tomatoes fresh? Do the coupons apply to the day-old bread? No, you can't have that, I saw it first. There is so much curiosity, so much of the small boy picking up pretty rocks, that you quickly begin to see personhood in the bear. Or you begin to see bearhood in yourself. It's all the same.

They can get used to the same things, too: cans with sharp edges, rubbery vegetables, a table too close to the kitchen fire. . . . Fire? Yes, fire, the great Bad Guy of all children's animal stories (along with Nasty Hunters and Wolves, of course). It seemed that some of the stuff the dump received every day was burnable, and desultory efforts to light it usually left a couple of hot spots at night. The bears pawed all around the flames, their noses so close they'd reflect orange. I understand that this happens at other bear dumps, and occasionally a bear gets too close and gets burned or singed. Adaptive omnivores indeed.

One night a supervisor asked us to satisfy his curiosity about a popular product then being touted in magazines as good defense against wild animals. It was an air horn, one of those little cannisters that otherwise sensible people blast into your ear at football games. People were apparently being suckered into buying them as protection against grizzly bears. If a bear charges you, just toot this thing at him and he'll run away. Sounds great, I'll take two.

People who believe that a good loud noise is sure to scare a grizzly bear away certainly couldn't be people who have ever heard grizzly bears making loud noises at one another. A loud noise, especially if the grizzly hasn't been having a good day or is just in the mood to match loud noises with someone, doesn't sound like a good way to protect yourself from a grizzly bear. Who knows what the bear will think about it? There's a lot to be said for loud noises when you're hiking; if you make them as you walk along you're much less likely to surprise some animal that's sleeping in the middle of the trail; most animals move off a ways if they hear you coming. But once you've surprised one, and it's checking you out on its hind legs or rolling toward you for a closer look (or worse), you might as well count on divine intervention as make a loud noise at it. Either might work, but I bet that if God does intervene he won't use an air horn.

Anyway, Les and I waited until there was a sow, about 250 pounds or so, with a big yearling, about half her size, right in front of the car. They were just getting involved in a huge pile of radishes (I can't imagine how anyone could come to have so many radishes as this to throw away at once), no more than thirty feet from the steering wheel. It was dark, and I wondered aloud at how *I* would react if someone cut loose behind my back with one of those horns at a time and place like this. The bears were chowing down with some enthusiasm when

Les, in the driver's seat, stuck the can out the window and gave it a short, piercing toot. Both bears gave a start, then resumed eating.

"Hmm. Not much response." We were whispering.

"No. Maybe you should try a longer blast." Les nodded, held the can out the window, and pressed the button for several seconds. At this point the patrol car windshield seemed to be as much protection as my Audubon Society membership. Les, a calm, sensible man, had his revolver in his other hand, just in case the air horn said something horribly insulting in bear talk, but the revolver didn't look up to stopping a grizzly bear if one decided to come through the windshield.

Luckily, bears are patient, and though they don't know that rangers are their friends, they don't know how much damage they can do, either. The second blast definitely disturbed them, because they stopped eating. They both looked around at the dark car. I was never sure what the bears thought of the car, or if they could see us well through the windshield, or if they knew that cars usually have people in them (I don't know as much as bears don't know). These two, after a minute of checking us out, wandered away. Either they were restless, or annoyed, or tired of the radishes, or something else. I couldn't say, for sure, but the air horn wasn't very convincing.

Outdoor writers, who have little to lose, get a lot of mileage out of talking about bear repellents that have been proven in some hunting camp or other. Paradichlorobenzene (moth balls) is mentioned frequently as a good bear repellent. Yellowstone grizzly bears have been observed *eating* paradichlorobenzene. I know of a number of scientists who are working very hard to come up with effective "aversive agents" that might lessen the risk of harm when humans and bears encounter one another. Studies of this kind are necessary, I know; with so many people insisting on using bear country, there has to be a way to keep the injury rate as low as possible if only so the bears won't get a lot of bad publicity and end up being killed off. But I regret that it's necessary. Hiking in grizzly country without risk is like kissing your sister. One of the most important parts of the grizzly country experience, besides its rareness, is that hackle-raising humility that comes from knowing one is in the presence of a superior predator. Of knowing that one is, for once, a potential prey species. I hope we never reach the point where we are not allowed to have that feeling, but, given the gloomy outlook for the grizzly bear in the lower forty-eight, we may not have to worry about the feeling in the first place before long.

Though I learned a lot at the dump, watching those grizzlies feed, search, nap, and occasionally square off for a few therapeutic loud noises, my basic convictions about the bear were only strengthened. Most basic of all is my belief that even though grizzly bears are capable of explosive devastation, they can be lived with in places like Yellowstone. Look at the facts. Here is an animal that can bite through your skillet, or dismantle your recreational vehicle (removing the side nearest the refrigerator), or kill an elk with a good swat (ask yourself how many times you'd have to hit an elk with your hand to kill it), or reduce a dead tree to sawdust to get some ants, and it hardly ever *kills* anybody. Grizzlies can kill people, and we give them plenty of chances, the way we crowd into their country; in recent years grizzlies have been killing more people, a sign that we've reached some limit of their tolerance and the capacity of their country. But they continue to show a restraint that amazes me, and that we hardly deserve.

I don't underestimate them, and I've had my share of memorable dreams involving me, a grizzly bear or two, and small crowded places; being mauled by a grizzly bear has always struck me as one of those wilderness experiences where the novelty wears off almost right away. But look at what the bears put up with: all the thousands of sweet- or sour-smelling, careless, bacon-frying hikers who intrude on them for every one "incident" (an unfortunate euphemism that probably can't be avoided) that results in tragedy. Like a nuclear reactor, or a heart, we take the grizzly bear for granted until it does something we weren't expecting. I think, in the bear's case at least, that the problem is in our expectations, not in the bear's behavior.

We certainly make too much of the viciousness of the bear. Any species that survives by eating its neighbors is bound to make the community jumpy, but keep in mind that most of the time bears do no more than eat their neighbor's lawn, or dig up his flower bed.

Partly because in modern America being killed and eaten by a wild animal is incredibly rare, and partly because such an event is great press, we have a distorted view of the ferocity of grizzly bears. Every precaution must be taken—I always carry some honest fear into grizzly country—but let's be realistic about what the grizzly is and isn't.

The grizzly *isn't* a man-eater in the traditional sense. Unlike the famous lions and leopards of Africa or the tigers of India, the grizzly doesn't make its living eating people (a population of brown bears once got reasonably good at it in an isolated part of Russia, but even then relatively few people were killed). Some of the big cats have killed over a hundred people *each*. Fifty years ago, when Jim Corbett was hunting down man-eaters in the Kumaon Hills of India, he wasn't just some rich white hunter off on a sporting jaunt. He was a national hero. Those people were being dragged from large settled villages, nightly, by tigers that lived in good part on human flesh.

Rare is the grizzly bear that has killed more than one person. Many became famous as stock killers, back before 1900, but even then some profitable exaggeration occurred to the advantage of aggrieved stockmen and glory-seeking hunters. Unlike the cats, the grizzly is primarily a vegetarian. Both grizzlies and blacks can and do kill people, and once in a while eat them, and even less once in a while kill them *to* eat them, but not as a matter of habit.

A friend of mine once outbluffed a young grizzly. She was hiking alone when the bear rushed toward her, apparently interested in dinner. She waved her arms, growled all manner of foul insults, and informed the bear in her biggest voice that he must understand that she was larger and meaner than he, and was in no way to be considered dinner. Each of his charges was met and stopped by a louder and more blustery one by her. Each time the bear backed off, just unsure enough of himself to chicken out. She doesn't remember how many charges there were, but knowing her normal calm I wish I could have been there. She's gifted with language, and I would have loved to hear her when *really* inspired. The bear finally went away.

Friends have seen bison, or elk, or their own horses, grazing in the same meadow with a bear. There are times of truce, apparently, as there seem to be times that the predator only preys when the prey "acts like dinner," that is, runs or panics. A ranger I know once saw a grizzly charge an unsuspecting elk. The elk continued grazing, even after the grizzly was clearly in view. The bear stopped, probably puzzled at this imperturbable ungulate. After studying the elk from a short distance for a moment, the bear wandered away (perhaps thinking, "Gee, I could have sworn that was dinner").

Now I don't recommend charging or bluffing grizzly bears, or even ignoring them. I find the whole thing delightfully confusing. Grizzly bear authorities tell us that if we are confronted by a grizzly bear and cannot escape by climbing a tree, we should play dead. It seems that the most damaging grizzly-hiker encounters (statistically speaking; there are exceptions) are unexpected, when a hiker surprises a bear on a kill or with a mate or young. In those circumstances the bear's response may be instinctive and quick defense, and a grizzly's defense puts most good offenses to shame. The idea behind playing dead is that an inert reclining being is not threatening. Though not a sure thing, playing dead has proven itself, statistically again, the best choice. Sometimes the bear will come over and roll the "body" around a little, or munch thoughtfully on an elbow (imagine lying quietly during this), but unless the hiker panics and struggles (acts like dinner?), the odds are good that the bear will go away.

What puzzles me is that grizzlies eat lots of dead bodies, feeding heavily on winter-killed elk in those springs when carrion is available. How is it that *this* dead body, a frightened hiker, doesn't get the same treatment? I suppose part of the answer is that at the moment of the encounter the bear wasn't looking for carrion, though I'd hate even more to be in that hiker's shoes in early spring, when elk carcasses are most available.

Like almost everything else about grizzlies (or many other things worth knowing about), we can't be sure we understand. We have to admit that their food habits surprise us. A few years ago scientists observed a Yellowstone grizzly passing up easily available dead meat to hunt and kill elk of its own. Even the carcass feeders are still teaching us. The prevailing attitude about bear food makes them "foul feeders." Any old-time hunter will tell you that "them bears don't get really worked up about a carcass until it's good and ripe." Actually, no one has proved that bears have a taste preference for rotten meat over fresh meat, but it has to be a lot easier for them to sniff out a rank carcass than a new one. For that reason they may feed more on the rank ones. They may also prefer a rank carcass because it will contain more maggots, a bear delicacy. What bears need and what people find disgusting tell us more about people than about bears. As the beggar and dump bears most dishearteningly demonstrated, willingness to try new foods is the bear's special blessing; even were the animal able to do so, it could not afford to worry that its diet causes people to suspect a character deficiency. Maggots, escargot; rancid elk meat, buttermilk; who's really deficient here? No one, I think, but I figure we're more suspect than the bears; at least bears never make judgments about people.

A 600-POUND GRIZZLY BEAR, a nearly black boar, was being held for helicopter relocation at the Fire Cache. His culvert trap, a circular metal tube about twelve feet long and four feet across (made from corrugated metal culvert tubing), mounted on a pair of wheels for towing, was parked in one of the long garage stalls. It was a cool dark tunnel, away from the prying eyes of tourists and most employees, a quiet and rather dank spot that I imagined might even be to the bear's liking were he not caged up in the trap.

I shuffled self-consciously the length of the passageway to the culvert at the far end—not sure whom I was afraid of disturbing—and took a seat on an upended bucket about a yard from the metal grill at the front end of the trap, the end the bear faced.

There was enough light from small high windows to see him well. He was resting on his belly, his paws drawn up near his chin, his nose a few inches behind the grill. He didn't move as I seated myself, or during the fifteen or so minutes that we sat staring at each other in that damp corner.

Bears don't have big eyes, so they are lost in that infinity of fur and fat and ripplingly smooth motion, two small dark sparks evolved to deal primarily in the nearby because what else need a 600-pound grizzly bear worry about? Like the Union officer who threw the auxiliary sails overboard shortly after his huge ironclad battleship was launched because nobody was going to make *him* hurry, this bear needed better eyes nowhere near so much as his neighbors did. If I'm too far away for him to see me, it's my responsibility to keep it that way. I try to look him over, but I keep coming back to the eyes. I have big hands, and his claws seem as big as my fingers; I am darkly amused that he could probably hook his claws into the grate that separates us and rip it from its welded frame. In this case, what the bear doesn't know won't hurt me. But from the claws I am drawn back to the eyes, steady, unblinking, either dull beyond my comprehension or perceptive beyond my imagination, staring with evident but unlikely calm back at me. His ears are reduced by the bulk of their surroundings—a massive round skull over heavily muscled jaws—to unimportance, like some anatomical afterthought stapled indecisively to the finished animal after it left the factory. Bears hear well, but, as with their eyesight, from my bucket in front of this one I figure that they don't really need to. I wouldn't insult *this* one if he was stone deaf.

When I'm not held accountable to human reason or scholarly

accuracy, which is to say when I'm alone, I lapse into a rather personal approach to what interests me; I talk to things, trying to calm a squirming fish as I struggle to free a hook and release it, reasoning vainly with a horse that is more interested in trailside clover than in getting to the corral by dark (then cussing him as I rein him in), or greeting the elk, bedded in the snow by my door, with a mixture of joy, respect, and fear. So I want to talk to this bear. I sit there wanting to *understand,* wanting to see something in those eyes besides my reflection (and not being seduced by the rhetorical opportunities of seeing oneself reflected in grizzly eyes), something in his passive still-ness besides brute patience. But I don't know how to start. What to say? I know that the trout doesn't understand my reassurances, I know the horse recognizes impatience in my voice and figures he can get one more mouthful of clover before the reins pull him away, and I never have figured out what those elk think of my silly greetings, but the talking is useful, at least for me. It's a kind of reaching out. But the bear is too much. I would ask questions if I thought the bear had answers, or if I thought that by asking them, out loud, I might sense an answer of my own. I most feel a need to express regret or apology for the circumstances of our meeting, to apologize for the idiot who baited the bear into a settled area where he had to be trapped before someone was hurt; again the bear would have no answer. I would express admiration for his size and power, or for his wildness . . . admiration, at last, for his utter independence of my admiration, or of anything else I think or want.

That is probably why he is so important to me; it's a one-way street of fascination, I caring most for his detachment and nearly alien disre-gard for me, caring that he can exist without caring about me. This bear is at my mercy, vulnerable to the moronic growth of commerce, the mindless pressures of human population, and the mechanical finality of a good rifle, and he doesn't even know it. He'll die some day, and all like him, never having grasped where he stood in relation to humans, never having sat on a bucket and studied one.

This is good, I decide, and it's also a little spooky. The bear in the trap suddenly seems a lot farther away, not just a yard but uncrossable distances, and I am chilled and uncomfortable on my bucket in the presence of so untouchable a spirit. I must stir uneasily, for suddenly the audience is over. From somewhere deep in the cavernous innards of the bear, like a train still far away in a mountain tunnel, a rumbling hum begins. Impatience. The menace in the sound is palpable, though the actual animal, eyes unblinking, claws at rest on the culvert floor, has not moved at all. I still can't talk to the bear, not even an "Okay, okay, I'm going," as I right the bucket, return it to its place by the wall, and with one last wishful look at those incredible eyes, hurry from the building and into the bright morning sun.

THOMAS McNAMEE WAS BORN in Memphis, Tennessee, and
educated at Yale University. He lives in New York City and has
written extensively on the grizzlies of Yellowstone National Park.
McNamee's 1984 book *The Grizzly Bear* met with instant critical
acclaim and was recently republished with a new epilogue in
which the author considers current developments in the park.
McNamee was a featured speaker at the "Fate of the Grizzly
Conference" in Boulder, Colorado, on April 5, 1986, and gave a
brilliant speech on the crisis facing the national parks. His
remarks were later published, in expanded form, as *Nature First*
(1987), a book that proposes an American system of national
biosphere reserves in which nature conservation would be the
primary goal of land management. These reserves would expand
park boundaries to conform with ecosystem boundaries, while at
the same time keeping existing management units intact.
McNamee would like to see Yellowstone designated as the first
biosphere reserve.

McNamee focuses in this selection on what is probably the
most difficult period in the annual life of the grizzly—the
emergence from hibernation. The season's difficulties are only
compounded by the presence of actively nursing spring cubs,
such as is the case here. But "these are perhaps exceptionally
lucky grizzly bear cubs, born in the prime of a conscientious and
experienced mother's life, in a good year for food, in a relatively
safe and undisturbed home range." Chances are, at least one of
them will survive to adulthood and possibly have a chance to
enter the reproductive cycle.

13. APRIL

THOMAS McNAMEE

STILLNESS. UTTER STILLNESS. MILES on snowy miles of it, of nothing moving, not a bird, not a deer, not a wind-quivered willow shoot—no wind—no one. Only stillness. A world dead beneath six months of snow, dead blinding absolute white. Above, fierce mid-April sun, and empty midday sky. Beyond, a black and white horizon, crags of ice and stone. Below, an ice-encrusted forest pocked with buried meadows. Here, a few black rocks, a clump of whitebark pine, a single ancient gnarled subalpine fir; a steep blank slope of snow.

There appears in that whiteness a darkness, a hole. There appears in the hole a wet black nose. Sniffing.

And with a sudden snow-explosion, where there was nothing there is all at once a lot of something. A grizzly bear. Three hundred fifty pounds thereof.

Sniffing, sniffing. It is still winter here at nine thousand feet, but, on a zephyr too faint to feel, the bear can smell spring from far down-mountain, and the tang of putrescent meat. Yet although she has eaten nothing for half a year, the bear is still not hungry. What she is is still sleepy. With a grunt, a long yawn, and a last dim squint at the lifeless winterscape she turns, and goes back through the hole in the snow beneath the snaggled roots of the old fir tree.

A week goes by. Snow falls, the den again disappears, and again the snow explodes to disclose a sudden outburst of bear. For several minutes she just stands there as if dazed, blinking, slowly waving her big head back and forth, sniffing the breeze; then she sits down. Hind legs splayed out on the snow, long-clawed forepaws limp in her lap, she sits up on her rear like a man, luxuriating in this lush beatitude of sun. She scratches her belly, even after six months' fasting still a stately pot. Now, turning toward the darkness of the den, she voices a soft *whuff.*

And out into the dazzling white world tumble two more grizzly bears, rather smaller than the first, perhaps five pounds apiece. They are every bit as cute and fuzzy as your great-aunt Alice could please, rollicking frolicking teddies, clumsy and goofy and gay.

They are hard to picture now as the terror of the wilderness. Indeed it is hard to picture even their mother as such. Still half in hibernation, she barely moves. Her gait, when she does, is drunken, unsteady, slow. If there were trouble now, her reaction might well be slow and clumsy. This posthibernation lethargy is one good reason why grizzly bears tend to choose such blizzard-blasted and remote places for their dens, and why for the next several days the family will not roam farther than a few seconds' travel from the safety of the den. The cubs are still unsteady on their feet, moreover, and the mother bear is still not hungry. Give her a week or so to shake this grogginess, though, and then watch out.

The cubs settle in for their first outdoor meal, of milk exceeded in richness only by that of coldwater marine mammals such as whales, seals, and walruses—grizzly milk being twenty-five to thirty-three percent fat, compared to three percent for cow or human milk. There are six nipples for the cubs to choose from, although grizzlies never bear that many young: litters are typically one, two, or three cubs, depending mainly on the nutritional status of the mother; litters of two are by far the commonest.

For almost three months now, nursing and napping have been the cubs' whole life. Their mother stirred and woke from her deep torpor from time to time—most notably near the end of January, to bring them into the world, eat the placenta, and clean them up a little—but the state of her consciousness even then was uncertain. The cubs, encircled in that massive furred insensibility, themselves not hibernating, have had nothing to do but grope and suckle and grow till their début today.

Pretty soon, though, they are going to be busy. Success in life for every grizzly bear depends on what that individual bear has learned in his cubhood; in the extent to which they rely on individual instruction, grizzlies are surpassed probably only by man and the great apes. Animals whose behavior is determined principally by their genetic inheritance tend naturally to be much alike; instinct is among the greatest of equalizers. Animals educated by their mothers, themselves the products of generations of individual instruction, tend to be individualists. Of the latter form there can hardly be a better representative than the grizzly bear. At least a year, more often two, and sometimes even three or more years of a grizzly's youth are spent in school. And in grizzly school the discipline is rigorous, and the lessons are many and hard. The mother grizzly is—must be—an exacting teacher.

Still a few days' respite remains, for the mother bear's hibernation wears off slowly. Basking, snoozing, nursing, frisking, all within a moment's dash of the den, the cubs pass a lazy homebound week in sweet far niente. Even in such seeming indolence, however, a crucial process is under way—the inculcation of the three fundamental rules of grizzly bear cubhood: follow mother; obey mother; have, within those constraints, as good a time as possible. They learn to see, they learn to walk. When, gaily wrestling, the cubs tumble downslope in the snow farther than that all-important moment's dash from the den, the big bear gently takes each cub's whole head in her jaws and carries him, dangling limp, back within the safety zone. When they bite too hard at her teats, they get a prompt flat-pawed boxing of ears. When she calls to them with a soft peremptory *woof* (they quickly learn), they by God come. They dig in the snow, they sniff at the multivariously aromatic breeze, they learn to keep their balance and run. They nurse, they grow. They play.

Meanwhile, as the last woozy sluggishness of posthibernation lethargy wanes, the mother bear is getting seriously hungry. Up here it is still winter, and there is nothing to eat. It is time to sally forth into spring.

With frequent stops for nursing, somersaulting, climbing, cavort-
ing, and every manner of exercise of the cubs' ebullient curiosity, the
three make their way desultorily down to death-redolent elk winter
range. The snowpack is deep this spring, and the elk—and deer and
moose and bighorn sheep—who have wintered in these sheltered valleys are down to the woodiest stubs of browse, and there is not enough
of even that to go around. Many are dying, many are dead.

The mother grizzly follows a scent to the edge of a seething
snowmelt creek, and there finds a carcass. Ravens squawk in the treetops. A coyote leaps from his covert and skulks into the forest to await
his chance to return. With a single slice of a single claw, the big bear
neatly opens the elk's abdomen. She clips the esophagus with a yank
of her teeth and pulls away the bulging rumen; this first of the elk's
four stomachs is full, despite the fact that this animal did starve to
death—so unnutritious are the winter's-end species of browse represented here. She lays the rumen aside. The cubs sniff fascinated at her
every motion and its consequence: when she lifts her head to sniff for
evidence of disturbance, their eyes are on her, and they, without the
least idea what they are doing or why, wave their heads back and forth
and sniff too; one waves his head so hard he falls over.

Although the elk may have died weeks ago, the body is barely
thawed, and the liver, while she would not especially care if it were
not, is still fresh. The mother bear lifts it out and presents it to the
cubs, to try their needly new teeth on. Clumsily they mouth at the
liver, tugging and growling fiercely. Even in play, even with such a
superabundance of food, the cubs make of every situation a contest.

The grizzly rips great chunks of flesh from the haunch and,
hardly chewing, half choking, wolfs them down. The cubs, not quite
ready yet for meat and already bored, want to play, and they hurl
themselves merrily at her head. With a gourmand's single-minded
snarl she bats them aside. She puts away an easy twenty pounds.

Done at last, licking her chops, she sits on her haunches and lazily
scratches an ear and yawns. At such moments her winter torpor still
threatens to reassert itself, but she cannot let it. There is work to do.
She excavates a shallow elk-sized hole and maneuvers the carcass in.
She shovels dirt, duff, mud, snow, sticks, rocks, whatever is handy, to
cover her property and warn off any interlopers; this covering will be
known to all as the signature of a grizzly bear, to be gainsaid only at
great peril. She even drags a good-sized tree trunk out of a logjam

downstream and heaves that over too.

There is a dense grove of Englemann spruce and lodgepole pine nearby, in a particularly dense part of which the mother bear scoops out a cozy bowl just big enough for her and the cubs. She rips down green spruce boughs and lines the depression to form a springy, heat-trapping mattress. Curled up here, concealed to perfection within defensive-charging distance of their meat cache, the bear and her young may sleep their breakfast off in watchful security. For the next several days and nights, as she gradually consumes the elk and teaches butchery to the cubs, this nest will be home.

Upstream, along ten feet of bank, a little seeping spring has melted through the snow, and there, thus warmed and sunny, the black alluvial soil has yielded tender shoots of sedge, the season's first green succulence. After their midday nap, the mother grizzly leads the cubs there to graze. Although she esteems no food more highly than meat—for there is none more nutritious—the grizzly bear instinctively seeks out a balanced diet. After the die-off of starving prey in early spring and then the stress of calving season, there will be progressively less meat available: the weakest ungulates (hoofed animals) and their most vulnerable young will already have died, and their survivors will be too fleet of foot to catch. Until fall, when prey and carrion again become available, the bears' livelihood will be progressively more dependent on their ability to recognize and harvest the most nourishing food plants.

In some springs less lucky than this one—when, for example, the winter kill of ungulates is low, perhaps because the snows have been light and hence more browse has been available—grizzly bears must subsist almost entirely on vegetation. Yet even in the best of springs, in the high, cold country where most grizzlies live, much of their range is still under snow, or still so frigid that nothing is growing yet, and what meager plants there are are few and far between. And then in late summer and on into fall, as the countryside dries up and the nights grow cold again, many plant species mature and wither and die. At these times, especially in dry years, a grizzly bear's knowledge of when to seek and where to find such superficially insignificant microclimates as that of this sedge-fringed seep may spell the difference between life and death.

Spring is unquestionably the hardest time of year for grizzlies to find food, and in a naturally regulated population the nutritional

deficits of spring are believed to be the principal cause of grizzly mortality—and, because spring nutrition directly affects fertility and cub
survival, it is a major agent limiting their reproductive success as well.
(A "naturally regulated population," by the way, is more a theoretical
ideal than an observed reality, since grizzly populations everywhere
but in the remotest Arctic tend to be at least partially regulated by
human factors such as killing or habitat destruction.)

A well-educated and experienced grizzly bear's knowledge of his
home range is astoundingly comprehensive and precise. Our mother
bear remembers not only where she found good things to eat last year
but also where, six years ago, in a summer of drought, a low moist spot
in an otherwise sere expanse of sun-parched timothy still held a
pocket of lush bluegrass. She remembers which slopes and ridgetops
are the first to be blown free of snow in spring. She remembers, even
before their aerial parts appear, where the richest starchy roots and
tubers may be dug. She knows the buried whereabouts of pocket
gopher populations. She remembers where, each fall, the squirrels
have harvested and hidden their hoards of pine nuts. She knows the
locations of all the avalanche chutes in her range, where the frequent
snowslides have limited the vegetation to that which can withstand all
that cascading snow—the grasses, supple-stemmed shrubs, and forbs
(soft-stemmed plants that die down to the ground in winter, most of
which are familiar as wildflowers)—and she remembers which of
those avalanche chutes, facing south, are first to catch the sun and
therefore first to green up. Even now, as they learn to grasp the blades
of sedge in their back molars and roll their heads to snap it off, the
cubs are storing up essential memories.

This is the first of many lessons to come in botany, which will be
the major subject of their primary education. Because grizzlies retain,
albeit in modified form, the short gut of their more carnivorous distant ancestors, and lack the cellulose-digesting ability of the ruminants
(cud-chewing, four-stomached animals like elk and deer and cows)
with whom they share their habitat, they must make the most of the
scant proteins which almost all their food plants contain in usable
form for only a short time—in the preflowering phase, when the
plants' reserves of solar energy and mineral nutrients are concentrated in the stem and leaves in preparation for the manufacture of
flowers and seeds. The cubs will learn to recognize this stage in the
lives of hundreds of species of plants, and they will learn precisely

where to go to find these items at their peak of succulence at every time of the year, under a wide range of climatic conditions, and throughout a great variety of habitat types. To a greater extent than any other factor, this process, of following their food plants' phenology, determines how and where grizzly bears live their lives.

And it may seem strange, but that is how the awesome grizzly, widely known as "the largest terrestrial carnivore," actually spends most of his waking time—placidly munching on grass and flowers.

The vegetarian life is nevertheless a precarious one. At least until high summer brings the berry crops, the caloric value of most grizzly bear plant foods, although substantially higher than that of the plants they do *not* eat, is quite low in relation to the plants' weight and bulk. The bear's digestive efficiency is also low, so every grizzly bear is constantly on the lookout for a quick shot of easily digestible, high-protein, high-calorie goodness—in other words, meat. The discovery of a network of pocket gopher or ground squirrel tunnels will often send a grizzly into a perfect frenzy of excavation. So great sometimes is a grizzly bear's lust for meat that he will expend far more energy in its pursuit than could possibly be gained; one ten-pound marmot, more often than not never caught, can account for the furious hurling downhill of two tons of talus. Digging, by the way—more than ripping open a moose's belly or your sleeping bag—seems to be what the grizzly bear's prodigious front claws have evolved for.

Grizzly bear food habits can be fairly neatly summed up in one word: opportunism. They will eat some of the lowliest crud in the world, but they still know a square meal when it comes along, and they will let little stand between it and themselves. Watch.

A week has passed. Nibbling daintily at the streamside sedge again, the cubs spot a field mouse zipping across the snow. They are instantly after it, all vegetarian thoughts instantly banished. Such pursuit they do not need to be taught: grizzly bears instinctively chase things that flee from them—which accounts for the puncture wounds in the fenders of some park rangers' trucks, as well as certain other more serious disfigurements. But the mouse is too quick for these still clumsy babies, down its burrow in a flash. Dig then they must, and impressively do. Sod-clods fly between their little back bow legs. But their coordination is not yet sufficient, and the mouse has escaped— until their mother moves in. She cocks an ear groundward, hears the faint rustle of the subterranean quarry, and with a single scoop of her paw brings up a hunk of turf from which squirts the mouse, straight into her jaws. Crunch, gulp, and it is gone. The cubs look on, dazzled, one lesson closer to competence.

IN 1987 JIM CARRIER, a writer for the *Denver Post,* spent the summer in Yellowstone National Park. His biweekly reports from the field, which appeared in the *Post,* explored some of the salient issues facing the world's first national park. "It was," as Carrier acknowledged in his first letter, "a dream assignment." In these three letters, Carrier focuses on the Yellowstone grizzly bear. His guide in the park is Steve French, an emergency room physician whose passion is the grizzly and who was featured in an Audubon Society television special on the bears. French shows Carrier the site of one of Yellowstone's infamous dumps and explains that the bears have now adjusted to natural food sources. Later they look for bears in Hayden Valley—one of the most beautiful places in Yellowstone—but the grizzlies prove elusive.

These "Letters from Yellowstone" (1987) by Jim Carrier are reprinted by permission of Jim Carrier and the Denver Post.

14. LETTERS FROM YELLOWSTONE

JIM CARRIER

June 24

I WENT LOOKING FOR BEAR THE OTHER DAY—GRIZZLY bear.

My guide was Steve French, a man who will see more bears in Yellowstone than anybody this summer, because he goes where they are. He agreed to let me come along.

We hit Hayden Valley, smack in the middle of the park, about 6:00 A.M. and were just up off the pavement when he showed me the first tracks. Dried in mud, one paw measured about 4 ¾ inches across. Another was slightly smaller.

As we walked west, we climbed sage-covered knolls, up and down. At the top of each, Steve would put his finger to his lips, take off his cowboy hat, and creep to the crest.

The valley was waking up. We heard coyotes, and the flutter of ducks on the Yellowstone River. Each hill we climbed was lit at the top by the sun rising behind us.

We stopped to rest often. I was carrying a huge wood tripod, and Steve was carrying a 16mm movie camera, with a lens about as long as his leg. We both shouldered backpacks, and carried binoculars. As we caught our breath, he talked about his favorite subject.

"I've seen 75 grizzlies this year, in three weeks of looking. I know 42 different bears," he said.

"The bears in Yellowstone are very healthy. We have a healthy breed that can be saved. We have a new bear that is not as fat. It's free and wild. It's behaviorally different than the garbage bears."

I had seen pictures in the 1960s of bears along the road, being fed everything imaginable by tourists. They poked their heads into cars, begged on their haunches. The scenes were known as "bear jams" and were as much a part of Yellowstone as Old Faithful.

I also had seen pictures of bears in the dumps of Yellowstone, waiting for the garbage trucks to show up. Up until 1941, the park had bleachers by dumps for nightly bear shows.

But the dumps were closed and the feeding stopped around 1970. A new philosophy swept wildlife managers. Not only was it aesthetically displeasing to see bears eating trash, it was dangerous.

Because they ate human food, carrying human scent, and sometimes held by a human hand, the bears became used to humans. And they lost their fear of man.

Aggressive bears would tear through campgrounds, coolers and tents looking for more food. Inevitably, there were conflicts with people.

Black bears, the bears along the road, would occasionally nibble a finger. Grizzlies did far worse damage.

Steve French was a surgical resident at the University of Utah hospital in the late 1970s when he told me he watched as plastic surgeons took a flap of skin from the shoulder of Barrie Gilbert, a Utah biologist mauled at Yellowstone, to cover the missing left side of his face.

After that, French got interested in studying bears. When the university contracted to run Yellowstone's clinic at Yellowstone Lake, French was sent for a two-week period.

"I learned about the grizzly bear, and I had the best teacher—the bear," he told me. "I read all the books and attended all the seminars. But the only way to observe and experience wildlife is to sit down and wait."

He showed me spring beauties popping their white flowers up after snowbanks receded, yellow bells and bisquit root—all bear food. And he grinned when he found evidence that a bear had dug into a cache of yampa, buried by a pocket gopher.

Every few minutes, we scanned the sage for bear. He pointed to the spot of the infamous Trout Creek dump, the last dump to close in Yellowstone. "Now bears are congregated at trout streams," he said. "Today's generation is rediscovering the old food sources. They're chasing elk everywhere." Just a few days prior, he had filmed a bear killing an elk calf.

I asked him why people didn't see bears along the road anymore.

French said he had heard stories. But he didn't care to mire in the politics of the bear.

"C'mon," he said, picking up his pack. "Let's go see some bears."

June 26

STEVE FRENCH LOOKED like no doctor I'd ever seen.

Mountain man, maybe, with a long scruffy beard, a beat-up Stetson and an aw-shucks way of talking, a truck driver's boy from Texas. But not a respected emergency room chief from Evanston, Wyoming, onetime medical chief of staff, member of the hospital board, a former nuclear engineer, marathon runner and all-around pillar of the community.

What better company, I thought, in bear country?

We had spent a futile morning in Hayden Valley looking for grizzlies, but it was getting hot and unlikely they would appear from their daybeds in the trees. We would return again at sunset.

On the way back to the pickup, French lectured me about bear attacks.

"A bear can kill a human at will," he said. "But they usually don't."

Bears attack when they're threatened: a mother protecting her cubs, a bear defending a carcass, a bear surprised. Rarely is a bear just trying to eat you.

In Yellowstone's history, there have been hundreds of injuries and four deaths from bears. Last year there were no injuries. But in 1984, a woman was eaten by a grizzly that never was found.

It was the kind of talk around a campfire that would send me to my bedroll with the willies—if I went at all.

That evening, a front was coming through. By the time we returned to the valley, rain was falling in sheets. I hunched beneath a parka and Steve crawled on the lee side of sagebrush.

"I hate to take out the poncho," he said. "It's still packed up in the way I bought it. I hate to mess it up." He said it in that good-ole-boy Texas drawl.

A few nights before, he had been caught out here after dark and stumbled onto a grizzly with cubs. The sow charged to within 50 feet, stood up, turned and left.

I told him the bear would have spit him out as too hairy. He told me I could take comfort in knowing a bear would return me to the nitrogen cycle.

"It's important for the grizzly bear to have the capacity to kill and eat us," he said. "That may seem paradoxical for a doctor. But the fact that they do keeps us humble. We should see ourselves not as top of the heap, but as a cohabitant.

"We hold the grizzly bear in awe, not because of mythology, not because it stands and walks, not for its speed or dexterity. The reason is that it can kill and eat us. If it didn't, it would be a 500-pound marmot."

Attempts to teach bears to fear man, he said, so-called aversive training being tried in Wyoming and Montana, were regrettable.

"They might as well take the gravity out of the mountains, the swiftness out of the streams, the heat out of the thermal areas. Let's pave it over so you won't turn an ankle. Let's sanitize Yellowstone."

Just then, the rain stopped and a rainbow appeared. The sky was so big that it was raining behind us and sunny ahead. Scattered throughout the valley, as far as we could see, were elk and buffalo, grazing.

"You see," Steve grinned. "Mother nature rewards those who suffer through harsher times."

Moments later we caught a glimpse of two bears in the distance. Just a tease in the glare of the setting sun. Then they were gone.

We watched instead an elk herd below us. "Here comes kindergarten," Steve said. From out of nowhere came four calves, romping in play. They moved through the herd and found their mothers.

I got home at midnight, 20 hours after I started the day. Steve apologized for not doing better, but I reminded him of something he had said earlier.

"My end point is not to count grizzlies. My love is to go and enjoy grizzly country. And it's darn good country—about the best thing we have left."

For that one day, I was a cohabitant.

June 29

MY SEARCH FOR BEARS in Yellowstone was more than a curious safari.

I wanted to see them because they are so rare, because they are the essence of wildness. But also because I was nagged by the question: where are the bears? A question everyone asks when they drive through the gate and see the sign: "This is bear country."

The answer was as elusive as the grizzlies Steve French and I tried to find in Hayden Valley.

No one really knows how many bears are in Yellowstone. The park's estimate is about 200 grizzlies, but they never have been counted. The black bear population is anybody's guess. It may be as low as the grizzlies', but the black is not considered threatened.

The first real study of the Yellowstone grizzly began in 1959 when biologists realized the bear was in trouble. It was hunted outside the park. It had been forced to live on a smaller range. When it tangled with man or man's livestock it usually lost.

Even within the park, "problem bears," those who had injured someone or were considered dangerous, were routinely killed. It always had been that way.

In 1937, a year in which there were 115 personal injuries and 81 cases of property damage, 41 black bears and 10 grizzlies were killed.

When the park closed the garbage dumps and stopped roadside feeding in 1968, the bears went wild. They rummaged through campgrounds, strolled into bordering towns, even walked onto the front porch of Old Faithful Inn. It began a period they called "Bear Wars." Again, the bears lost.

Many were transplanted, trapped and drugged, carried away by trucks or helicopter. Most came back. They got two or three chances. After that they were killed.

No one knows how many black bears were killed, but it is likely in the hundreds. Local people say the roads in the park went from being "lousy with bears" to bearless in one season.

As for the less visible grizzly, more than 100 were killed in the name of "control" between 1968 and 1984. Another 200 died in and around Yellowstone, mostly from hunting and poaching.

The last two of the garbage dump grizzlies were killed in Montana last year, 15 years after the park decided to create a wild and free-ranging bear. It was a dark period in wildlife management.

In Yellowstone now, every bear counts. Grizzlies have become a gauge of the biological health of the park.

They have also become a measure of the park's success in carrying out its mandate to preserve the park while providing for the pleasure of man.

As a result, the bear exerts an influence far beyond its number.

Five to 7 percent of Yellowstone's budget is devoted to the grizzly. A special office keeps track of bear sightings. Trails are closed to prevent bears from being chased away by hikers.

Extraordinary efforts are taken to keep the park clean. Garbage is picked up twice a day. Rangers and a forest of signs warn visitors to keep their food away from bears. All-night patrols watch for coolers left out in campgrounds.

"Once rewarded with food, then it is only a matter of time before the bear is destroyed," said John Varley, the park's chief biologist.

"Human-bear conflicts translate directly into dead bears."

RICK BASS, A NATIVE OF Houston, Texas, felt the lure of the Rockies in his late teens, and in 1976 entered Utah State University, where he played football and majored in petroleum geology. He also took some English courses from Thomas Lyon, who encouraged him to continue writing. After graduating, Bass worked in the oil industry in Mississippi, Louisiana, and Texas, and eventually—in 1987—moved with his wife, Elizabeth Hughes, an accomplished artist, to a ranch in Montana, where he has since devoted himself to writing. Rick Bass's books include *Wild to the Heart* (1987), *The Deer Pasture* (1988), *Oil Notes* (1989), and, most recently, *Winter: Notes from Montana* (1991). He is currently finishing a novel about wolves and a wolf biologist entitled *Where the Sea Used to Be*.

In this essay from *Wild to the Heart*, Rick Bass describes a trip he made into the Yellowstone grizzly country. He is purposefully vague as to the exact location—mentioning only the Tetons and St. Anthony, Idaho. Bass touches on many of the important issues: the Craighead study, the controversial decision to suddenly close the park dumps, the problem of livestock grazing on the surrounding national forest lands. Bass is by no means optimistic as to the future: "Both sides are trying hard, with transgressions of course in either camp. . . . The larger grizzlies are being selected against. . . . They *are* becoming smaller, less aggressive, more furtive; it is just a quickly downhill race to see if they run out of individuals before they get there." Whether the bears can adapt, by becoming smaller and more accommodating like the bears of Europe, is the key to their survival in Yellowstone.

15. THE GRIZZLY COWBOYS

RICK BASS

I

I GOT THIS LETTER, FROM THE FOREST SERVICE. THEY
said they would send me out with some of their people, in a forest
where grizzlies used to be, and sheep now are, if I'd write about it, and
draw the picture.

So in July this girl from Mississippi and I are out on horses and
this big old silver-bearded mountain man named Jenkins is pulling a
pack-string of government mules with one forearm while the other
tugs the reins of his black horse, Dime, who is twenty years old and
muscled, very large, and spirited, too much so. Mountain air. Jenkins
(Wayne) himself is sixty-one. He calls the mules wicked names when
they are bad.

A camera hangs around Elizabeth's neck. There is a notepad in
my pocket. The Forest Service wants me to tell people what bears are
like, sheep too. I know my assignment, and frown, and concentrate on
it, but it's the people I keep seeing, even out here.

There are, in this one wilderness area, almost two million acres
and hundreds of black bears, but only six (maybe) grizzly bears. On
the horses, there's Elizabeth and me, and Wayne, and Gary and Bob.

They've got us outnumbered by one. It would be nice to say we are all on the same side, but that's not entirely correct. We would like to be, but the bear doesn't want us, won't take us. Like the wisest of our dreams, surely the grizzly realizes that to depend on us would doom him; to depend on anything, even a lucky break in the winter, would doom a grizzly, and make him a thing less than he fully is.

These woods are different, riding through a field, buck-and-rail fence behind us, just before we enter the trees; the last bit of mountains we see are the Tetons—and the horses step over fallen trees, downed and rotting timber. There are slow streams, backed up from the workings of beaver, and we splash through these, and we shift and creak in our saddles, that good noise, and the woods are different because there are bears in them. Grizzlies. I don't, didn't, know that six of anything could make as much of a difference as can six grizzly bears, even spread through an entire state, a whole country.

It's good policy, to keep around a thing that knows how to keep from dooming itself. When birds called, or fluttered in the brush, we were conscious of the noise, the sound. All sounds were important. We listened to everything. I knew the big mountains were above me, ahead and high through the trees, and I could feel the different air masses, sliding down off of them, at different times in the day. I could feel everything. I felt like an Indian, and was glad and grateful for everything, and cannot explain why.

IF ONE OF THOSE six bears was a female, and had cubs, we could have eight bears in these woods, this forest, if both cubs lived, and survived.

EVERYTHING HAPPENED too fast. It is now one year since that trip and I am writing this, as Barry Hannah says, only as an obligation to the people who put the trip together, and who are waiting to see what I have to say, something that has never been said before. Which can't be done. "It's the crown jewel of American wildlife, fierce, noble, instills fear, respect," etc., *magnificent;* you can lay the words out as if on a Scrabble board, or put them in a bag and shake them up. Be sure and include *majestic.*

Instead I will write about the people I was with, who are trying to save the bear, those six bears. They're not a mirror of the grizzly, but close. You can sit around with them and watch them whittle or talk about camp cooking or shoeing a horse and then, sometimes, you can almost see the bear, if he is indeed still out there. The way the moon would sometimes come up over the mountains: I *thought* I could kind of picture what one would look like, in the wild. I have to confess that it was a feeling, as seemingly transparent as it was, that nonetheless you could hold on to. Miraculous. Sleeping in those woods was new. Do we have much left that is new? You can't forever do away with your old, either. What I am saying is that I just wish we would move a little more carefully, with our grizzly bears.

AS BEAUTIFUL AS the mountains were, and as real as the saddles creaking and dusk rising seemed and felt—it was still the nights that were the smoothest, clearest, and purest. In the tent, I would lie awake, after Jenkins and Foli and Bob had cooked for us, and cleaned up, and were preparing the horses for the night, feeding them a little oats—and I would look up at my tent ceiling and know pretty well that there could be a grizzly nearby—they saw one, not twenty miles from the very creek we're above, last summer! Never mind the creek's name—and if you think we, humans, didn't come out of those woods too, in our past, then you're disowning something. There was steak caught in my teeth one night and I broke off a twig and picked it free.

THERE WERE STARS and muted campfire noises down by the horses, and at night I was often up on a little hill, and over in the next valley I suppose sheepherders were watching the sheep and I was reaching back to my past, because it had to be pretty much as it was a hundred years ago, and it wasn't sliced away from the rest of us yet. I was *doing* it. There was bacon and egg and fried potatoes in my stomach, and the taste of them still there.

You could write your congressmen, and western congressmen. You could probably find their addresses, and sit down and write. You could rent a helicopter, too. You could fly over the wilderness before first snow, even in late summer, sprinkling dead sheep, far into the wilderness, sailing them down, spiraling, into the treetops below. There is the theoretical and then there is the pragmatic. One tastes better and is more comfortable and the other keeps you alive. It's no secret which of the two the grizzlies would prefer.

THE HORSES WERE beautiful, even for horses. They would put these things on them, as dusk fell and fireflies began to dance, called Mormon hobbles, magician-style handcuffs that were quite simple to snap loose, if you knew the trick—neither the horses nor the Indians ever figured the trick out, only the Mormons—the harder you pulled, the tighter they got, but when you pushed against them (on them) in a certain and light way, they literally fell off, mystically, and the horses stepped free—and in the evenings the horses, when first hobbled, would take off in great prancing leaps, front and back legs bound together, so that it looked like a new species of animal, unicorns, perhaps, the green meadows in which they were hobbled were that beautiful, and their odd lunges, and the clanking sounds, leaping, gathering, leaping, gathering, trying to outleap the hobbles . . . Wayne and Gary and Bob sitting around, tired, watching them, holding their coffee cups, just watching them . . . after a while the horses would quiet down, and gather, and commiserate, and begin grazing. . . .

Elizabeth and I could smell those stars and cold air currents rolling down off the mountains. I wanted more of it, all I could get.

In the morning there was sun. Those bastards back at work were probably milling around with their noses in each other's behinds, like dogs. Sons of rotting bitches! It was good to be tightening a horse's cinch strap, in the morning. It was great. I pulled it real tight; slapped him in the belly, to make him suck up harder, and pulled quickly tighter, again.

IT WAS GARY'S (Foli's) turn to make breakfast. It was the second day. We were to ride very deep into the wilderness, days and days. Jenkins and Bob were older, and were easing into the trip. You could tell it took them two days and a certain amount of miles to relax. Leaving something behind: going back to another thing. Having the opportunity, the availability, option, to do so.

Jenkins lights a pipe. There aren't any bears in this story. He begins to sing, and has not even been drinking.

You know the way dust rises on a trail, from a horse's hooves. One of the mules, the chief and balky one, was named "Hooger." To hear Jenkins get mad and bellow: Hooger! Go out in the woods sometime and pretend the mule is being a real ass, say he has bitten you, or emptied your post all over the mountain because a butterfly has startled him, or pretend he is merely wreaking havoc on the other mules, biting and kicking them for pleasure. Pretend black blinding anger, and cut loose: yell that Hooger word. It will scare the bears off, but it sounds good, coming up out of your chest and out your throat. This is sort of what the woods were like, with Wayne, and Bob, and Gary.

BOB WAS FROM Vietnam—not born there—born in Idaho, his brother guides a raft on fishing trips down a river. Bob used to be a cowboy, the kind that holds on to bulls—and he's the range expert. He looks at plants and knows their name, and how much water they require, can tell you what's been eating them and if there's a dearth or abundance of it.

You can't look at Bob and not know that he wasn't in Vietnam. Somehow, it is a part of him, and in his gaze, even when he does something simple, like watches the fire, or cleans dishes, or puts his foot in the stirrup of a saddle. But, he is very happy. You can tell this too, by these same things, same sights. He deserves this. The word is dues. I am sure that he thought about this Idaho place, often, over there. It probably doesn't even matter if the old bear survives or not. I know that is not what they wanted me to say and it is not what I believe or wish in my heart and I didn't even have any intention of saying it myself but now I am thinking of Bob, over there, thinking about these mountains, and rivers, and the way fires smell, and cold mornings, and though yes, the woods are better for him because he knows there are grizzlies in them, the other part ain't too bad, and could have maybe brought him around on his own. Maybe. Probably. Not as quickly, for sure, but probably, and just as far. Maybe. I think.

People who have been through tough times but are finally at peace sure do have that look about them.

II

THERE'S A MAN named Emry Davis up in these mountains. That is how his name is spelled. He wears red suspenders and is short and chesty and chews. His dogs, being sheepdogs, each have one yellow eye and one blue eye. He is his father's father's grandson, and is sixty. They've always herded sheep in these mountains, since the 1800s. There are blue lakes up above tree line, with scattered moraine, and flowers.

The grass in the meadows is like a carpet. You want to roll in it, on your back, and there are hawks above you. It is a good country. Emry Davis runs three thousand sheep through this wilderness early in the summer. His family used to run thirty thousand, then ten thousand. The three thousand still sounds like a lot. It's a pretty big piece of country, though.

If Emry Davis kills a grizzly he goes to jail along with everyone in his outfit: nephews, sons. They aren't the sort of men who would like that kind of action. The movie *Tom Horn*. Gary and Bob and Wayne ride herd on the sheepherders. The thing is working. The sheep thing. Everything clicks. If only there were bears to thunder across the tall grass, down through the creeks. Chasing elk. Ripping at logs, roaring. Being bears.

Emry rides through the aspen, the breezes, doing his job up here. The sheep do gain, on these rich cool high meadows. He's never seen a grizzly up here. His father used to see them often, and had stories.

They, the sheep, never stay in one place for more than a night. Bob doesn't let them take the range down. Gary rides through the night, with field glasses, watches the herders, the sheep, ranges back and ahead, looking for sign, tracks, fur, kills. He calls if he finds even the suspicion of grizzly and everybody—sheep, rangers, FBI agents lurking in the woods (seriously: Emry displays some of the business cards they tack to trees in his camp, during the day, while he is out herding—to let him know he is being watched—Hello, Crockett, Tubbs? This is Castillo. We've got a problem)—Emry shakes, as he shows the cards, creased and old and accumulated, in his wallet—he is only a man who lives in the woods and fields and raises his sheep in the wilderness—if a bear is sighted, or sign thereof—grizzly, not black—all of these people, players in the mountains, get the hell out of the woods. Make way for the bear.

I think Wayne is there because he is older, gruff, knows all about horses, the woods, and life. He doesn't know the Latin names of the plants as does Bob and can't fix the communications equipment like Gary can, but Wayne directs things nonetheless.

The man who understands horses is in charge of the mission.

THE PLOT AND COUNTERPLOT is sinfully human and complex to take place back in the good old mountains. Gary is trying to undo the damage an ambitious grad student, who was the bear monitor before him, has done, with what are now obviously false reportings of grizzly sign. Gary spends five to ten times the amount of hours in the woods that the previous monitor did, and lives day and night looking, not just eight-hour days as was the previous monitor's schedule, in the forest; and in three years he has seen grizzly tracks once. The grad student who reported the plethora of grizzly fur, scratchings, scat, etc., has a very comfortable job now. It looked damn good on his resume.

Oh well. The bears can take this, must, along with all the other bullshit. They have been shot at, poached, lied to, tranquilized, dropped from helicopters during transplanting (a process whereby the federal government tells an eight-hundred-pound animal used to feeding on thousand-pound elk and mountainsides of green vegetation where it needs to go, and to stay put). Jenkins has seen a wild bear up here once in seventeen years—coincidentally, seventeen years ago, his first year on the job—and she was on a streamside, a long way off, in the morning sun—his hands move as he describes it, and it was almost a religious experience, you sense—flipping over boulders with one paw, boulders that three or four strong men wouldn't ever be able to budge, and the little cubs (two) would then rush in and pounce on mice, chase crickets and beetles, whatever was beneath the boulders. Wayne and his father, who was eighty then, watched the mother move all the way down the streamside and into the woods; the meadow looked afterward as if it had been mined: boulders strewn, some having tumbled all the way down into the stream. The sun on her long claws. Wayne said he was a hundred yards away, up in the trees, on a ledge, and was terrified. His father said he used to see them pretty often like that, as a young man.

Can you define the bear, in his absence, by the people, and country, around him? Probably not. But for me, they are the only clues. The little clickety 16mm films in the Forest Service headquarters: I watched them for eight hours, one Sunday—they take your breath away, but after a while, all the muscle, all the carnage—the two bears fighting over a dead elk they have found, racing back and forth across the stream with it in their jaws, dragging its half ton like a dog pulling his bedding around—becomes hypnotic. It isn't until you step back out of the building and look up at the mountains that you can ever consider what the bear is like.

ON THE SECOND DAY, Elizabeth is walking oddly: when we mount up, she winces, and rides bravely for two minutes before giving up and pulling her down sleeping bag out of the pack and piling it up around her saddle.

"We'll rub a little whiskey on your behind tonight, and it'll be fine," Wayne assures her, seriously. She looks at me, then at Wayne, but Wayne is looking straight ahead, then back at the mules, tugging, urging Hooger on.

"He is probably kidding," I tell her, later. These mountains. We had pancakes for breakfast.

"WHAT DO YOU DO for a living anyway, Rick?" Gary asks sleepily. Lunch: peanut butter sandwiches. Warm water. My eyelid flickers; my left hand jumps. For some reason I'm unable to answer him. Elizabeth watches me cautiously, hands me a piece of her candy bar. Finally, instead, I just tell him this:

"At work, they make up stories about each other, and tell them to the bosses, trying to get each other in trouble, trying to get ahead by putting someone else down. They hardly ever do anything *productive*. They just make up these horrible stories, and rumors."

Wayne shakes his head and looks disgusted. Bob looks off at the woods. Gary is incredulous. The woods feel suddenly different. I should not have mentioned it, put it into words. A horse stamps, nickers, paws; dust rises.

WE ARE ABOUT THIRTY miles into the woods before they are able to begin talking about the office part of their own lives. I think about my office life, and ride, and listen. They have named some of the mules in the string for people in their office.

Fortunately Hooger is not one of them. And we can't even flip boulders over—but expect the bear to coexist, to fit where we tell it to fit? To not go along a certain stream? We can roast sheep over a fire out here at night, ten thousand feet up, but expect the grizzly to not even wander across any of the three thousand that have come into his high green country this summer?

Surprisingly—or perhaps not—he does not. The thick presence of all the black bears is as condemning a sign as any. Radio-collar studies have shown that black bears, when a grizzly moves into their area, fall over themselves getting out of the territory. They don't even wait for daylight. They flee. One collared black bear made fifty miles before dawn.

I like to think that if from anywhere on their range the grizzlies can see a road, a town, smoke rising, they leave: the true wild bears, the ones that have not been tampered with, experimented upon.

Some people say the various "bear teams" have committed two major mistakes—the first understandable, the second unforgivable— done sheerly out of politics and meanness, knowing full well the consequences—it surprises me that none of the slain campers' families ever filed suit, for manslaughter, or worse—have been one, trying to transplant drugged, tranquilized bears to places less distant than the moon or its equivalent, and two—simply not wanting to back down from a memo—closing the dumps at Yellowstone. It doesn't even need discussing. The Craighead brothers—John and Frank, for a long time the foremost and only grizzly experts in the country—told the Park Service to close the eyesore dumps slowly, and for office reasons, the Park Service didn't, and instead shut them down entirely, overnight, taking them away—and the fat and healthy and numerous bears spilled, like prizes from a cereal box, hungry and aggressive and sassy and portly, accustomed to being around people, into the general lowland countryside. Hello, pilgrims.

This occurring about the time Bob was going over the big pond in a bomber, wearing camouflage. It shocked the bears' system, and if they are to recover from it, the dumps, so runs the argument, will need to be re-established—not the hideous park refuse centers, but their nutritive equivalents, back deep in the wild high alone places, where the bear belongs, where he deserves to be, where he came from. So that he can help define what is still high and alone. The dumps lured nearly all the grizzlies out of the mountains; the Park

Service took the dumps away, and killed the bears; there aren't many left—not enough females left in Yellowstone to field a healthy football team. . . .

Sheep carcasses, cattle, road-killed elk and deer; the great winterkills of the Madison River elk—by dropping these things a hundred miles into the woods, the bears might meet each other, reproduce, feed, and survive, and grow back into the system from which they came in the first place, a system that *could* hold them, but doesn't, because they're down, reproductively speaking, to zero. (About twenty-five breedable females in the Yellowstone ecosystem—forty-three cubs.) This idea might not work, and should be filed away somewhere for the horrible, possible future—no one is in favor of it, at present—but it should be filed, should be heard, and considered. If the bears don't come out of it themselves, it could be the next thing to try.

Even Emry Davis, the pragmatic old sheepherder, admits that it is a way to save them, the bears, what one might at first suppose is his enemy. Every bear that is shot by black bear hunters, every bear that is killed by humans, seems to be a female, as their exposure is so much greater than that of the males: gathering more food, for the demands of reproduction, of saving the species.

There is frustration on Wayne's (and Bob's and Gary's) part. They want to see action, effort, not debate. Too many stuffed shirts: too many people afraid of making a mistake, creating controversy, and losing their "jobs," as did the Craigheads (what a lovely name). I think of my office. No purity left—not where it counts. Or not where it's effective. Gary, riding out on his horse, searching for fur. A hundred and fifty miles from a pay phone.

"The biggest problem is that the line of control is not narrow enough," says Wayne. It is a growl. There's sun: we're on a ridge, looking out over the western United States. We saw a cigarette pack by an old campfire a while back. We're not deep enough yet. Not for me, not for them, and certainly, then, not for the bear.

"A few years ago there were too damn many bosses, always working against each other, following different plans. Now there's another group—the Interagency Grizzly Bear Committee—since 1983—which is trying to work together with everyone—coordination—the Fish and Wildlife people, the Forest Service, the Park Service, the BLM. . . ."

There's still squabbling. But it will get better. It has to.

Wayne is getting windy. He's been thinking about it for years, and sees it like a vision. "You always do best when one man—just one, a good one—is in charge of it. That one man might make a mistake here and there, but it's the staticness, and neutrality of the situation, that can be fatal."

The bear is perfectly capable of just fading away; it's a thing we know, and fear.

We ride. Hawks soar on warm currents. We are in short sleeves. Elizabeth's camera snicks, taking pictures of ripped-up logs, scratches on trees—black bears, black bears, tame and wan. It seems that along the trail every third tree is scratched by bears; deep scratches, that make you stare. One set extends above our heads, even seated on the horses. The smell of black bear does not alarm the horses, the mules. How they know to fear the grizzly, an animal they have never seen, I do not understand, but would like to learn. Bears freeze to death in the winter, from the hard conditions, and nutrition is so critical that even one good three-day meal—an elk, a deer, a couple of sheep— can make the difference, and carry them through, roll them across the winter of sleep, and into the spring, one more year of many.

III

SHEEP LOVE TO DIE, it seems to me. I'm listening to John Burns. This man is the boss. We're in St. Anthony, before the trip. There seems to be an itching almost-anger, practiced resignation, that he cannot go, that he cannot be in two places at once, and do more. He has met me at 6:00 A.M. to talk about the problem, and the forest, and he deploys men and women, cuts trees as he thinks they, the cuttings, will best aid the grizzlies (six), rather than the Forest Service—this in the times of cutting back. There are computers in every office, but John Burns deploys the people. It's a nice small Idaho town.

John Burns is talking about sheep, about the ways they can die. He begins to tick them off on his fingers, but gives that up. "They run up to coyotes, wanting to play. They fall over in stream crossings and forget to get back up, and drown. They die giving birth. They die of fright, of thunder. The sight of lightning kills some. They blunder into large black bears. Their most famous and practiced trick is suffo- cation: they get bottlenecked somewhere, a place too narrow for them to all fit, but they keep pouring in anyway, *trying* to fit; they climb up on top of each other's backs, and crush those below, and suffocate them. You can lose two-thirds of your herd inside five minutes, that way." And I think: they worship death.

The grizzly has killed people before, the grizzly has killed sheep. It takes an expert to keep a herd alive in the mountains, and sometimes bears get blamed for losses they didn't cause. But they will kill sheep. They like to eat them.

John Burns has an ashtray made from the plaster cast of a grizzly track taken several years ago. It is the size of a tennis racquet. His forest totals 1,837,000 acres. The six or less bears are his number-one priority. An American hero. It is possible that all six are males. I think, leaving his office, that I wish he had at least a hundred to work with— to start over, and correct mistakes. There were seven, but someone shot and wounded a radio-collared mother, who died in her den over the winter from malnutrition. Which was fortunate, because her cubs consumed her, in the den, and didn't die from same. But what will they do next year? There have been several sightings of these cubs around a certain lake, which is heavy black bear hunting country. Over in Yellowstone, the count is twenty-five sows and forty-three cubs. We've got to hold tight, do the right thing, there. The forty-three cubs is a good number; but the twenty-five sows—that worries me. And that's the *highest* sighting in years—an improvement.

More. I want more. More chaos, more anarchy.

More honor, more strength. We can get it right. We can go into the woods without being mauled, without ruining things. I want the bear to give us one more chance.

Can you doom a grizzly, by touching him: by allowing him to have nonfatal interaction (tranquilization, capture) with humans, and be released? It appears no amount of cannons and fireworks, rifle shots, even pain, can deter a grizzly after surviving a human handling. Does he remember the fact that he escaped, and was therefore stronger? And is no longer afraid? Certainly, he's not afraid. You have to admire their straight-ahead belief in themselves. It has gotten them further than we have gone, yet. Almost all of the "problem bears" have been created by human touch—garbage in camps, in towns—at one time or another. It is time to stop handling bears. The Interagency Grizzly Bear Committee, for example, is trying to limit the number of radio-collared grizzlies in the wild to ten.

If you see a little bear, a cub, in the woods, and you've got a tree, you could go up it—because the mother will never be far away, and she'll be very, very angry, if and when she discovers you nearby. Or, because grizzlies (and blacks) can climb, you could instead lie down, and try to present as harmless a presence as possible. The bear can hit thirty miles an hour; running is never an option.

Maybe if she sees you, and you lie down, or stand very still, she'll leave. Or she might charge, bluffing. Or she might charge, not backing off, and then do some chewing, some swatting. Be very quiet, and cover your vital organs by crouching, one hand over the back of your neck. Some people make it out this way, some don't. A game warden up in Glacier killed a radio-collared male at point blank with six shots from a .357 magnum. It was the sixth shot he got lucky on, snapping the neck. Big gun. (He was letting the bear out of a cage.)

So I don't think much of weapons, with regard to grizzlies. I say, let him chew. Because if you start firing away and don't get lucky with that fifth shot, or sixth, then he'll eat you for sure, all of you, and then deposit you in his scat, all over the West.

If you lie still, and don't fight, he might take only a rib; a piece of shoulder. I had a professor once who got up on a meadow with the wind all wrong, and cubs in the area, and he was mauled. A research graduate student was with him, down below the meadow, and he saved the professor's life by sneaking up behind some bushes and roaring—like another bear—and frightening her away. The professor said it was a sound like the cracking of an egg—the bear's jaws, popping his skull; and the heat, and the breath.

They got the professor out by helicopter. A lot of people—most of them—do live through a grizzly attack. The professor lived, and teaches. He acknowledges, gratefully, that it was his fault. And he doesn't go out in the meadows, up high like that, with a strong breeze behind him, anymore.

In fact, he says, all strong breezes like that one rattle him.

DON'T TAKE A DOG with you into bear country. The dog runs around, sniffs up a bear, surprises it, is frightened, and runs back to you. With a surprise hot on his tail. Look what I have brought you, Dad. And human menstrual periods seem to provoke investigation, as do sexual odors.

We are dealing with an animal that came from Europe and Asia in the Ice Age, over the Bering Strait, like the rest of us, and into the tundra and glaciers; as wide and open a country as has ever existed, a world of ice. Increased size and aggression were the only ways to defend oneself, to develop with such a country; nowhere to hide. Every cell of a grizzly remembers his past, those times, and we will have to be very patient, letting him develop again, in response to yet another new environment: furtiveness, and avoidance. Both sides are trying hard, with transgressions of course in either camp. It is just that the bear's camp is so much smaller. The larger grizzlies are being selected against; the plots of their average weight are declining, plummeting, down over ten pounds a year. They are getting there. They *are* becoming smaller, less aggressive, more furtive; it is just a quickly downhill race to see if they run out of individuals before they get there.

VEINS RACE ACROSS the horses' legs and chests, standing in sun. "Everyone is so nice," says Elizabeth. It is the day before we leave.

There are spurs, on the grizzly cowboys out here, Wayne and Bob and Gary. The mules and horses have *U.S.* branded on their flanks. In the winter, Wayne travels to Tennessee, to shop for stock. We sit in the shade; the horses stand in the sun, and fidget. It is another century.

Off in the woods, the sandhill cranes begin to howl and flap; birds of tremendous size, happy in a country of great size. There is a breeze. Bob and Wayne talk awhile. We are closer to the valley again, looping around, heading back. In two days we will be in a car, driving, on a road. Wayne is talking about retirement, figuring out the logistics. Please no.

"Oh, I'm so big, so old, so tired," Wayne groans, that night. "Used to be I'd dance eight of ten dances." He has told his wife that when he gets back, he will take her dancing. "Now I'm only good for two out of ten." He shakes his head mournfully, but then, brightening, asks us if we have heard the story about the man who used to have this job of his, of being a grizzly cowboy, before he did.

"No," we tell him.

Wayne chuckles. "He was a tough old booger: he would definitely dance ten out of ten. First and only time we ever met him, we were camped up above Boone Crick with the herders, about sundown, and this guy comes racing down through the woods and downed timber riding a sow grizz, whipping her with a rattlesnake, and he grabs a cup and scoops up a gulp of sheep dip, downs it, tosses the cup away and takes off again, saying, 'Sorry to eat and run, boys, but I've got to go, there's a mean sucker after me.' "

IV

ONE THING IS FOR certain: after the second day, you do not ever want to come out. Bob tells me about whortleberry plants, points them out. If I were a bear, I would eat them. They look delicious. Summer.

"HOW'S THE LOAD?" Wayne, leading the string, calls back. He means are any of the tents or packs slipping off. Hooger is bad about crow-hopping: turning sideways and bucking, in a tight little prance, until all the pans spill. Coffee and beans, and tin cans and pots. Perhaps he likes the noise.

"Fine," comes the answer, Bob, immediately, comfortably. Bob in the back, watching, instinctively, also judging the range. A team. Gary off alone, casting, youngest, much energy: riding across and back, up and ahead, back, looking. The horses and mules break into trots at seemingly regular intervals. The woods are right this morning. There are yellow flowers. Gary points out claw marks on a tree.

THE LAST DAY. Hooger misbehaving, trying to run all the way. A cabin up ahead; we're riding through deep green grass, crossing beaver streams. The mountains tall and white behind us. I twist, turn in my saddle, and look back; even while looking, plodding slowly away. The mules break into a run when they see the cabin. Wayne cries out angrily, but their will is loosed: they thunder foolishly across the meadow, stumbling and stepping into holes. Wayne goes racing by me, spurring Dime; his saddle's creaking madly, his spurs are bouncing up and down and jingling wildly. He's riding hard, cursing, and we watch him and the mules spread out across the meadow, all of them galloping, and check our own horses severely, rein back, to keep from following.

PART IV

THE SOUTHWEST

"Permanent grizzly ranges and permanent wilderness areas are of course two names for one problem. Enthusiasm about either requires a long view of conservation, and a historical perspective. Only those able to see the pageant of evolution can be expected to value its theater, the wilderness, or its outstanding achievement, the grizzly. But if education really educates, there will, in time, be more and more citizens who understand that relics of the Old West add meaning and value to the new. Youth yet unborn will pole up the Missouri with Lewis and Clark, or climb the Sierras with James Capen Adams, and each generation in turn will ask: Where is the big white bear? It will be a sorry answer to say he went under while conservationists weren't looking."

—Aldo Leopold
"Wilderness for Wildlife,"
A Sand Country Almanac, with Essays on Conservation from Round River, 1949

GRIZZLY BEARS ONCE ROAMED ACROSS the Southwest. Their range included

mountainous regions and major watercourses in southern Colorado, southern Utah, Arizona, New Mexico, southern California, and northern Mexico. The decline of the grizzly in the region can be directly linked to the rise of the livestock industry, which waged an unremitting war on predators from the 1870s through the 1930s, by which time the grizzly had become extinct in all areas but Colorado and Mexico. What also doomed the southwestern grizzly was the fact that there were no large national parks in the desert uplands to protect it (in California there were large parks but hunting grizzlies was permitted in them, for some reason).

Black bears continue to thrive in the Southwest, which has some of the best bear habitat in North America. Whether grizzlies remain in southwestern Colorado and northern Mexico is an open question. Grizzlies were killed in Mexico in the 1960s and a grizzly was killed in Colorado in 1979. In the three wild areas thought to have grizzlies— the San Juans of Colorado, and the Rio Yacqui headwaters and Sierra Del Nido of Mexico—reports of grizzly activity and occasional sightings persist. At present the U.S. Fish and Wildlife Service's official grizzly bear recovery plan (1991) states that the San Juans are under consideration for further grizzly study and possible restoration of the bear population; the situation in Mexico is less hopeful.

In addition to these three ecosystems, there are several other areas in which grizzly reintroduction could be considered. All previously had grizzlies in the twentieth century. Among these are, first, both the Blue Range Primitive Area in Arizona and the combined Gila Wilderness/Aldo Leopold Wilderness in New Mexico, which offer large, integrated units of pristine grizzly habitat. Grazing allotments have for the most part been retired or purchased by state game and fish departments for wildlife. In the case of the Gila, the Forest Service commissioned a biological study in 1974 that concluded the wilderness area could support a grizzly bear population. Like the vast San Juan ecosystem to the north, the Gila region contains over 1,000 square miles of designated wilderness area for such a project. Second, the 500-square-mile Gray Ranch—newly acquired by The Nature Conservancy—provides an ideal opportunity to restore grizzlies to the Animas Mountains. The ranch is located in the bootheel of southwestern New Mexico; three of its last grizzlies were killed in 1911 by famed hunter Ben Lilly. Third, any discussion of regional reintroduction would be incomplete without mentioning the southern Sierra Nevadas of California, a little to the north of the traditional Southwest. Grizzlies thrived in these mountains through the early twentieth century; black bears are still plentiful. From Yosemite National Park south to Sequoia National Park, there are over 3,600 square miles of contiguous parkland and wilderness area waiting for the grizzly to return. A further motivation is the fact that California calls itself the Golden Bear state, and the grizzly is featured on the California state flag.

As the livestock industry declines in the Southwest and else-where—a result of more efficient and profitable feedlots and growing trends to eat poultry and fish instead of red meat—there is some reason to have genuine hope that the grizzly can be restored to its ancestral range here. Other countries around the world with dry mountain environments—Spain, Italy, Greece, Turkey, Syria, Iran— have managed to protect their native brown bear populations, and it would certainly seem within our capability to do the same, particularly in light of our frontier and wilderness traditions. Hopefully by the year 2000 there will be wild grizzlies somewhere in the Southwest again, adding their magic and majesty to the mountains. Perhaps one day, hiking along some old pack trail in the Southwest, you will be one of those lucky souls who spots, in the green avalanche slides on the north side of some mountain with a Spanish name, a mother grizzly frolicking with her new spring cubs in the last of the winter snow.

ALDO LEOPOLD WAS ONE of the Renaissance figures of the
twentieth century: a scientist who practically invented modern
game management, a philosopher who created the concept of the
land ethic, a nature writer whose work can stand beside any
volume of Beston or Krutch, a Forest Service manager who almost
single-handedly formed the world's first wilderness area—the
Gila—in 1924, and a university professor who served as mentor to
hundreds of fledgling wildlife biologists. Leopold's literary and
philosophical reputation rests solely on a small, posthumously
published collection of essays: *A Sand County Almanac, with Essays
on Conservation from Round River* (1949). "Escudilla," an essay from
the book, was inspired by Leopold's early days as a forester
assigned to the Apache National Forest in southcentral Arizona.
While in the Southwest, Leopold saw the federal government
virtually wage war on the grizzlies at the behest of the powerful
livestock interests who used—some would say abused—the public
lands. Writing in the late 1940s of the misunderstood grizzly,
Leopold was one of its first defenders. He realized that the bear
was an indicator species, and that as the major mountain masses
lost their resident silvertips, so did they also lose their wildness. In
fitting testimony to Leopold's lifetime of service to the cause of
conservation, the federal government two decades ago set aside
nearly a quarter of a million acres of the Black Range in
southwestern New Mexico as the Aldo Leopold Wilderness area.
The grizzly may one day roam these mountains again.

16. ESCUDILLA

ALDO LEOPOLD

LIFE IN ARIZONA WAS BOUNDED UNDER FOOT BY grama grass, overhead by sky, and on the horizon by Escudilla.

To the north of the mountain you rode on honey-colored plains. Look up anywhere, any time, and you saw Escudilla.

To the east you rode over a confusion of wooded mesas. Each hollow seemed its own small world, soaked in sun, fragrant with juniper, and cozy with the chatter of piñon jays. But top out on a ridge and you at once became a speck in an immensity. On its edge hung Escudilla.

To the south lay the tangled canyons of Blue River, full of white-tails, wild turkeys, and wilder cattle. When you missed a saucy buck waving his goodbye over the skyline, and looked down your sights to wonder why, you looked at a far blue mountain: Escudilla.

To the west billowed the outliers of the Apache National Forest. We cruised timber there, converting the tall pines, forty by forty, into notebook figures representing hypothetical lumber piles. Panting up a canyon, the cruiser felt a curious incongruity between the remoteness of his notebook symbols and the immediacy of sweaty fingers, locust thorns, deer-fly bites, and scolding squirrels. But on the next ridge a cold wind, roaring across a green sea of pines, blew his doubts away. On the far shore hung Escudilla.

The mountain bounded not only our work and our play, but even our attempts to get a good dinner. On winter evenings we often tried to ambush a mallard on the river flats. The wary flocks circled the rosy west, the steel-blue north, and then disappeared into the inky black of Escudilla. If they reappeared on set wings, we had a fat drake for the Dutch oven. If they failed to reappear, it was bacon and beans again.

There was, in fact, only one place from which you did not see Escudilla on the skyline: that was the top of Escudilla itself. Up there you could not see the mountain, but you could feel it. The reason was the big bear.

Old Bigfoot was a robber-baron, and Escudilla was his castle. Each spring, when the warm winds had softened the shadows on the snow, the old grizzly crawled out of his hibernation den in the rock slides and, descending the mountain, bashed in the head of a cow. Eating his fill, he climbed back to his crags, and there summered peaceably on marmots, conies, berries, and roots.

I once saw one of his kills. The cow's skull and neck were pulp, as if she had collided head-on with a fast freight.

No one ever saw the old bear, but in the muddy springs about the base of the cliffs you saw his incredible tracks. Seeing them made the most hard-bitten cowboys aware of bear. Wherever they rode they saw the mountain, and when they saw the mountain they thought of bear. Campfire conversation ran to beef, *bailes,* and bear. Bigfoot claimed for his own only a cow a year, and a few square miles of useless rocks, but his personality pervaded the county.

Those were the days when progress first came to the cow country. Progress had various emissaries.

One was the first transcontinental automobilist. The cowboys understood this breaker of roads; he talked the same breezy bravado as any breaker of bronchos.

They did not understand, but they listened to and looked at, the pretty lady in black velvet who came to enlighten them, in a Boston accent, about woman suffrage.

They marveled, too, at the telephone engineer who strung wires on the junipers and brought instantaneous messages from town. An old man asked whether the wire could bring him a side of bacon.

One spring, progress sent still another emissary, a government trapper, a sort of St. George in overalls, seeking dragons to slay at government expense. Were there, he asked, any destructive animals in need of slaying? Yes, there was the big bear.

The trapper packed his mule and headed for Escudilla.

In a month he was back, his mule staggering under a heavy hide. There was only one barn in town big enough to dry it on. He had tried traps, poison, and all his usual wiles to no avail. Then he had erected a set-gun in a defile through which only the bear could pass, and waited. The last grizzly walked into the string and shot himself.

It was June. The pelt was foul, patchy, and worthless. It seemed to us rather an insult to deny the last grizzly the chance to leave a good pelt as a memorial to his race. All he left was a skull in the National Museum, and a quarrel among scientists over the Latin name of the skull.

It was only after we pondered on these things that we began to wonder who wrote the rules for progress.

SINCE THE BEGINNING, time had gnawed at the basaltic hulk of Escudilla, wasting, waiting, and building. Time built three things on the old mountain, a venerable aspect, a community of minor animals and plants, and a grizzly.

The government trapper who took the grizzly knew he had made Escudilla safe for cows. He did not know he had toppled the spire off an edifice a-building since the morning stars sang together.

The bureau chief who sent the trapper was a biologist versed in the architecture of evolution, but he did not know that spires might be as important as cows. He did not foresee that within two decades the cow country would become tourist country, and as such have greater need of bears than of beefsteaks.

The Congressmen who voted money to clear the ranges of bears were the sons of pioneers. They acclaimed the superior virtues of the frontiersman, but they strove with might and main to make an end of the frontier.

We forest officers, who acquiesced in the extinguishment of the bear, knew a local rancher who had plowed up a dagger engraved with the name of one of Coronado's captains. We spoke harshly of the Spaniards who, in their zeal for gold and converts, had needlessly extinguished the native Indians. It did not occur to us that we, too, were the captains of an invasion too sure of its own righteousness.

Escudilla still hangs on the horizon, but when you see it you no longer think of bear. It's only a mountain now.

"EL OSO GRANDE" offers the editor's views on the North American grizzly, based on his explorations and experiences in both the San Juan Mountains of southwestern Colorado and the Gila Wilderness of southwestern New Mexico, as well as in northwestern Wyoming and in Denali National Park and Preserve, Alaska. The essay emphasizes the need to restock both the Gila Wilderness and the San Juan Mountains with grizzlies in the 1990s. It is fitting to end this anthology with a selection that speaks to the issue of reintroduction, for the restoration of predators in American wilderness areas is one of the major challenges facing conservationists in the 1990s.

17. EL OSO GRANDE

JOHN A. MURRAY

WHEN I WAS A BOY IN OHIO, MY CLASSMATES and I took yearly field trips to the Cincinnati Museum of Natural History. Toward the end of these tours, we inevitably gathered around a large glass case near the gift shop, and were reluctant to leave that spot for the bright yellow school buses waiting outside in the rain. This exhibit housed the fossilized 13,000-year-old skull of a grizzly bear that had been unearthed in Welsch Cave, just west of the Cumberland Plateau in central Kentucky. According to the descriptive placard, the Midwest had been at that time a boreal woodland and cool taiga parkland not unlike the Interior of present-day Alaska, and had supported a diverse array of now-vanished mammals. The climate then changed, and *Ursus arctos horribilis* remained only in the major watercourses and mountainous regions of the Far West.

Everything about the skull was impressive. To this day I recall it vividly: the thickly armored plate protecting the frontal lobes of the brain, the massive arches and supports around the eye orbits, the sculpted tunnels through which vessels and nerves once traveled, the densely stitched sutures over the surface of the cranial vault, the polished ivory canines that were built more like tusks than teeth. On either side of the skull at the base of the jaw—almost like carrying handles—two great lateral arches flared out to accommodate the powerful crushing muscles that evolution has bestowed upon the grizzly. Elsewhere, elegant running grooves and angular supports gave further evidence of where the living jaw muscles had once been laminated to the bone.

There was something else about that skull. Looked at from the front—so that the ursid elongation was not apparent—it faintly resembled the skulls of the older primates we had seen on another floor of the museum. I have always believed that we children gathered around that mineralized chunk of the glacial past in part because we intuitively sensed a distant kinship with the bear. In fact, at some point in the late Mesozoic age, down the ever-unifying branches of the evolutionary tree, our species probably did share a common ancestor. It did not surprise me when I learned, later in life, that the bear had been worshipped in prehistoric times, at first in a mother-son cult and later in a bear-father cult, and that the bear skull was at the center of both religions.

The opportunity to finally explore grizzly country arose when I was seventeen and the family moved to Colorado. Here I soon located large integrated relics of grizzly habitat, but the grizzlies were all gone, except for the shaggy prisoners pacing defiantly at the Denver Zoo and the last indefatigable holdouts still at large in the San Juan Mountains. To this day I find it an incredible historical fact that in less than one century the U.S. Biological Survey, obediently serving the orders of the livestock industry, extirpated a species that had shared the Southern Rockies and the Southwest with a series of vibrant human cultures for at least 120 centuries. How the once-plentiful grizzly was eradicated from Rocky Mountain National Park, which our civilization presumably established for wildlife preservation, is a story that has never been told. If only—I have often wished—bears could be given voices, so that they could provide their version of modern history.

Perhaps because reliable sources—old-timers, mostly, who knew the country well and were advanced enough in years to religiously tell the truth—kept reporting that there were grizzly bears in the San

Juans, I spent most of my free time there. Recent events, including the grizzly killed at Blue Lake in 1979, have indeed confirmed the veracity of their once-discounted stories. It was easy to see why this isolated mountain mass served as the last refuge for the species south of Yellowstone. The valley trails ran 15 to 20 miles up to the Continental Divide, and a maze of side canyons on either side of the primary drainages provided self-contained microhabitats for the increasingly secretive bears. Further, the refugium was enormous: from Stony Pass south along the Divide to Cumbres Pass, the mountains are to this day crossed by only one paved road in over 150 miles.

As might be expected, the grizzly place names were more plentiful in the San Juans than elsewhere in the state. Here the bears made their last stand, and wherever they fell some thoughtful sheepherder or cattleman had named a prominent landform for their latest victim. There was, for example, Grizzly Peak (13,695 feet) at the head of Grizzly Gulch on the upper reaches of Vallecito Creek north of Durango. And there was Mount Oso—*oso* is Spanish for bear—and the Rincón la Oso and La Oso Creek a few miles to the east near Weminuche Pass, in alpine mountains so high, wild, and open you knew the Basque sheepherders of the early 1880s were speaking of El Oso Grande, or the grizzly bear, a circumpolar species they knew from the Pyrenees, and not El Oso Negro, the forest-dwelling American black bear.

For many years, I packed into the country around Weminuche Pass, and other areas on the headwaters of the Rio Grande, looking not so much for grizzlies as for the remnants of their ancestral range. On the tundra slopes above Ute Lake, for example, I found vast white nebulae of alpine bistort (*Polygonum bistortoides*) in full blossom, at the exact location where government trapper Lloyd Anderson spotted a sow grizzly and two cubs feeding in the summer of 1967. Grizzlies are known to have a penchant for bistort roots, which the Cheyenne and Blackfeet Indians ate much as we eat the potato. Just over the ridge from Ute Lake, in Starvation Gulch, trapper Ernie Wilkinson killed a two- or three-year-old grizzly in a cubby trap in September 1951. I visited Ernie once in his taxidermy shop in Monte Vista and he pulled the withered right front paw of the grizzly from a drawer. The rest of the bear had rotted in the sun before he could get to it. Five long bone-colored foreclaws protruded from the last intact metacarpal joints and the fur was thick, black, kinky, and silvertipped. The dried-up foot was all that remained of a once-magnificent Colorado grizzly, and Ernie seemed genuinely sorry he killed the bear.

That same year sheepherder Al Lobato killed a grizzly bear near Blue Lake, at the headwaters of the East Fork of the Navajo River about 60 miles to the southeast of Starvation Gulch. Lobato packed the head skin out and gave it to Ernie, who mounted the bear, a young blond grizzly, with its mouth open and its teeth bared, looking as ferocious as possible. Wilkinson gave the head to his friends at Platoro Lodge, which is located near Blue Lake on the Conejos River, and I have often sat there in the dining hall and watched the people as they watched the grizzly. No one ever really looks at the deer and elk heads, only the grizzly. Once a sheepherder stopped by for coffee and told a table full of fishermen about the grizzly he had seen a week earlier on the North Fork, feeding on cow parsnip "in the snowslide by the waterfall," and when they looked at him in disbelief, he walked out disgusted, certain of what he saw. Nearly thirty years after the Lobato grizzly, on September 23, 1979, outfitter Ed Wiseman killed a grizzly in the high timber about one mile from Blue Lake. I've examined the skull and pelt of the Wiseman grizzly at the Denver Natural History Museum—the pelt is variegated in color and the skull is medium-sized—and I've hiked up the South Fork Canyon to Blue Lake to explore the country where the bear lived. Both experiences filled me with a great sadness, at what had been lost, and with a great hope, at what can one day be. As much as I loved the San Juans, which remain to this day some of the finest grizzly habitat on the continent, I realized early on that in order to see genuine grizzly country—that is, mountains with a significant population of bears in them—I would have to get up to Yellowstone.

The summer after my sophomore year at the University of Colorado I worked as a wrangler at a family-owned dude ranch near Yellowstone. Here, at last, were wild bears. Early in the season, as I brought the riding stock down from the night pasture, I often found fresh grizzly tracks along the horse trail in the swamp by the river. There were scat piles, too, that told me the bears were eating everything from willow catkins to grass to butterfly hatches. As hungry as they were, though, the grizzlies never bothered the Herefords that were camped out in the same bottomland, nor did they disturb the beehives, the pig yard, or the chicken coop. Later in July, while cutting lodgepole pines in one of the canyons to fix broken fence, my buddies and I came across some shed grizzly fur in the wild rose bushes, scattered like discarded bundles of sun-bleached knitting yarn. We tried the rose hips and found them just as tasty as the mother grizzly and her cub had the day before, and we followed their almost human tracks through the forest to a beautiful running spring up in the rocks where they had stopped to take a nap. It was at this spring, in the green moss near a decayed stump, that I saw for the first time the rare Calypso orchid (*Calypso bulbosa*).

All through August, leading wealthy saddlesore easterners on afternoon rides, we rode past milk bucket–sized scat piles on the back ridges, near excavated areas where the resident grizzlies had harvested biscuit-root (*Lomatium ambiguum*). These sites literally looked like a gardener with a strong back had recently been hard at work, digging holes for a good-sized rose garden. Once, while out alone for a Sunday ride, I followed a scent trail into the timber and found a mule deer carcass covered with newly cut spruce branches and overturned sod, and was foolish enough to dismount and poke around the buried meat hoard for a minute before realizing what it was. The high point of the summer came with a fleeting glimpse of a grizzly as it bolted from a tundra snowbank for a pocket of high timber, the sun glinting off its hump as the bear plunged down the far green slope. "My god," one man with binoculars said, "what a piece of work he is." The grizzly vanished all too quickly into the Douglas firs, and we were left to stand there silently on the steep granite ridge as the cold white clouds passed by so very near.

Stories of Old Bruin abounded during the long, dull stretches we spent shoeing horses down at the corral, practicing the double-diamond hitch in the tack shed, or playing cards in the bunkhouse. The foreman—I still have the elk bugle he made for me out of a section of garden hose—told of waking up in a remote camp early one morning to see a grizzly bear a few yards away eating oats from a canvas pannier, and of waiting very quietly in his sleeping bag while the bear finished his breakfast and then lumbered off into the quaking aspen. It took him and his hunter—who had slept soundly through the entire affair—several hours to round up the horses, which had broken loose from their makeshift rope corral at the first scent of the bear. Doc, who owned the spread and was one of the most colorful characters in Park County, regaled us with doubtful accounts of close enounters with Old Silverback, a thousand-pound rogue grizzly that terrorized the timberline basins at the head of the Lamar River and once—or so he said—intentionally stampeded a herd of wild buffalo through Doc's trout fishing camp.

Doc also claimed that Ernest Hemingway had hunted from the ranch before he discovered Sun Valley in Idaho, but years later, when Carlos Baker edited Hemingway's letters, I investigated this and it turned out that Hemingway had only hunted from the Nordquist Ranch up near Cooke City. In September of 1935, to give one example, Hemingway brought along his millionaire playboy friend Tommy Shevlin—one of the hedonistic crowd which was slowly unraveling him—and the two of them killed three grizzlies (among other things) while hunting from the Nordquist Ranch. Hemingway's two bears consisted of a mother and a cub. He wrote Archibald MacLeish: "The grizzly hide was very beautiful like a silver fox but thicker and longer and blow [sic] beautifully in the wind. Finest hide I'd ever seen." Unfortunately, Hemingway didn't properly flesh out and salt the big hide, so the hair slipped and the whole thing had to be thrown away. The meat had been left to rot in the field. It is surprising that someone so keenly aware of irony didn't see the irony of a mother grizzly and her cub dying for the sake of a few sentences in a letter to Archibald MacLeish. Both Hemingway and Shevlin were hunting grizzlies over bait, the same way Hemingway hunted leopards along the Mara River in British East Africa.

One morning I was called into the ranch house to help move an upright piano and noticed the outstretched pelt of a grizzly hanging over the fireplace. I asked Doc's wife about it—she was at a rolltop desk fussing over a red-inked account book—and as I recall one of Doc's sons had shot the bear in a dispute over who owned a freshly killed bull moose, or at least that was the officially published version of the incident. The most impressive thing about the grizzly pelt was its size. It was so small. The years had not been kind to the trophy. Moths had burrowed into the fur, the claws had disappeared, a spark-ignited forest fire had severely charred one leg, and even the glass eyes—the crowning indignity—had apparently found their way into some child's marble collection. There appeared to be seven well-aimed bullet holes in the hide, scattered like the stars of Ursa Major from the hindquarters to the head. That sorry piece of fur has always symbolized for me the state of the grizzly in northwestern Wyoming in the 1970s. Doc has been dead for over a decade now and I sincerely hope that someone has had the common decency to take that sad little hide up into the North Absaroka Wilderness and give it a proper burial.

During the late seventies and early eighties I often made trips to the Gila Wilderness in southwestern New Mexico, the former stomping grounds of notorious grizzly hunters such as British aristocrat Montague Stevens, who owned the enormous S. U. Ranch, Ben Lilly, the most famous professional grizzly hunter of the twentieth century, and Bear Moore, a prospector who devoted his life to killing grizzlies after a disfiguring attack. One of the local ranchers once told me that another well-known grizzly hunter—President Theodore Roosevelt— "almost came out to hunt one year" at the old Lyons hunting lodge on the East Fork, but decided to hunt black bears in Mississippi instead. Roosevelt would have certainly liked the Gila grizzly country. It was as full of silvertips in 1902 as the Dakotas were in 1883 when T. R. began ranching there. But the desert grizzlies would not last much longer. They simply could not withstand the relentless assault of the cattlemen's poison baits, set-gun traps, no. 6 Newhouse steel traps, and repeating rifles. The last grizzly in the Gila Wilderness, which Aldo Leopold founded in 1924, was killed on Rain Creek in April 1931, about five miles west of Tepee Canyon, where Geronimo spent his last winter of freedom before surrendering to General Miles in September 1886.

These ancient volcanic mountains were different, as grizzly habitat, in almost ever respect from the Rockies. For one thing, the country was much drier—only about twelve inches of annual precipitation at the lower elevations—and there were no running streams in the uplands, only scattered seasonal springs and dry washes. Here the dominant tree was the ponderosa pine, and mature open-canopied stands stretched like cultivated parkland for hundreds of square miles. At the bottom of the deep barrancas, the habitat was almost subtropical, and the broad-leafed trees, overhung with wild grape vines and poison ivy, formed a nearly impenetrable jungle inhabited by black-tailed rattlesnakes, Gila monsters, scorpions, tarantulas, and other privacy-loving animals. Although decades of fire suppression had resulted in a decline of the pioneer edges and grassy clearings that the grizzly depends on for various food items, the habitat was still rich, with acorns, prickly pear cactus fruit, manzanita berries, piñon nuts, juniper berries, and squealing javelina in almost every canyon. The quality of the Gila Wilderness as grizzly habitat was dramatically underscored in 1974 when the U.S. Forest Service, feeling guilty for having played a role in the persecution of the species, commissioned a feasibility study on grizzly bear restoration. Not surprisingly, the scientists concluded that "the Gila Wilderness [is] sufficiently large to satisfy the spatial requirements" of restocked grizzlies. This controversial study was quickly buried in the back of a dusty file cabinet. Everyone I talked to in New Mexico about the issue wanted grizzlies back in the Gila, not to mention jaguars and Mexican wolves. The local people understand that these high-profile vertebrates attract tourists as much as cliff dwellings, white-water rafting, and the burgeoning herds of restored elk (also wiped out earlier in the century but later reintroduced).

Black bears are still thick in the Gila and are still hunted because their higher reproductive rate makes them less susceptible to eradication than grizzlies, which have the lowest reproductive rate of terrestrial mammals. Becky Campbell, a hunting guide in Gila Hot Springs, once showed me the pelt of a black bear she had killed with a single shot from her Hawken in Turkey Park, and the hide was enormous, like a swirling dark map of the known universe. The health of the black bear population in the Gila told me this area could still support grizzly bears. I loved this area so much, and saw so much potential for it in terms of grizzly reintroduction, that I wrote a book about it. A few people didn't like that. I received a letter, for example, from a woman working as a fire-lookout in the Gila National Forest, stating that books like mine "are more often than not damaging to the land in that they bring people to remote areas." I take the completely opposite view. Without popular support, bear sanctuaries like the Gila or the San Juan Mountains are doomed. Special interests will develop and dilute them to the extent that it will be impossible to protect black bear habitat—particularly the precious wet acreage—let alone restock the grizzlies. This was made painfully clear to me in 1991 when I learned that a developer has filed a plan to build a 1,790-acre ski resort deep inside the Gila Wilderness on Hummingbird Saddle, a location that is essential habitat for the resident black bears and would be critical habitat for any restored grizzlies. Like John Muir, I believe that people need to see these wild areas so they can appreciate their beauty and challenge developers who would otherwise proceed with their plans undeterred by public outcry.

Interestingly enough, Hummingbird Saddle is the one location in the Gila Wilderness where I saw a bear. It was not a grizzly, of course, for they are all gone (for now), but a fine mature black bear. After setting up camp on the Saddle, I had hiked down the little side trail to Hummingbird Spring, which emerges in the forest on the south side of Whitewater Canyon about fifteen minutes from the Saddle. A very light rain was falling from a single cloud directly overhead, and at the same moment this lens-shaped cloud was reflecting the red light of the setting sun down into the green aspen forest, creating a vivid modulated effect of red and green lighting. As I was filling my canteens at the spring, which consists of a narrow pipe dripping a steady stream of cold water into a basin of ferns, bluebells, and red columbines, I noticed some fresh bear tracks in the mud next to a bunch of freshly cropped bighead clover. Nearby some bear hairs were caught in a deadfall, unmistakable in their ebony color, smooth texture, and faint ursine odor. Glancing into the forest, I realized I was not alone. A bowshot into the trees, as black as the charred stump of a lightning-struck spruce, a black bear studied me intently with both round ears pressed forward and wet nose bobbing up and down on the drafts. There were some green clover leaves protruding from the gape of its mouth, giving it the appearance of a black angus steer disturbed in its grazing. Our eyes met for a heartbeat and then, with a plaintive "baww," the bear turned and vanished into the trees. How someone could turn a four-mile-long wilderness trail into a paved road and then construct a ski resort in the last good bear habitat west of the Pecos, particularly considering the marginal snow conditions of the desert uplands, is beyond me. I am tempted to say "over my dead body."

Sometimes, driving back to the Rockies over the Plains of San Agustin just north of the Gila, I stopped the old green Volkswagon Rabbit along the side of the road and looked out over the enormous bank of fixed-array radio telescopes, their huge white parabolic dishes attentively scanning the silent blue New Mexican sky for signs of intelligent life. How ironic, I often thought, that we had in this century a fairly intelligent life form just a few miles to the south—the grizzly has the greatest cranial capacity relative to body size of any predator—and we chose to wipe the species out instead of live in peaceful coexistence with it. If the grizzly were discovered on another world—with its rotating forearm, its ability to use its foreclaws like fingers, and its phenomenal memory of plant phenology—all of our resources would be applied to preserving and understanding this impressive form of life. And yet here in the Far West our institutions systematically tried to destroy the species. The only good thing is that the 1,000-square-mile Gila Wilderness grizzly bear ecosystem is still intact, thanks to the pioneering efforts of Aldo Leopold, and could easily support the grizzly again.

More and more, through the 1980s, my eyes turned north, past the beleaguered bears of Yellowstone, past even the once-pristine wildlands of Alberta, toward Alaska, where the wildlife refuges were the size of New England and the bears were outnumbered only by the mosquitoes. In the late summer of my thirty-fourth year I finally moved up to the old Russian colony. For two summers now, three by the time you read this, I have spent considerable time among the grizzlies of Denali National Park and Preserve, have spent whole days and weeks with them, often at close range, and through patient observation have become better acquainted with their world. In this process I have put aside much of what I learned in the books of my youth—all that *Hunting Trails of a Ranchman* and *Meeting Mister Grizzly*—because too much of what was written was, if not untrue, too sensationalized for someone who has sat on the ground for whole seasons, with a camera instead of a rifle, and simply watched grizzlies go about their daily affairs. The myths that have been perpetrated on this species—the bear's formidable strength notwithstanding—are a credit to the human imagination, if not a comment on human integrity. My view of the grizzly is now based for the most part on scientific studies I respect and on personal experience, the latter of which is always, as Aristotle was fond of reminding Plato, the most reliable source of truth.

The first thing I noticed about the grizzly habitat in the Alaska Range is that it is somewhat similar to the Southwest. Ansel Adams said as much in 1947, when he traveled to the park to take his famous picture of Mount McKinley (Denali). Adams said the mountains of Interior Alaska reminded him of the mountains of southern California. Exactly. There are no standing trees up out of the river bottoms and stream drainages and so, as in the desert, the lines of all the major landforms are readily apparent. One would not think that anything larger than a grasshopper could live in this country—miles and miles of barren ground as empty as if a prodigious forest fire had swept everything away—and yet this region supports as many grizzlies as the Upper Missouri did when Lewis and Clark first explored that area in 1805. The first time I hiked over this pristine grizzly habitat, I felt as uplifted as Aldo Leopold did in September 1936 when he finally packed into the Sierra Madres of Mexico. "It was here," Leopold later wrote, "that I first clearly realized that land is an organism, that all my life I had seen only sick land, whereas here was a biota in perfect aboriginal health." In the wide open valleys and still-trailless mountains of Denali National Park—coming from the Rockies, I was delighted to find not one developed trail—the grizzlies live much as they did before the first human foot stepped over the Bering Land Bridge into the New World. I also found that Denali was a perfect place to observe grizzlies, with continuous light from about mid May through early August, and unobstructed views in all directions encompassing dozens of square miles.

What I would most like to tell you about the grizzlies I've gotten to know in the park is how very different, in terms of personality, each bear is. These individual variations are often most evident in the facial expressions. Traditional grizzly iconography—the paintings of George Catlin, Charles Russell, and Carl Rungius—generally represents the grizzly as having one look, a menacing, monolithic visage like something emblazoned on a Saxon war shield. What I have found in the field, however, is that the grizzly bear has a highly mobile face—as expressive as any of the canids and felids and some of the primates—and that it is in the face, particularly in the subtleties of movement around the eyes and mouth, that you find the essence of emotion and personality.

I keep one whole notebook in which I record only these facial expressions, many of which I've also captured on videotape and on slide film. Here are a few: happy (when a mother watches her cubs nap after an afternoon nursing session), sad (when a three-year-old cub is rejected by its mother and must go off to live away from her), baffled (when a parka squirrel disappears down a secret escape hole in the tundra), amused (when a mother watches her cubs play with a captured wood frog), curious (when a bear hears a strange new sound), alert (when a bear sees another, as yet unidentified, bear approaching), worried (when a bear smells a nearby wolf pack), sleepy (particularly in September and October before denning), playful (when a grown cub runs into its former sibling and they begin to cavort over the tundra), frightened (when a low-ranking bear suddenly encounters a high-ranking bear), guilty (when a cub steals a parka squirrel from its mother and knows it is about to be punished), lustful (males in particular get glazed eyes and drool copiously when chasing a female in estrus), startled (when bears hear a sudden loud noise), pensive (when they spot a wounded caribou out in the open but stop to study the nearby wolves), angry (when a wolf pack takes over a carcass). And there are many others, a notebook full.

The myth is that all grizzlies are pretty much alike—they are intolerant of people, they reflexively attack anything that wanders into their ken, they are almost exclusively carnivorous, they lack the intelligence of the members of the dog and cat families, and they are solitary to the extent that they even avoid the company of their own species. But by watching many different bears in a variety of situations over a period of years, I have come to realize that this is a socially complex animal more similar in diet and behavior to the plant-eating primates than to the wholly carnivorous canids and felids, and that it has a surprising ability to adjust to environmental changes and to modify its behavior in accordance with human activities. Above all, you will see that each grizzly is as behaviorally unique as each human being is, and that they, like us, have their Hotspurs and their ordinary citizens. George Schaller, a zoologist with the New York Zoological Society, once observed, in studying the behavior of the African lion, that we can look to the lions more for insights on human behavior "than the tree-dwelling vegetarian monkeys and gorillas that behaviorists often study." I would say that the same is even more true for the grizzly, which, like our species, is both a predatory hunter and a major consumer of plant food sources.

My acquaintance with the grizzlies of Denali has convinced me, more than ever, that it is both appropriate and desirable to restore the grizzly to places like the San Juan Mountains, the Gila Wilderness, and even the Sierra Nevadas of California. The San Juans, I should make clear, are unique in this group because a grizzly was killed there in 1979. This means that the San Juan grizzly ecosystem, unlike the other two, is formally protected by the 1973 Endangered Species Act, and that the federal government has a legal responsibility to preserve the habitat and augment the population. Experts tell me it will take from seventy to ninety bears to restock the ecosystem, and that some revolutionary new techniques could be used, such as "interspecific cross-fostering," a process in which newly born grizzly cubs are placed with lactating black bear sows in their natal dens. Highly detailed satellite photographs could help with habitat evaluation and management decisions. Released grizzlies could be radio-collared and radio-mapped. Time of entry in drainages could be manipulated, as it is in Yellowstone, Glacier, and Denali, to avoid conflicts. The same safeguards used in these other grizzly areas could help in public education, to ensure that people don't do foolish things, like sleep next to a canvas pannier full of oats or poke around a covered mule deer carcass.

My experience with the public while doing research on this subject in the late 1980s tells me that, if the issue were put to a popular referendum, the constituency is there to approve restocking. The historic resistance is from the livestock interests, but, for better or worse, the industry is no longer the powerful hegemony it once was. Feedlots are replacing cattle ranches, consumers are choosing poultry and fish over red meat, federal land managers are finally increasing grazing fees, and inactive grazing allotments are being retired or purchased by the states for wildlife use. All this bodes well for the grizzly in Colorado, New Mexico, and elsewhere. Hiking through the San Juans or the Gila country without the grizzly—and I've hauled my wellworn Universal backpack over hundreds of miles of trail in both areas—is about like seeing *Hamlet* without Hamlet ever appearing on the stage. The theater is still standing, and the setting is definitely intact. There are some interesting supporting characters, and there is a vague sense of a plot line, but the main action, the finest flights of lyric poetry, and the whole *raison d'être* of the production are gone.

Not far from the grizzly skull in the Cincinnati Museum of Natural History was another glass case, and I often stood by that one for a long moment in captive fascination, after my classmates had run for the school bus. This exhibit housed the last passenger pigeon, a female named Martha that died in the Cincinnati Zoo in 1914. "How could this happen?" I asked my teacher. "How could they kill a billion birds?" The sheer magnitude of the crime was incomprehensible. I made a promise to myself that when I grew up I would try to make the world a place where such things did not happen; if we could not save the passenger pigeon, then perhaps we could save other species like the grizzly bear. So when I hear people say that six grizzly ecosystems in the Lower 48 are sufficient, that Fishing Bridge and Grant Village pose no threat to the grizzlies of Yellowstone, and that this new mining development or that new forest road improvement won't affect the overall situation, I know better. The grizzly in the contiguous United States faces a "death by a thousand cuts" as its habitat is insidiously rendered depauperate through recreational home building, timber clear-cuts, oil and gas exploration, ski resorts, and a myriad other money-making schemes euphemistically sold to the public as progress. Only eternal vigilance—mountain after mountain, generation after generation—will save the grizzly and all that the grizzly represents.

EPILOGUE

MUCH OF THE FINEST WRITING about grizzly bears has appeared since Aldo Leopold's landmark essay "Escudilla" was first published in *A Sand County Almanac, with Essays on Conservation from Round River* in 1949. "Escudilla" pays tribute to Old Bigfoot, a grizzly that was killed on 10,912-foot Escudilla Mountain in Apache County, Arizona, in June 1910. Leopold was well acquainted with both the mountain and its population of grizzlies from the fifteen years (1909–1924) he spent as a forest manager in the Southwest. "Escudilla" represents a radical departure from previous writings about the species, both in terms of point of view—Leopold's espousal of the biocentric perspective—and in terms of prose style—a lean, muscular prose as spare as the land on which the desert grizzly lived. To those who have labored through the previous century and a half of writings on the North American grizzly—and these essays are well represented in F. M. Young's anthology *Man Meets Grizzly* (1980) and in B. D. Haynes' *The Grizzly Bear* (1966)—"Escudilla" is refreshingly modern in other ways. Gone is the dry factual reportage of the government surveys, the picaresque quality—so often lapsing into self-parody—of the early adventure narratives of James Pattie and Washington Irving, the adolescent braggadocio of the Victorian hunting accounts of Charles Sheldon and Theodore Roosevelt, and the sentimentality of the premodern naturalists like Ernest Thompson Seton and Enos Mills. All these literary precursors are entertaining, to be sure, and valuable insofar as they collectively advanced the cause of conservation and contributed to the development of the genre, but their integrity is too often subverted by apocrypha and exaggeration.

Aldo Leopold, unlike any previous writer to address this uniquely American theme, was a professionally trained scientist, federal land manager, and university professor who believed in the sanctity of facts. As he wrote in "The Land Ethic" (in *A Sand County Almanac*): "[Science's] . . . great moral contribution is objectivity. . . . This means doubting everything except facts." Leopold was also a disciplined writer who respected the power of words. Rather than resurrect the old myths of the grizzly as rapacious cattle thief (Enos Mills' solemnly telling us that Colorado's "Old Mose" killed eight hundred cattle) or bloodthirsty man-killer (Washington Irving's notorious account of a hunter and a grizzly duking it out at the bottom of a prairie sinkhole), Leopold gave posterity the rather ordinary truth. The grizzly was a fellow life-form struggling to survive with dignity in a world that often degrades and destroys that which is natural and free. All the bear required was "a cow a year, and a few square miles of useless rocks." The grizzly posed no threat to human life; in fact he enhanced it aesthetically and morally. But because the Arizona spring of 1910 brought little rain, and the bear had to eat a cow in order to live, the cattle barons decreed he should die. A government trapper was summoned and within a month the bear had been slain by a set-gun trap in a gorge. After his rotting pelt had been nailed to the side of a barn and his skull sent off to the National Museum, Leopold observed that "Escudilla still hangs on the horizon, but when you see it you no longer think of bear. It's only a mountain." Leopold wrote with insight, craft, and sympathy about grizzlies at a time when few intellectuals had the courage to defend predators, and in so doing he raised the topical essay to the level of a literary art form.

Many distinguished essayists, both from the sciences and the humanities, have followed Aldo Leopold's pioneering trail into this subject over the last forty years. The older writers—Frank Craighead, Jr., Ed Abbey, John McPhee—will be familiar to most readers, and the younger ones—Rick Bass, Doug Peacock, Rick McIntyre—will soon be familiar to most. Because of their efforts, the grizzly bear essay is now a distinctive genre that has grown in sophistication and maturity. Although these writers share a common topic, their approaches vary greatly. On the one hand, for example, we have the formal voice and discursive mode of the scientist, as in Frank Craighead's essay on the Yellowstone grizzly Marian, and on the other we have the conversational voice and digressive mode of Rick Bass's essay on a horse-packing trip he made into the Yellowstone grizzly country. The essays are similarly diverse in terms of structure. Some of the authors have written straightforward linear narratives, as in John Haines' account of a trip on which he had to shoot a grizzly in self-defense, while others have worked with more complex literary structures, as in the parallel narrative of Doug Peacock's *Grizzly Years* (1990). Although it is not evident in the selection included here, those who read

Peacock's entire book—the most unusual tribute ever written to the grizzly bear—will find the author shifts back and forth from his experiences as a Green Beret medic in Vietnam to his later life with grizzlies in a daring, highly successful counterpoint. Most of the essays fall somewhere between these outer boundaries.

What unifies these selections, in addition to subject and point of view, are the level of literary craft brought to the task and the extent to which the authors are informed on the natural history of the grizzly bear. Two of the authors are wildlife biologists—Adolph Murie and Frank Craighead—and they have an expected level of professional expertise. What is most impressive here, though, is the mastery of grizzly ecology shown by the nonscientists, such as Thomas McNamee, who walks us with encyclopedic detail through the complete yearly cycle of a Yellowstone grizzly in his book *The Grizzly Bear* (1984), and Paul Schullery, who explains the equally erudite management context in which the Yellowstone grizzly exists in his book *Mountain Time* (1984). Readers familiar with earlier grizzly writings will also notice that these essays do not follow the time-honored, predictable motif of "man surprises bear at close quarters, man is charged by bear, man empties rifle into bear, man clubs bear over the head with rifle, man kills bear in ferocious struggle with Bowie knife." In fact, Alaskan poet John Haines parodies this format in the closing paragraphs of his essay "Out of the Shadows." Rather, these are finely crafted personal essays. Frequently the essayists have added dialogue and character development to their plot lines, further enlivening the discourse, as in Rick Bass's "The Grizzly Cowboys." Where the craft is most evident, though, is in the closing paragraphs. William Kittredge, for example, ends his essay, "Grizzly," with a moving epiphany:

> Up there on Huckleberry Mountain, I couldn't sleep. . . . As the sky broke light over the peaks of Glacier, I found myself deeply moved by the view from our elevation, off west the lights of Montana, Hungry Horse, and Columbia Falls, and farmsteads along the northern edge of Flathead Lake, and back in the direction of sunrise the soft and misted valleys of the parklands, not an electric light showing: little enough to preserve for the wanderings of a great and sacred animal who can teach us, if nothing else, by his power and his dilemma, a little common humility.

There are three persistent themes in these contemporary essays: communion, liberation, and renewal. The first involves the sense of the bear as a sacred animal, and has its roots in the Amerindian cultures, and in the Græco-Roman and Paleolithic cultures in which brown bears—the European version of the grizzly—were deified. This theme is evident in "Escudilla," as Leopold infers the sacredness of the grizzly by declaiming its killing. The government trapper, a deadly emissary of the secular world, made the sacred mountain "safe for cows" but "did not know he had toppled the spire off an edifice a-building since the morning stars sang together." Leopold portrays the bear as an avuncular "god of the place," and the essay is written as an almost biblical parable of how we diminish ourselves and our world by choosing the profane—money profits—over the sacred—the grizzly. Like a latter-day Jeremiah, Aldo Leopold deplores the fallen, apostate social order that in destroying the resident wild spirit of the mountain has annulled the wildness of the holy mountain.

This communion or religious theme is particularly evident in Richard Nelson's selection. Nelson, a cultural anthropologist, writes of the Koyukon Athapaskan people of Interior Alaska in his book *Make Prayers to the Raven: A Koyukon View of the Northern Forest* (1983). To the Koyukuk River villagers, the grizzly bear, as well as the black bear, "[take] us near the apex of power among spirits of the natural world" and are second only to the wolverine in power. The bears "are conspicuous, imposing, sometimes even awesome personages" and "their remains [are] vibrant and electric with spiritual energy." Nelson recalls a story the village elders once related to him:

> Some old-timers—Chief John, Old Thomas, Big John—told me this a long time ago: Every hair on the brown bear's hide has a life of its own. Every hair moves, vibrates by itself when something surprises the bear. . . . It takes a few years for all that life to be gone from a brown bear's hide. That's the kind of power it has.

Similarly, Doug Peacock, who is particularly knowledgeable about the Blackfeet Indians of northern Montana, on whose reservation he has tracked grizzlies, writes:

> To the ancient Blackfeet the grizzly, whom they called Real

Bear, was the most esteemed of all animals. Many surviving tales evolved from elements of the much older traditions of the Spirit Bear, the most common of which are variations in the story of the Medicine Grizzly. The great bear was a healer and the source of power of the medicine pipe . . . the Blackfeet revered the grizzly. . . .

Again, bears are seen as sacred animals having special spiritual power.

For John McPhee, the sighting of a Barren Grounds grizzly bear along the Salmon River in northwestern Alaska is tantamount to a conversion experience in its intensity: "The sight of the [grizzly] bear stirred me like nothing else the country could contain. . . . He implied a world." That night, in his sleeping bag, McPhee closed his eyes:

> There he was, in color, on the side of the hill. That vision was indelible. . . . It was a vision of a whole land, with an animal in it. This was his country, clearly enough. To be there was to be incorporated, in however small a feature, into its substance.

A second theme that shapes these essays is liberation—the sense of the bear as a symbol for political freedom. This theme is present early on in "Escudilla," as Leopold declaims "the Congressman who voted money to clear the ranges of bears" and inveighs against the forest officers (himself among them) who "were the captains of an invasion too sure of its own righteousness." The bureau chief did not "foresee that within two decades the cow country would become tourist country and as such would have greater need of bears than of beefsteaks." Having lost its reigning grizzly, Escudilla was no longer a wilderness and Leopold wondered "who wrote the rules for progress." The answer to that rhetorical question was simple—the wealthy cattlemen whose capital interests were marginally affected by the predators on the public lands were the ones who wrote "the rules for progress." Leopold here allies himself with the larger democracy of nature, and employs the bear as a rallying point for his shallowly buried subversive message, although his career and life attest to the fact that he believed in evolution over revolution as a means of changing the status quo.

The political theme runs strongly through many of the later selections. Edward Abbey—the quintessential iconoclast—comes to mind first, as he has written in his essay, "Thus I Reply to René Dubos" in *One Life at a Time, Please* (1988): "It is my fear that if we allow the freedom of the hills and the last of the grizzly to be taken from us, then the very idea of freedom may die with it." In this statement, Abbey directly links the wilderness with political freedom. There is no more potent a symbol of the North American wilderness than the grizzly, as Abbey argues:

> We must not allow our national parks and national forests to be degraded to the status of mere public playgrounds. . . . Enter Glacier National Park and you enter the homeland of the grizzly bear. We are uninvited guests here, intruders, the bear our reluctant host. Those who prefer, quite reasonably, not to take such chances should stick to Disneyland in all its many forms and guises.

In his selection, Montana novelist A. B. Guthrie attacks the special interest groups, chiefly the wool growers, whose activities on the public range threaten the grizzly. He relates a telling anecdote:

> The question arose as to what should be the official Montana animal, the grizzly or the elk. It appeared that the state legislature might designate the elk. But then the hundreds of schoolchildren showed up last spring to demand that the bear be chosen. The legislators had no choice. . . . It is just this sort of action that is the key to the grizzly's survival. . . . Only *the people* [emphasis added] can make it happen.

Only by forging coalitions and uniting resources can supporters of the bear contend equally with the moneyed interests. Prominent writers like Guthrie serve as natural leaders for such movements. There is little doubt, for example, but that John McPhee's best-selling Alaska book *Coming into the Country* (1977) had a tremendous influence on the country and on the U.S. Congress, which three years later passed the comprehensive Alaska lands bill. This wide-reaching piece of legislation doubled the national park system and tripled the national wilderness system, thus affording unprecedented protection for the grizzly bear. Similarly, the ground-breaking work of Frank and John Craighead, which has been critical of federal management policy of the grizzly in Yellowstone, has strongly impacted how the government manages both grizzly bears and scientists.

All of Aldo Leopold's great Southwestern essays—"On Top," "Thinking Like a Mountain," "Escudilla," "The Green Lagoons," "Guacamara," and "Song of the Gavilan"—celebrate renewal, the restoration of inner order through contact with the regenerative forces of nature. For Leopold, the desert mountains were healing places where "every living thing sang," where wolves "howled in wild defiant sorrow," and prodigious thunderstorms recharged "the high solitudes." In these sanctuaries, Leopold learned the true meaning "behind Thoreau's dictum: In wildness is the salvation of the world." This psychological theme is evident in Doug Peacock's *Grizzly Years*, in which the author explicitly links his recovery from the Vietnam War with his pursuit of the grizzly. Peacock writes:

> Bears provided the original model of spiritual renewal. The bear showed early man how to get through the little death of winter by burial, emerging from the cold in spring, sometimes with new life in the form of bear cubs. The bear showed the way of survival and renewal as part of the cycle of life.

Peacock's extended forays into grizzly country, like war-injured Nick Adams' fishing trip to Hemingway's Big Two-Hearted River, assume the dimensions of a session with the therapist. And his writings, which are intensely personal and forthcoming, achieve the penitential catharsis of confession. Through this process, Peacock comes to identify with one grizzly in particular, the Bitter Creek Grizz: "The old bear was, like me, in the autumn of his life," and "was a holdover from the days when bears could afford to be bold and aggressive." In the end, Peacock states emphatically that the grizzlies "saved my life." There are, to paraphrase Herman Hesse's famous description of Steppenwolf, two worlds in a human being, the world of culture and sublimated nature—the man—and the world of instinct, impulse, and raw, wild nature—the grizzly bear. In seeking out and communing with the grizzlies, Peacock and others, including Jim Carrier's Wyoming grizzly aficionado Steve French and Denali's devoted ranger Rick McIntyre, reconcile the dichotomous spheres of being. Their writings bear witness to the overwhelming sense of renewal that accrues from making contact with all that is repressed by civilization and is symbolized so perfectly in the grizzly.

What is the status of the grizzly in North America at the present? Currently the grizzly bear is maintaining much of its historic range in the western Canadian provinces and in Alaska, although there is cause for concern in several local situations. For example, a proposed mining development and a proposed salmon fishery seriously threaten the brown bears of the McNeil River bear sanctuary on the Alaska Peninsula; grizzlies throughout the Anchorage basin are being lost to urban growth; and the grizzlies of Denali National Park are imperiled by increased tourist development in the Kantishna region, by potential mining developments, and by a meteoric rise in the number of visitors using the park. Maintaining current automobile restrictions on the Denali park road in the 1990s will be absolutely essential to preserving grizzly bear viewing opportunities in the park. Elsewhere, clear-cutting of coastal rain forests in British Columbia and Alaska has inflicted serious damage on brown bear habitat (coastal grizzlies are called brown bears, as are the conspecific bears of Asia and Europe). Experts believe that there are around 5,000 grizzlies in Alaska and about the same number in Alberta, British Columbia, the Yukon Territory, and the Northwest Territories combined. Hunting is permitted in all of these locations and currently does not pose a danger to the species.

Only a handful of grizzly populations, a total of perhaps 1,000 grizzlies, remains in the Lower 48: in Yellowstone National Park, the northern Continental Divide in Montana, the Selway-Bitterroot Wilderness Area in Idaho, the North Cascades of Washington, the Selkirk Mountains of Idaho, and the Cabinet Mountains of Montana. Grizzlies are considered marginal in some of those areas, such as the North Cascades, the Selkirks, and the Selway-Bitterroot country. At the present time, the grizzly is a federally listed threatened species in all six of those ecosystems, and is a federally listed endangered species in the San Juan Mountains of southwestern Colorado. The agency charged with protecting the grizzly—the U.S. Fish and Wildlife Service—will concentrate over the next decade on improving the situation for the bear in the first six ecosystems mentioned. Additionally, the most recent Grizzly Bear Recovery Plan (1991) gives tacit approval to the restoration of the grizzly in Colorado by stating that the objective of the plan is "to reach viable populations of grizzly bears in each of the areas where grizzly bears are present or were suspected in 1975 in the states of Montana, Washington, Idaho, Wyoming, and Colorado where the habitat is able to support a viable population." Grizzly habitat in Colorado is some of the finest in North America, and about 900 square miles of designated wilderness area exist for the restocking project in the San Juan Mountains. Reports of grizzly sightings and activities persist in this remote mountainous area.

Grizzlies are also possibly found in the Sierra del Nidos and Sierra Madres (Rio Yaqui headwaters) of Mexico. The first is an island mountain system with intensive livestock grazing and a history of the use of Compound 1080, a deadly predacide; grizzlies were killed there through 1960, and sightings persist. The Rio Yacqui is the more remote region of the two and could afford grizzlies somewhat better protection, should the Mexican government choose to preserve or restore the bear. Worldwide, brown bears—and, again, the grizzly is part of a holearctic species—are holding their own in a surprising diversity of countries, from northern Japan's Hokkaido Island, through China and the Soviet Union, to the high mountains of southwest Asia, and in a few of the more rugged mountain masses of Europe. Brown bears are still plentiful enough to be hunted in some of the eastern European countries, as they are in the Soviet Union. Spain has recently expanded its protection of the last tiny brown bear ecosystems along the Pyrenees Mountains, and Italy has long been proud of its surviving brown bears in Abruzzo National Park. Austria surprised the international community in 1991 by announcing that it had recently released five brown bears into the Austrian Alps, where the bears have been extinct since 1842, and that it planned to release forty more bears into the mountains over the next few years.

We shelter these bears in their preserves and parks, finally, as the ancient Greeks honored their sacred mountains, groves, and animals, as refuges of the spirit, testifying that our greed is not unrestrained, our growth not without limit, our grasp of the holy not entirely lost. Those who have packed far up into grizzly country, as have these authors, know that the presence of even one grizzly on the land elevates the mountains, deepens the canyons, chills the winds, brightens the stars, darkens the forests, and quickens the pulse of all who enter it. They know that when a bear dies, something sacred in every living thing interconnected with that realm, including those resident human souls, also dies. History judges civilizations not only by their pyramids and cathedrals, social programs and legislatures, judicial codes and symphonies, but also by their stewardship of the earth. Hence the Holy Roman Emperor Charlemagne is forever damned for issuing the decrees that deforested half of Western Europe, and the North American Indians are forever praised for living on the land for 10,000 years without having significantly changed it. The brown bears of Germany are long gone, but almost twenty-five centuries after the Periclean Golden Age, brown bears still freely roam the wild mountains of Greece. The essayists in this book, like the oracles of old, remind us of what is important and what is not, of what endures and what does not, and of what, as Aldo Leopold would say, is progress and what is not.

THE GRIZZLY BEAR IN NORTH AMERICA: A CHRONOLOGY

1540—Spaniard Francisco Coronado explores the central Rio Grande Valley of New Mexico and ventures onto the short-grass plains of Colorado. He is the first European to travel extensively through grizzly habitat.

1602—Spanish explorer Sebastian Viscaino describes grizzlies feeding on a whale carcass near Monterey, California.

1690—Henry Kelsey, exploring the Canadian prairies for Britain's Hudson's Bay Company, kills a grizzly bear and eats its meat. The Indians are distraught, telling him, "It was god."

1770s—Russian naturalists report brown bears in Alaska.

1789—Canadian statesman and explorer Alexander MacKenzie records presence of grizzly bears in western Canada.

1805—Explorers Meriwether Lewis and William Clark describe grizzlies in what is today eastern Montana. They also kill numerous grizzlies and return with skulls and pelts for Peale's Philadelphia Museum.

1808—Lieutenant Zebulon Pike returns from his survey with two "pet" grizzlies, which are placed in a Philadelphia zoo.

1815—Naturalist George Ord, in Philadelphia, gives the grizzly bear the scientific name *Ursus horribilis.*

1815—Naturalist Adelbert von Chamisso theorizes that the grizzly bear of Alaska is the same species as the European brown bear.

1819—The government expedition of Major Stephen Long explores Colorado and returns with grizzly bear specimens.

1821—Lewis Dawson, a member of the Fowler expedition seeking a viable overland route to Santa Fe, is killed by a grizzly near the Purgatoire River in eastern Colorado.

1823—Frontiersman James Ohio Pattie kills numerous grizzlies in Colorado.

1835—Washington Irving describes grizzlies in Oklahoma in his travel narrative *A Tour on the Prairies.* He is the first professional writer to do so.

1838—Artist George Catlin exhibits his western paintings, which include now-famous paintings of grizzly bears, in Washington, D.C. He later exhibits in London and Paris.

1851—Naturalist Von Middendorf recognizes the grizzly as a holarctic species, and gives it the name *Ursus arctos horribilis.*

1856—Grizzly Adams comes out of the California mountains with his pet grizzly bear "Ben Franklin."

1867—Territorial legislature of Colorado closes hunting season on grizzlies for two years.

1872—Yellowstone National Park is established.

1890—Last grizzly in Texas is killed.

1897—Grizzly is reported as rare in Colorado. Last grizzly in North Dakota is killed.

1899—Ernest Thompson Seton writes *The Biography of a Grizzly.*

1904—Old Mose is killed near Canon City, Colorado.

1905—While hunting in Colorado, Theodore Roosevelt reports the grizzly has become rare in the state.

1906—Charles Russell paints *A Wounded Grizzly.*

1908—Ben Lilly moves west from Louisiana and kills his first grizzly; he will single-handedly kill dozens of grizzlies throughout the Southwest during his years as a professional hunter and trapper.

1913—Naturalist William Wright publishes *The Grizzly Bear.* His book includes some of the first published photographs of grizzlies in the wild.

1919—Naturalist Enos Mills publishes *The Grizzly,* and reports the grizzly is no longer found in northern Colorado.

1920—U.S. Government begins campaign to eradicate grizzlies.

1922—Last grizzly in California is killed.

1923—Old Ephraim, a famous Idaho grizzly, is killed. Last grizzly in Utah is killed.

1931—Last grizzly in New Mexico is killed. Last grizzly in Oregon is killed.

1935—Last grizzly in Arizona is killed. Ernest Hemingway kills two grizzlies, mother and cub, near Cooke City, Montana.

1948—Over the next two years, at least five grizzlies are killed in southwestern Colorado.

1951—Two grizzlies are killed in San Juan Mountains of Colorado.

1952—Grizzly killed in Colorado, the last for 27 years.

1954—Authorities create the Rio Grande–San Juan Grizzly Bear

Management Area in southwestern Colorado, in hopes of preserving the last southwestern grizzlies.

1959—Biologist brothers John and Frank Craighead begin historic long-term study of grizzlies in Yellowstone National Park.

1960—Grizzly is killed in Sierra del Nido Mountains of Mexico.

1962—National Geographic television program focuses international attention on the Craighead study.

1964—The Wilderness Act is signed into law, giving formal protection to last vestiges of grizzly habitat in many western states.

1964—The Rio Grande–San Juan Grizzly Bear Management Area in Colorado is dissolved. Officials discount numerous reports of grizzly sightings in the San Juan Mountains.

1971—The Craigheads part company with the National Park Service, citing numerous disagreements over policy and procedure.

1972—Centennial celebration of Yellowstone Park. Nearly 100 grizzlies are killed in the park ecosystem during the early 1970s (this from a population of less than 200 members), as officials close dumps suddenly, despite the warnings.

1973—The Endangered Species Act is signed into law. The grizzly bear is soon listed as endangered in the Lower 48 states.

1975—John Craighead submits proposal to reintroduce grizzlies into Colorado's San Juan Mountains. Idea rejected by Colorado Wildlife Commission.

1976—Officials in Colorado Division of Wildlife recommend restoration of grizzly to the San Juan Mountains in an internal study.

1977—Businessman/philanthropist Malcolm Forbes offers his 262-square-mile ranch in southwestern Colorado as a site for grizzly restoration. Idea rejected by Colorado Wildlife Commission.

1979—Big-game outfitter kills a 16-year-old female grizzly bear in Colorado's San Juan Mountains. Necropsy indicates she probably had borne cubs in the past, revealing the possible presence of a male and the cubs in the area. Government continues to permit black bear hunting and livestock grazing in the area. Both are historic sources of conflict with grizzlies.

1980—Alaska National Interest Lands Conservation Act is signed into law. Protects vast regions of grizzly habitat throughout the state.

1980—Colorado biologist Tom Beck begins three-year study of the area in which female grizzly was killed in San Juan Mountains (1979). Finds recent dig sites, a location at which a marmot was unearthed, and a grizzly den. Outfitter reports seeing grizzly sow and cubs on East Fork of the Navajo River on the Banded Peak Ranch. Beck later finds a large quantity of blond bear hairs at this site, and a dig for the roots of spring beauty, a wildflower. Program is terminated in its second year because of funding shortages. No change in management policy with respect to black bear hunting and livestock grazing in the area.

1985—Arizona wildlife manager Dave Brown publishes *The Grizzly in the Southwest* (University of Arizona Press), recommending grizzly restoration in the Gila/Blue Range area.

1986—"Fate of the Grizzly" Conference is held in Boulder, Colorado, as the Park Service reveals there are fewer than 35 breeding females left in Yellowstone. Some scientists in attendance predict the grizzly will be extinct in Yellowstone by the year 2000.

1988—Wildfires destroy much timberland in Yellowstone, possibly improving the long-term habitat situation for grizzlies.

1990—Scientists confirm grizzly bears are present in northern Washington.

1991—Sightings of grizzlies and reports of grizzly activity in southwestern Colorado persist. Federal and state land managers continue to ignore these reports; black bear hunting (over bait) and livestock grazing continue in this area. The grizzly remains a federally listed endangered species in Colorado.

FURTHER READING

Adams, James Capen. 1860. *Mountaineer and Grizzly Bear Hunter of California.* Boston.

Associated Press. 1980. "Guide who says he slew grizzly with handheld arrow is disputed." *The New York Times,* February 29.

Beck, T., *et al.* 1982. South San Juan Mountains grizzly bear survey. Colorado Division of Wildlife Project SE-3-4. Endangered Wildlife Investigations. Colorado Division of Wildlife nongame files. Photocopy.

Bissell, S. J. 1980. Grizzly bear incident, September 1979 summary report. Compendium of reports, maps, photographs, correspondence, and newspaper columns. Colorado Division of Wildlife nongame files.

Brown, David E. 1985. *The Grizzly in the Southwest: Documentary of an Extinction.* Norman: University of Oklahoma Press.

Chapman, J. A., and G. A. Feldhammer. 1982. *Wild Mammals of North America.* Baltimore: The Johns Hopkins University Press.

Craighead, Frank C., Jr. 1979. *Track of the Grizzly.* San Francisco: Sierra Club.

Craighead John J., J. S. Sumner, and G. B. Skaggs. 1982. *A Definitive System for Analysis of Grizzly Bear Habitat and Other Wilderness Resources.* University of Montana Foundation, Missoula, Wildlife-Wildlands Monograph.

Craighead, John J., J. Varney, and F. C. Craighead, Jr. 1974. *A Population Analysis of the Yellowstone Grizzly Bears.* Montana Forestry Conservation Experimental Station Bulletin No. 40, School of Forestry. Missoula: University of Montana.

Dobie, Frank. 1950. *The Ben Lilly Legend.* Boston: Little Brown.

Dufresne, Frank. (1965) 1991. *No Room for Bears.* Bothell, Washington: Alaska Northwest Books.

Erickson, A. W. 1974. Evaluation of the suitability of the Gila Wilderness for re-establishment of the grizzly bear. Report to the U.S. Forest Service, Southwestern Regional Office, Contract 6-369-74. Typescript.

Haynes, B. D., and E. Haynes. 1966. *The Grizzly Bear: Portraits from Life.* Norman: University of Oklahoma Press.

Herrero, Stephen. 1985. *Bear Attacks: Their Causes and Avoidance.* New York: Nick Lyons.

Hittel, Theodore H. 1860. *The Adventures of James Capen Adams, Mountaineer and Grizzly Bear Hunter of California.* Boston.

Mills, Enos A. 1919. *The Grizzly, Our Greatest Wild Animal.* New York: Houghton Mifflin.

Murray, John A. 1987. *Wildlife in Peril: The Endangered Mammals of Colorado.* Boulder: Roberts Rinehart.

Murray, John A., and Dave Brown. 1988. *The Last Grizzly, and Other Southwestern Bear Stories.* Tucson: University of Arizona Press.

Roosevelt, Theodore. 1983. *American Bears.* Ed. Paul Schullery. Boulder: Colorado Associated University Press.

Russell, Andy. 1967. *Grizzly Country.* New York: A. Knopf.

Schneider, Bill. 1977. *Where the Grizzly Walks.* Missoula: Mountain Press.

Schullery, Paul. 1980. *The Bears of Yellowstone.* Yellowstone Park, Wyo.: Yellowstone Library and Museum Association.

Seton, Ernest Thompson. 1899. *The Biography of a Grizzly.* New York: Grosset and Dunlap.

Storer, Tracy I., and Lloyd P. Tevis, Jr. 1955. *California Grizzly.* Lincoln: University of Nebraska Press.

Wright, William H. (1909) 1977. *The Grizzly Bear.* Lincoln: University of Nebraska Press.

Young, F. M., and C. Beyers. 1980. *Man Meets Grizzly: Encounters in the Wild from Lewis and Clark to Modern Times.* Boston: Houghton Mifflin.

INDEX

ABOUT JOHN A. MURRAY

JOHN A. MURRAY is Assistant Professor of English at the University of Alaska, Fairbanks. He has published nine other nature books, including *A Republic of Rivers: Three Centuries of Nature Writing from Alaska and the Yukon* and *The Islands and the Sea: Five Centuries of Nature Writing from the Caribbean.* His previous writings on the grizzly bear can be found in *The Last Grizzly, and Other Southwestern Bear Stories, Wildlife in Peril: The Endangered Mammals of Colorado,* and *The South San Juan Wilderness Area.* During the summers of 1989, 1990, and 1991, he studied and photographed the grizzly bears of Denali National Park and Preserve.

Alaska Northwest Books™ proudly recommends several of its outstanding books on nature and the environment:

Grizzly Cub: *Five Years in the Life of a Bear,* by Rick McIntyre.
Grizzly Cub is the true account of a bear's first five summers, as recorded in words and color photographs by Denali National Park and Preserve ranger Rick McIntyre. The book is endearing and thoughtful reading for young and old alike. With 56 color photographs.
104 pages, softbound, $14.95 ($18.95 Canadian), ISBN 0-88240-373-7

Wild Echoes: *Encounters with the Most Endangered Animals in North America,* by Charles Bergman.
In *Wild Echoes,* the author writes of his experiences with the gray wolf, the Florida panther, the trumpeter swan, and several other species, and explores mankind's role in the survival of these gravely threatened creatures.
With 17 photographs.
336 pages, softbound, $12.95 ($15.95 Canadian), ISBN 0-88240-404-0

No Room for Bears: *A Wilderness Writer's Experiences with a Threatened Breed,* by Frank Dufresne, with a foreword by Roger Caras.
No Room for Bears is a moving tribute to the bear. Dufresne's adventure tales are woven among natural history sketches and folklore. This classic is for all readers who believe in the bear's right to room on the planet.
With 17 illustrations by Ruth Darling.
256 pages, softbound, $12.95 ($15.95 Canadian), ISBN 0-88240-414-8

Where the Sea Breaks Its Back: *The Epic Story of Early Naturalist Georg Steller and the Russian Exploration of Alaska,* by Corey Ford.
This book is the dramatic portrait of naturalist Georg Wilhelm Steller, who sailed with Vitus Bering on his tragic final voyage of exploration along Alaska's coast in 1741-42 documenting wildlife species unknown to Europeans. This compelling account is full of adventure and discovery.
With 14 illustrations, 1 map.
218 pages, softbound, $12.95 ($15.95 Canadian), ISBN 0-88240-394-X

Ask for these books at your favorite bookstore, or contact Alaska Northwest Books™ for a catalog of our entire list.

Alaska Northwest Books™
A division of GTE Discovery Publications, Inc.
P.O. Box 3007
Bothell, WA 98041-3007
1-800-343-4567